Table of Contents

Chapter 1: Introduction to NFTs and Game Development 1
   1.1. The Evolution of Gaming and Digital Ownership 1
   1.2. Understanding NFTs: Beyond the Hype 2
   1.3. The Synergy between NFTs and Video Games 4
   1.4. Legal and Ethical Considerations in NFT Usage 6
   1.5. Future Trends: NFTs Reshaping Gaming Economies 9

Chapter 2: Basics of NFT Technology 12
   2.1. Blockchain Fundamentals for Gamers 12
   2.2. Decoding Smart Contracts and Their Role in NFTs 14
   2.3. Token Standards: ERC-721 and ERC-1155 Explained 16
   2.4. The Mechanics of Minting NFTs 19
   2.5. Understanding NFT Marketplaces and Exchanges 21

Chapter 3: Designing NFTs for Games 24
   3.1. Conceptualizing NFT Assets in Gaming 24
   3.2. Artistic and Technical Considerations 25
   3.3. Creating Unique and Desirable NFTs 27
   3.4. Balancing Game Economy with NFT Integration 29
   3.5. Case Studies: Successful NFT Integrations in Games 32

Chapter 4: NFTs and Game Development Platforms 35
   4.1. Selecting the Right Blockchain Platform 35
   4.2. Integration of NFTs in Popular Game Engines 36
   4.3. Utilizing NFT APIs and SDKs 39
   4.4. Cross-Platform Compatibility and Challenges 42
   4.5. Security Aspects in NFT-based Games 44

Chapter 5: Programming NFTs for Gamers 48
   5.1. Basics of Writing Smart Contracts for Gaming NFTs 48
   5.2. Implementing Gameplay Mechanics with NFTs 50
   5.3. User Authentication and Ownership Verification 53
   5.4. Managing NFT Transactions Within Games 55
   5.5. Enhancing Player Experience through NFTs 58

Chapter 6: Monetizing Games with NFTs 62
   6.1. New Revenue Models with NFTs 62

6.2. Pricing Strategies for In-Game NFTs 64
6.3. Auctions and Secondary Markets 67
6.4. Royalties and Continuous Earning Models 70
6.5. Case Studies of Monetization Success 74

Chapter 7: Building NFT Game Communities 77
   7.1. Engaging Players with NFT Collectibles 77
   7.2. Community Building on Blockchain 79
   7.3. Leveraging Social Media for NFT Gaming Promotion 81
   7.4. Organizing Online Events and Tournaments 83
   7.5. The Role of Influencers and Streamers 85

Chapter 8: NFTs in Multiplayer and Online Games 88
   8.1. NFTs in Massively Multiplayer Online Games (MMOGs) 88
   8.2. Creating Shared Economies in Online Worlds 90
   8.3. Player-to-Player Trade and NFT Market Dynamics 93
   8.4. Building Persistent Worlds with NFTs 96
   8.5. Case Study: NFT Integration in an MMOG 100
      Case Study: "CryptoWorlds" 100

Chapter 9: NFTs in Mobile Gaming 105
   9.1. Opportunities and Challenges of NFTs in Mobile Games 105
   9.2. User Experience Considerations for Mobile 107
   9.3. Integrating Wallets and NFTs in Mobile Games 110
   9.4. Mobile Gaming NFT Marketplaces 114
   9.5. Future Prospects of NFTs in Mobile Gaming 118

Chapter 10: NFT Artwork and Digital Assets 121
   10.1. The Art of Creating NFTs for Games 121
   10.2. Collaborating with Digital Artists 124
   10.3. Licensing and Copyrights in NFT Art 126
   10.4. 3D Models and Virtual Assets as NFTs 128
   10.5. Ensuring Authenticity and Rarity in NFT Art 132

Chapter 11: Smart Contract Development for Gaming NFTs 135
   11.1. Advanced Smart Contract Coding Techniques 135
   11.2. Testing and Deploying Smart Contracts 138
   11.3. Smart Contract Optimization for Efficiency 141
   11.4. Security Best Practices in Smart Contract Development 144

11.5. Auditing and Quality Assurance of Game Smart Contracts 147

Chapter 12: The Future of Gaming NFTs 151
12.1. Emerging Trends in NFT and Game Technology 151
12.2. NFTs in Augmented and Virtual Reality Games 153
12.3. The Impact of AI on NFT-Based Games 154
12.4. Predictions: The Next Decade of Gaming NFTs 156
12.5. Ethical and Social Implications of Future NFT Gaming 158

Chapter 13: User Experience and Interface Design for NFT Games 161
13.1. Designing Intuitive NFT User Interfaces 161
13.2. User Experience Principles in NFT Integration 163
13.3. Accessibility and Inclusivity in NFT Gaming 165
13.4. Personalization and Customization with NFTs 168
13.5. Feedback Loops and Player Engagement Strategies 171

Chapter 14: Marketing and Promoting NFT Games 175
14.1. Crafting a Unique Selling Proposition for NFT Games 175
14.2. Digital Marketing Strategies for Blockchain Games 176
14.3. Community Engagement and Loyalty Programs 179
14.4. Collaborations and Partnerships in the NFT Space 181
14.5. Navigating Regulatory Compliance in Marketing 183

Chapter 15: Legal Considerations in NFT Game Development 186
15.1. Intellectual Property Rights in NFTs 186
15.2. Legal Frameworks Governing Digital Assets 187
15.3. Privacy and Data Security in NFT Transactions 189
15.4. Consumer Protection Laws and NFTs 192
15.5. Global Regulatory Landscape for NFT Gaming 194

Chapter 16: Economics and Financial Analysis of NFT Gaming 197
16.1. Economic Models in NFT Gaming 197
16.2. Financial Planning and Budgeting for NFT Projects 199
16.3. Analyzing Market Trends and Player Spending Habits 201
16.4. Risk Management in NFT Investments 203
16.5. Valuation of NFTs in the Gaming Context 204

Chapter 17: Community and Social Impact of Gaming NFTs 207
17.1. Building Inclusive Gaming Communities with NFTs 207
17.2. Social Dynamics and Player Interaction in NFT Games 209

17.3. NFTs and Their Role in Digital Identity 211
17.4. Ethical Gaming Practices and Player Welfare 212
17.5. The Role of NFTs in Charitable Initiatives and Social Causes 215
Chapter 18: Technical Challenges and Solutions in NFT Gaming 218
18.1. Scalability Issues in Blockchain Games 218
18.2. Interoperability Challenges with NFTs 220
18.3. Overcoming Latency and Performance Hurdles 222
18.4. Ensuring Game Continuity and NFT Persistence 224
18.5. Advanced Solutions in Blockchain Technology for Gaming 227
Chapter 19: Player Analytics and Data in NFT Gaming 230
19.1. Tracking Player Behavior in NFT Games 230
19.2. Utilizing Analytics for Game Improvement 231
19.3. Data Security and Privacy in Player Analytics 234
19.4. Personalizing Player Experiences with Data 236
19.5. Ethical Data Usage in Blockchain Gaming 239
Chapter 20: Case Studies and Real-World Applications 242
20.1. Analysis of Successful NFT Games 242
    Case Study 1: Axie Infinity 242
    Case Study 2: Decentraland 242
    Case Study 3: CryptoKitties 243
    Case Study 4: Gods Unchained 243
    Case Study 5: The Sandbox 243
20.2. Lessons from Failed NFT Game Projects 244
    Case Study 1: FOMO3D 244
    Case Study 2: CryptoCelebrities 244
    Case Study 3: BitconnectX 244
    Case Study 4: EtherTulips 245
    Case Study 5: CryptoCountries 245
    Lessons Learned 245
20.3. Innovative Use Cases of NFTs in Indie Games 246
    Case Study 1: Neon District 246
    Case Study 2: MyCryptoHeroes 246
    Case Study 3: CryptoSpaceX 246
    Case Study 4: Axie Infinity 247

- Case Study 5: Gods Unchained 247
- Lessons Learned 247
- 20.4. Corporate and Big Studio Approaches to NFT Gaming 248
  - Case Study 1: Ubisoft - Quartz 248
  - Case Study 2: Electronic Arts (EA) 248
  - Case Study 3: Square Enix 249
  - Case Study 4: Atari 249
  - Case Study 5: Zynga 249
  - Lessons Learned 249
- 20.5. Future Directions and Experimental Concepts in NFT Gaming 250
  - 1. Metaverse Integration 250
  - 2. AI-Generated Content 250
  - 3. Dynamic NFTs 250
  - 4. Decentralized Autonomous Worlds (DAWs) 250
  - 5. NFT-Driven Ecosystems 251
  - 6. Virtual Reality (VR) and Augmented Reality (AR) Integration 251
  - 7. Cross-Game Quests and Events 251
  - 8. Sustainable NFT Practices 251
  - 9. Gamified DeFi (GameFi) 251
  - 10. Real-World Asset Integration 251
  - Experimental Concepts 251

Chapter 1: Introduction to NFTs and Game Development

1.1. The Evolution of Gaming and Digital Ownership

The gaming industry has undergone significant transformations since its inception. From the early days of arcade machines and simple console games to the modern era of immersive virtual reality and massively multiplayer online games (MMOGs), the evolution has been driven by technological advancements and changing consumer preferences. One of the most revolutionary developments in recent years is the advent of non-fungible tokens (NFTs), which are reshaping digital ownership in the gaming world.

NFTs are unique digital assets that represent ownership of a specific item or piece of content, secured by blockchain technology. Unlike traditional in-game items that are often controlled by the game developers and cannot be traded outside the game's ecosystem, NFTs can be bought, sold, and traded on various marketplaces. This breakthrough is changing the way players perceive and value digital assets.

Historically, gamers have invested significant time and money into acquiring in-game items, characters, and achievements. However, these assets were typically confined to the game in which they were obtained, with no real-world value. The introduction of NFTs changes this paradigm by enabling true ownership and transferability of digital assets, creating new economic opportunities for players and developers alike.

Blockchain technology, the backbone of NFTs, ensures that each token is unique and cannot be duplicated or tampered with. This security and transparency are crucial for establishing trust and value in digital assets. By leveraging blockchain, NFTs provide a decentralized and immutable record of ownership, which is accessible to anyone with an internet connection.

One of the most significant impacts of NFTs in gaming is the creation of player-driven economies. Players can now monetize their in-game achievements and assets, leading to a new era of play-to-earn models. In these models, players can earn NFTs through gameplay, which can then be sold or traded for real money. This shift has the potential to transform gaming from a hobby into a viable source of income for many.

The integration of NFTs into gaming also opens up new possibilities for game design and development. Developers can create games with unique, scarce items that hold real value, fostering a deeper sense of investment and engagement among players. Additionally, NFTs can facilitate cross-game compatibility, allowing players to use their digital assets across multiple games and platforms.

Despite the promising potential of NFTs in gaming, there are also challenges and concerns that need to be addressed. One major issue is the environmental impact of blockchain technology, particularly the energy consumption associated with proof-of-work systems. Developers and blockchain networks are exploring more sustainable solutions, such as proof-of-stake, to mitigate these concerns.

Another challenge is ensuring legal and regulatory compliance in the emerging NFT market. As digital assets gain value and popularity, governments and regulatory bodies are increasingly scrutinizing their use and implications. It is crucial for developers and players to stay informed about the evolving legal landscape to avoid potential pitfalls.

The rise of NFTs also raises ethical considerations, particularly regarding the potential for speculative behavior and market manipulation. As with any new technology, there is a risk of bad actors exploiting the system for personal gain. Ensuring transparency, fairness, and accountability in NFT transactions is essential to maintain trust and integrity in the market.

Looking ahead, the future of NFTs in gaming is filled with exciting possibilities. As technology continues to evolve, we can expect to see even more innovative uses of NFTs, from virtual real estate and digital art to new forms of interactive entertainment. The convergence of gaming and blockchain technology is poised to create new paradigms of digital ownership and value, fundamentally changing the way we interact with virtual worlds.

In conclusion, the evolution of gaming and digital ownership through NFTs represents a significant shift in the industry. By providing true ownership and transferability of digital assets, NFTs are empowering players and developers with new economic opportunities and creative possibilities. While challenges and concerns remain, the potential for NFTs to reshape the gaming landscape is undeniable, marking the beginning of a new era in digital entertainment.

1.2. Understanding NFTs: Beyond the Hype

Non-fungible tokens, or NFTs, have become a buzzword in both the tech and gaming industries. However, to truly understand their potential, it's essential to look beyond the hype and grasp the fundamental aspects of what NFTs are and how they function.

At their core, NFTs are digital assets that represent ownership or proof of authenticity of a unique item or piece of content. Unlike cryptocurrencies such as Bitcoin or Ethereum, which are fungible and can be exchanged on a one-to-one basis, NFTs are distinct and cannot be exchanged equivalently. This uniqueness is what makes NFTs valuable in various applications, especially in gaming and digital art.

NFTs are built on blockchain technology, which provides a decentralized ledger that records all transactions and ownership changes. This ensures that the provenance of each NFT is transparent and traceable. The most common blockchain for NFTs is Ethereum, utilizing standards like ERC-721 and ERC-1155, which define how NFTs are created and managed on the blockchain.

The creation of an NFT, known as minting, involves converting a digital file into a blockchain-based asset. This process typically requires a smart contract, which is a self-executing contract with the terms of the agreement directly written into code. Smart contracts facilitate the automation of transactions and ensure that the rules governing the NFT are enforced without the need for intermediaries.

For example, here's a simple Solidity code snippet for an ERC-721 contract:

```solidity
pragma solidity ^0.8.0;

import "@openzeppelin/contracts/token/ERC721/ERC721.sol";

contract MyNFT is ERC721 {
    uint256 public tokenCounter;

    constructor() ERC721("MyNFT", "MNFT") {
        tokenCounter = 0;
    }

    function createNFT() public returns (uint256) {
        uint256 newItemId = tokenCounter;
        _safeMint(msg.sender, newItemId);
        tokenCounter++;
        return newItemId;
    }
}
```

This basic contract allows the creation of unique NFTs by incrementing a token counter each time a new NFT is minted, ensuring each token has a distinct ID.

One of the most compelling aspects of NFTs is their ability to provide true digital ownership. In traditional digital ecosystems, ownership is often illusory; users might have access to digital items, but they do not truly own them. NFTs change this by embedding ownership directly into the blockchain, allowing users to buy, sell, and trade digital assets freely, independent of any single platform's control.

The gaming industry stands to benefit immensely from this capability. In-game items, characters, and achievements can be tokenized as NFTs, granting players actual ownership. This not only enhances the player experience but also introduces new economic dynamics where players can monetize their skills and assets. The concept of play-to-earn is gaining traction, where players can earn valuable NFTs through gameplay, which can then be sold or traded in open markets.

NFT marketplaces, such as OpenSea and Rarible, play a crucial role in this ecosystem by providing platforms where users can list, buy, and sell NFTs. These marketplaces operate similarly to e-commerce sites but are powered by blockchain technology, ensuring that all transactions are secure and transparent. The emergence of these platforms has democratized access to NFTs, allowing creators and players from around the world to participate in the market.

Despite their potential, NFTs are not without challenges. The environmental impact of blockchain technology, particularly the energy-intensive proof-of-work consensus mechanism, has raised concerns. Some blockchain networks are transitioning to more sustainable models, like proof-of-stake, to address these issues. Additionally, the high costs associated with minting and transacting NFTs, often referred to as gas fees, can be a barrier to entry for many users.

Another significant challenge is the legal and regulatory landscape surrounding NFTs. As digital assets, NFTs occupy a gray area in many jurisdictions, leading to uncertainties regarding their classification, taxation, and legal protections. Developers and users must stay informed about the evolving legal context to navigate potential risks effectively.

The speculative nature of the NFT market also poses risks. The rapid increase in NFT popularity has led to inflated prices and market bubbles. While some NFTs have sold for astronomical sums, others may lose value quickly, leading to financial losses for investors. It is crucial for participants to approach the market with caution and conduct thorough research before making investments.

NFTs also raise important ethical considerations. Issues such as copyright infringement, where digital content is tokenized without the creator's consent, are prevalent. Ensuring that NFTs respect intellectual property rights and promoting fair practices within the ecosystem are vital for maintaining integrity and trust.

Looking ahead, the potential applications of NFTs extend far beyond gaming and digital art. Industries such as real estate, music, and even identity verification are exploring the use of NFTs to enhance transparency and efficiency. The ability to tokenize physical and digital assets opens up new possibilities for innovation and economic growth.

In conclusion, understanding NFTs requires delving into the technology and principles that underpin them. While the hype surrounding NFTs can be overwhelming, their potential to transform digital ownership and create new economic models is undeniable. By addressing the challenges and embracing the opportunities, NFTs can pave the way for a more inclusive and dynamic digital future.

1.3. The Synergy between NFTs and Video Games

The intersection of NFTs and video games is creating a new paradigm in the gaming industry, transforming how players interact with digital assets and how developers design game economies. This synergy between NFTs and video games is not merely a technological integration but a fundamental shift in the gaming experience and economic model.

NFTs bring a new level of ownership to in-game items. Traditionally, in-game assets such as skins, weapons, and characters are controlled by the game developers. Players can earn or purchase these items, but their ownership is limited to the game's ecosystem. NFTs change this by allowing these digital assets to exist on a blockchain, giving players true ownership and the ability to trade these items outside the game.

For example, in a game where rare items are represented as NFTs, players can trade these items on open marketplaces like OpenSea or Rarible. This opens up a secondary market where the value of in-game assets is determined by supply and demand, similar to physical collectibles or art. Players can potentially earn real money from their gaming efforts, incentivizing longer engagement and deeper investment in the game.

The integration of NFTs into games also allows for the creation of interoperable assets. An NFT representing a sword in one game could be designed to be used in another game, provided both games support the same standards. This cross-game compatibility enhances the value of NFTs, as players can carry their investments across different virtual worlds.

Smart contracts play a crucial role in managing these NFTs. They ensure the authenticity, ownership, and transfer of NFTs without the need for intermediaries. Here's a basic example of how a smart contract for a game item might look in Solidity:

```solidity
pragma solidity ^0.8.0;

import "@openzeppelin/contracts/token/ERC721/ERC721.sol";
import "@openzeppelin/contracts/utils/Counters.sol";

contract GameItem is ERC721 {
    using Counters for Counters.Counter;
    Counters.Counter private _tokenIds;

    constructor() ERC721("GameItem", "GMI") {}

    function mintItem(address player, string memory tokenURI) public returns (uint256) {
        _tokenIds.increment();
        uint256 newItemId = _tokenIds.current();
        _mint(player, newItemId);
        _setTokenURI(newItemId, tokenURI);

        return newItemId;
    }
}
```

In this example, the mintItem function allows the creation of new game items as NFTs, assigning ownership to a player and setting a unique token URI that points to the item's metadata.

The economic implications of NFTs in games are profound. Play-to-earn models, where players earn NFTs through gameplay, are becoming increasingly popular. These models create a symbiotic relationship between players and developers. Players are motivated to spend more time in the game, while developers benefit from increased engagement and the potential for secondary market transactions generating royalties.

Furthermore, NFTs can enhance game design by introducing scarcity and exclusivity. Developers can create limited-edition items or events that generate unique NFTs, driving demand and creating a sense of urgency among players. This can lead to higher engagement levels and increased revenue opportunities.

Despite the promising potential, integrating NFTs into games comes with challenges. Ensuring the security and integrity of NFTs is paramount. Blockchain technology is secure, but smart contract vulnerabilities and user error can lead to asset loss or theft. Developers must implement robust security practices and educate players on safe NFT management.

The environmental impact of blockchain technology is another concern. Proof-of-work blockchains, such as Ethereum, consume significant amounts of energy. As the gaming industry adopts NFTs, the demand for energy-intensive blockchain transactions will increase. Transitioning to more sustainable blockchain solutions, like proof-of-stake, is essential to mitigate this impact.

Additionally, there is the issue of accessibility. Not all players are familiar with blockchain technology or have access to cryptocurrency. Simplifying the process of acquiring, storing, and using NFTs is crucial to ensure broad adoption. User-friendly interfaces and seamless integration with existing gaming platforms can help bridge this gap.

Regulatory and legal considerations also play a significant role. The classification of NFTs, their taxation, and compliance with local laws are complex issues that both developers and players need to navigate. Staying informed and proactive about regulatory developments is essential to avoid legal pitfalls.

The community aspect of NFTs in gaming is another important factor. Players are not just consumers; they become part of a broader ecosystem where they can create, trade, and interact with digital assets. This sense of community can drive engagement and loyalty, fostering a vibrant and dynamic gaming environment.

In conclusion, the synergy between NFTs and video games is opening up new possibilities for digital ownership, economic models, and player engagement. By leveraging blockchain technology, developers can create more immersive and rewarding experiences, while players gain true ownership and new opportunities to monetize their gaming efforts. As the industry evolves, addressing the challenges and embracing the opportunities will be key to realizing the full potential of NFTs in gaming.

1.4. Legal and Ethical Considerations in NFT Usage

The integration of NFTs into gaming introduces a myriad of legal and ethical considerations that developers, players, and regulators must navigate. As with any emerging technology, the adoption of NFTs brings about new challenges related to intellectual property, consumer protection, regulatory compliance, and ethical practices.

One of the foremost legal concerns is the issue of intellectual property (IP). NFTs often involve the creation, distribution, and sale of digital assets, which may include art, music, characters, and other creative works. Ensuring that these assets do not infringe on existing copyrights or trademarks is critical. Developers must secure proper licenses and permissions when using third-party content to avoid legal disputes.

For instance, if a game developer wants to include popular music tracks as NFTs within their game, they must negotiate the appropriate rights with the music's copyright holders. Unauthorized use can lead to litigation, financial penalties, and damage to the developer's reputation. Ensuring clear and transparent agreements with IP owners is essential.

Another significant consideration is consumer protection. NFTs, being a new and rapidly evolving market, can be prone to speculative behavior and scams. Developers and marketplace operators must implement measures to protect users from fraud and ensure fair practices. This includes verifying the authenticity of NFTs, providing accurate information about the assets, and offering mechanisms for dispute resolution.

Regulatory compliance is also a crucial aspect of NFT usage. The regulatory landscape for digital assets varies significantly across jurisdictions, and staying compliant requires continuous monitoring and adaptation. In many countries, NFTs may be subject to securities regulations, anti-money laundering (AML) laws, and tax reporting requirements. Developers and platforms must work with legal experts to ensure adherence to these regulations.

For example, in the United States, the Securities and Exchange Commission (SEC) has indicated that certain types of NFTs could be classified as securities, subjecting them to federal securities laws. This classification hinges on whether the NFTs are marketed as investment opportunities or involve profit-sharing arrangements. Developers must be cautious in how they structure and promote their NFT offerings to avoid inadvertently falling under securities regulations.

Data privacy and security are also paramount. As NFTs often involve transactions on blockchain networks, they can expose sensitive user information. Developers must implement robust data protection measures to safeguard user data and comply with privacy laws such as the General Data Protection Regulation (GDPR) in Europe. This includes ensuring that personal data is securely stored and that users have control over their information.

Ethical considerations extend beyond legal compliance. The environmental impact of NFTs, driven by the energy consumption of blockchain networks, has garnered significant attention. Developers and platforms are exploring more sustainable blockchain solutions, such as proof-of-stake, to reduce their carbon footprint. Transparent communication about the environmental impact of NFTs and efforts to mitigate it is essential for maintaining trust with users.

Moreover, the speculative nature of the NFT market can lead to issues of fairness and accessibility. The high prices and volatile nature of NFTs can exclude many players from participating or result in significant financial losses. Developers should strive to create balanced and inclusive systems that allow a broader audience to benefit from NFTs without encouraging reckless speculation.

Community governance and the role of decentralized autonomous organizations (DAOs) can also play a crucial role in addressing ethical considerations. DAOs enable community-driven decision-making, giving players a voice in how NFT projects are managed and developed. This can help ensure that the interests of the broader community are considered and that the project aligns with the values and expectations of its users.

Transparency and accountability are key principles that developers should uphold. This includes clear communication about the nature of NFTs, the mechanics of the underlying blockchain, and the risks involved. Providing educational resources and support can help users make informed decisions and engage responsibly with NFTs.

Additionally, ethical considerations include the fair distribution of profits and recognition. Artists and creators should be fairly compensated for their work, with mechanisms such as royalties embedded into smart contracts to ensure ongoing earnings from secondary sales. This promotes a more equitable distribution of value within the NFT ecosystem.

For example, a smart contract can be designed to automatically allocate a percentage of each secondary sale back to the original creator:

```solidity
pragma solidity ^0.8.0;

import "@openzeppelin/contracts/token/ERC721/ERC721.sol";
import "@openzeppelin/contracts/token/ERC721/extensions/ERC721URIStorage.sol";
import "@openzeppelin/contracts/access/Ownable.sol";

contract RoyaltyNFT is ERC721URIStorage, Ownable {
    uint256 public tokenCounter;
    mapping(uint256 => address) public creators;
    mapping(uint256 => uint256) public royalties;

    constructor() ERC721("RoyaltyNFT", "RNFT") {
        tokenCounter = 0;
    }

    function mintNFT(string memory tokenURI, uint256 royaltyPercentage) public returns (uint256) {
        tokenCounter++;
        uint256 newItemId = tokenCounter;
        _mint(msg.sender, newItemId);
        _setTokenURI(newItemId, tokenURI);
        creators[newItemId] = msg.sender;
        royalties[newItemId] = royaltyPercentage;
        return newItemId;
    }

    function transferFrom(address from, address to, uint256 tokenId) public override {
        super.transferFrom(from, to, tokenId);
```

```
        _payRoyalty(tokenId);
    }

    function _payRoyalty(uint256 tokenId) internal {
        uint256 salePrice = msg.value;
        uint256 royalty = (salePrice * royalties[tokenId]) / 100;
        payable(creators[tokenId]).transfer(royalty);
    }
}
```

This contract ensures that the original creator receives a percentage of the sale price whenever the NFT is resold, promoting long-term benefits for artists.

In summary, while NFTs offer exciting opportunities for innovation and economic growth, they also bring significant legal and ethical challenges. By addressing these challenges proactively and transparently, developers and platforms can create a sustainable and equitable NFT ecosystem that benefits all participants.

1.5. Future Trends: NFTs Reshaping Gaming Economies

The integration of NFTs into gaming is not just a fleeting trend but a significant shift that promises to reshape gaming economies in profound ways. As the technology matures and more developers and players embrace it, several key trends are emerging that will define the future of NFT gaming.

One of the most exciting trends is the rise of play-to-earn (P2E) models. Unlike traditional gaming, where players invest time and money without tangible returns, P2E games reward players with NFTs or cryptocurrency for their in-game achievements. This model transforms gaming from a pastime into a potential source of income, enabling players to monetize their skills and time. Games like Axie Infinity have already demonstrated the viability of this model, where players earn tokens that can be traded for real money.

Another trend is the development of metaverse ecosystems, where NFTs play a central role. The metaverse is a collective virtual shared space, created by the convergence of virtually enhanced physical reality and physically persistent virtual space. NFTs can represent ownership of virtual real estate, avatars, and other assets within these worlds, allowing users to create, trade, and interact in entirely new ways. Companies like Decentraland and The Sandbox are pioneers in this space, offering virtual worlds where every asset is an NFT.

Interoperability between games is becoming increasingly important. NFTs enable assets to move seamlessly across different games and platforms, fostering a more connected and cohesive gaming ecosystem. This interoperability is facilitated by standardized token protocols like ERC-721 and ERC-1155, which ensure that NFTs can be universally recognized and utilized. Players can carry their NFTs from one game to another, enhancing the value and utility of their digital assets.

The role of decentralized autonomous organizations (DAOs) in gaming is also gaining traction. DAOs allow for community governance and decision-making, giving players a direct say in the development and management of games. This democratization can lead to more player-centric game design and foster stronger community engagement. In a DAO-governed game, players might vote on new features, rule changes, or the allocation of resources, ensuring that the game evolves in ways that benefit its community.

Innovations in smart contract technology are further enhancing the functionality of NFTs. Smart contracts can automate complex processes, such as royalty payments, revenue sharing, and asset transfers. For instance, a game developer might implement a smart contract that automatically distributes a percentage of secondary sales to the original creator whenever an NFT is resold. This ensures ongoing revenue for creators and encourages the production of high-quality content.

```solidity
pragma solidity ^0.8.0;

contract RevenueSharing {
    address public creator;
    uint256 public royaltyPercentage;

    constructor(address _creator, uint256 _royaltyPercentage) {
        creator = _creator;
        royaltyPercentage = _royaltyPercentage;
    }

    function distributeRoyalty(uint256 salePrice) external {
        uint256 royalty = (salePrice * royaltyPercentage) / 100;
        payable(creator).transfer(royalty);
    }
}
```

The environmental impact of NFTs is also being addressed through advancements in blockchain technology. With growing awareness of the energy consumption associated with proof-of-work blockchains, there is a shift towards more sustainable solutions like proof-of-stake and layer 2 scaling solutions. Ethereum's transition to Ethereum 2.0, which employs a proof-of-stake mechanism, is a significant step towards reducing the carbon footprint of NFTs.

Furthermore, the integration of artificial intelligence (AI) and machine learning with NFTs is opening up new possibilities. AI can be used to create dynamic and adaptive NFTs that evolve based on player interactions or external data. For example, an AI-generated NFT character could learn and develop new abilities as it participates in different games, providing a unique and personalized gaming experience.

The social and cultural impact of NFTs in gaming is also noteworthy. NFTs enable the creation of unique digital identities and communities centered around shared interests and assets. This fosters a sense of belonging and pride among players, as they own a piece of the game's history or exclusive items that reflect their achievements and status. Social platforms and forums dedicated to NFT gaming communities are proliferating, enhancing player interaction and engagement.

Regulatory developments will continue to shape the future of NFTs in gaming. As governments and regulatory bodies around the world recognize the growing importance of digital assets, they are formulating frameworks to ensure fair practices, consumer protection, and compliance with financial laws. Staying abreast of these regulatory changes is crucial for developers to operate within legal boundaries and build trust with their user base.

Lastly, the concept of fractional ownership is gaining popularity. Fractional NFTs allow multiple individuals to own a share of a high-value asset, making it more accessible to a broader audience. In gaming, this could apply to rare items, virtual real estate, or collective investments in game development projects. Fractional ownership democratizes access to valuable assets and enables collaborative investment models.

In conclusion, the future of NFTs in gaming is marked by innovative trends that are transforming the industry. From play-to-earn models and metaverse ecosystems to interoperability, DAOs, and sustainable blockchain solutions, NFTs are redefining the economic and social dynamics of gaming. As technology and regulatory landscapes evolve, the synergy between NFTs and gaming will continue to create new opportunities and reshape the digital entertainment landscape.

Chapter 2: Basics of NFT Technology

2.1. Blockchain Fundamentals for Gamers

Blockchain technology forms the backbone of NFTs, providing the infrastructure needed for secure, transparent, and decentralized digital asset transactions. Understanding the fundamentals of blockchain is essential for gamers looking to engage with NFTs effectively.

A blockchain is a distributed ledger that records transactions across multiple computers in a way that ensures security and transparency. Each transaction is grouped into a block, which is then added to a chain of previous transactions. This structure makes it nearly impossible to alter past records without changing all subsequent blocks, thus providing robust security.

One of the key features of blockchain is decentralization. Unlike traditional centralized systems where a single entity controls the database, blockchain relies on a network of nodes (computers) to validate and record transactions. This decentralization enhances security and trust, as no single point of failure or manipulation exists.

Consensus mechanisms are critical to blockchain's operation. These mechanisms ensure that all nodes agree on the state of the blockchain. The most common consensus mechanisms are proof of work (PoW) and proof of stake (PoS). PoW, used by Bitcoin and currently by Ethereum, requires nodes to solve complex mathematical problems to validate transactions. PoS, which Ethereum is transitioning to, relies on validators who stake their cryptocurrency to secure the network.

Smart contracts are self-executing contracts with the terms of the agreement directly written into code. They run on the blockchain, automatically enforcing the contract's terms when predetermined conditions are met. Smart contracts are fundamental to NFTs, as they manage the creation, ownership, and transfer of these digital assets.

For example, a simple smart contract for transferring an NFT might look like this in Solidity:

```solidity
pragma solidity ^0.8.0;

contract SimpleNFT {
    mapping(address => uint256) public balances;
    address public owner;

    constructor() {
        owner = msg.sender;
    }

    function mint(address to, uint256 amount) public {
        require(msg.sender == owner, "Only the owner can mint tokens");
        balances[to] += amount;
    }
```

```
    function transfer(address to, uint256 amount) public {
        require(balances[msg.sender] >= amount, "Insufficient balance");
        balances[msg.sender] -= amount;
        balances[to] += amount;
    }
}
```

This contract allows the owner to mint tokens and users to transfer them, illustrating the basic principles of NFT creation and transfer.

Blockchain's immutability ensures that once a transaction is recorded, it cannot be altered or deleted. This feature is particularly important for NFTs, as it guarantees the provenance and authenticity of digital assets. Each NFT's history, including its creation and ownership transfers, is permanently recorded on the blockchain.

Interoperability is another crucial aspect of blockchain technology. It enables different blockchains and their assets to interact seamlessly. For NFTs, this means that a digital asset created on one platform can be recognized and used on another, provided both platforms support the same standards, such as ERC-721 or ERC-1155.

Blockchain also supports decentralized applications (dApps), which run on a blockchain network rather than a centralized server. dApps leverage smart contracts to provide services without intermediaries, enhancing transparency and reducing costs. Many NFT marketplaces and games operate as dApps, offering users decentralized access to their digital assets.

Despite its advantages, blockchain technology faces challenges, particularly regarding scalability. As the number of transactions increases, the network can become congested, leading to slower transaction times and higher fees. Solutions like layer 2 scaling, sharding, and transitioning to PoS aim to address these issues and improve blockchain efficiency.

Security is paramount in blockchain technology. While the decentralized nature of blockchain enhances security, smart contract vulnerabilities and hacking attempts remain concerns. Developers must adhere to best practices in smart contract development and conduct thorough audits to mitigate risks.

Blockchain's transparency is a double-edged sword. While it ensures trust and accountability, it also raises privacy concerns. Public blockchains expose transaction details to anyone with access to the network, potentially compromising user privacy. Solutions like zero-knowledge proofs and privacy-focused blockchains aim to address these concerns by enabling private transactions.

In conclusion, blockchain technology provides the foundational infrastructure for NFTs, offering security, transparency, and decentralization. Understanding these fundamentals helps gamers appreciate the significance of NFTs and navigate the evolving landscape of digital assets effectively.

2.2. Decoding Smart Contracts and Their Role in NFTs

Smart contracts are the backbone of NFTs, automating the creation, ownership, and transfer of these unique digital assets. To fully grasp their role, it's essential to decode what smart contracts are and how they function within the blockchain ecosystem.

A smart contract is a self-executing contract with the terms of the agreement written directly into code. These contracts reside on a blockchain, where they automatically enforce and execute the terms when predetermined conditions are met. This automation eliminates the need for intermediaries, reducing costs and enhancing efficiency.

Smart contracts operate on blockchain platforms that support programmable transactions. Ethereum is the most prominent blockchain for smart contracts, using its native programming language, Solidity. Solidity allows developers to write complex smart contracts that manage various functions, from simple transactions to intricate decentralized applications (dApps).

For instance, an NFT smart contract typically includes functions for minting (creating) new tokens, transferring ownership, and verifying authenticity. Here's a basic example of an NFT smart contract in Solidity:

```solidity
pragma solidity ^0.8.0;

import "@openzeppelin/contracts/token/ERC721/ERC721.sol";

contract MyNFT is ERC721 {
    uint256 public tokenCounter;

    constructor() ERC721("MyNFT", "MNFT") {
        tokenCounter = 0;
    }

    function createNFT() public returns (uint256) {
        uint256 newItemId = tokenCounter;
        _mint(msg.sender, newItemId);
        tokenCounter++;
        return newItemId;
    }
}
```

This contract defines a simple NFT where each new token is minted with a unique identifier, ensuring its uniqueness and ownership.

The decentralized nature of smart contracts ensures that they are not controlled by any single entity. Once deployed, they run autonomously on the blockchain, with their code and transactions visible to all network participants. This transparency fosters trust and accountability, as anyone can verify the contract's behavior and transactions.

Security is a critical aspect of smart contracts. While the blockchain itself is secure, vulnerabilities in smart contract code can lead to exploits and financial losses. Developers must follow best practices in coding, conduct thorough audits, and employ formal verification methods to ensure the security of their contracts.

Smart contracts facilitate the interoperability of NFTs across different platforms and applications. Standards like ERC-721 and ERC-1155 define the structure and behavior of NFTs, ensuring they can be recognized and used by various dApps and marketplaces. This interoperability enhances the utility and value of NFTs, as they are not confined to a single game or platform.

In addition to basic functionalities like minting and transferring, smart contracts can incorporate complex features such as royalties and programmable behaviors. For example, a smart contract can be programmed to automatically pay a royalty to the original creator whenever the NFT is resold. This ensures that creators continue to benefit financially from their work even after the initial sale.

```solidity
pragma solidity ^0.8.0;

import "@openzeppelin/contracts/token/ERC721/ERC721.sol";
import "@openzeppelin/contracts/access/Ownable.sol";

contract RoyaltyNFT is ERC721, Ownable {
    uint256 public tokenCounter;
    mapping(uint256 => uint256) public royalties;

    constructor() ERC721("RoyaltyNFT", "RNFT") {
        tokenCounter = 0;
    }

    function createNFT(uint256 royalty) public onlyOwner returns (uint256) {
        uint256 newItemId = tokenCounter;
        _mint(msg.sender, newItemId);
        royalties[newItemId] = royalty;
        tokenCounter++;
        return newItemId;
    }

    function transferFrom(address from, address to, uint256 tokenId) public override {
        super.transferFrom(from, to, tokenId);
        _payRoyalty(tokenId);
    }

    function _payRoyalty(uint256 tokenId) internal {
        uint256 salePrice = msg.value;
        uint256 royalty = (salePrice * royalties[tokenId]) / 100;
        payable(owner()).transfer(royalty);
```

```
    }
}
```

This example shows a smart contract that mints NFTs with an embedded royalty mechanism, ensuring creators receive a percentage of resale proceeds.

The programmability of smart contracts extends to creating dynamic NFTs, which can change based on external conditions or interactions. For example, an NFT representing a game character could evolve and gain new abilities as the player progresses, with these changes encoded in the smart contract.

The potential applications of smart contracts go beyond gaming and NFTs. They can be used in various industries for automating transactions, managing supply chains, handling legal agreements, and more. The flexibility and automation they offer can revolutionize how contracts and transactions are managed in the digital age.

However, the widespread adoption of smart contracts also raises legal and regulatory considerations. Since they operate autonomously and are often cross-border, determining jurisdiction, enforceability, and compliance can be complex. Legal frameworks are evolving to address these challenges, ensuring that smart contracts can be integrated into existing legal systems.

In conclusion, smart contracts are integral to the functionality and utility of NFTs. They provide the automation, security, and transparency needed to manage digital assets effectively. By understanding and leveraging smart contracts, developers can unlock the full potential of NFTs and create innovative, decentralized applications that reshape various industries.

2.3. Token Standards: ERC-721 and ERC-1155 Explained

Token standards are essential for ensuring the interoperability, functionality, and widespread adoption of NFTs. Two of the most important standards in the Ethereum ecosystem are ERC-721 and ERC-1155. Understanding these standards is crucial for developers looking to create and manage NFTs effectively.

ERC-721 is the original standard for non-fungible tokens (NFTs) on the Ethereum blockchain. It defines a minimum interface for smart contracts to manage, track, and transfer unique tokens. Each ERC-721 token has a unique identifier, distinguishing it from other tokens, making it ideal for representing unique assets like art, collectibles, and in-game items.

An ERC-721 contract includes functions for transferring tokens, approving third parties to manage tokens, and querying token details. Here's a basic example of an ERC-721 contract in Solidity:

```solidity
pragma solidity ^0.8.0;

import "@openzeppelin/contracts/token/ERC721/ERC721.sol";
import "@openzeppelin/contracts/access/Ownable.sol";
```

```
contract MyERC721Token is ERC721, Ownable {
    uint256 public tokenCounter;

    constructor() ERC721("MyERC721Token", "M721") {
        tokenCounter = 0;
    }

    function mintToken(address to) public onlyOwner returns (uint256) {
        uint256 newTokenId = tokenCounter;
        _mint(to, newTokenId);
        tokenCounter++;
        return newTokenId;
    }
}
```

This contract allows the owner to mint unique tokens, each with a distinct ID, which can be transferred and tracked.

ERC-1155, on the other hand, is a multi-token standard that supports both fungible and non-fungible tokens within a single contract. This versatility makes ERC-1155 more efficient and flexible, particularly for gaming and complex applications where different types of assets are required.

An ERC-1155 contract can manage multiple token types, reducing the need for multiple contracts and saving on deployment costs. It also introduces batch operations, allowing multiple tokens to be transferred in a single transaction, enhancing efficiency.

Here's an example of an ERC-1155 contract in Solidity:

```
pragma solidity ^0.8.0;

import "@openzeppelin/contracts/token/ERC1155/ERC1155.sol";
import "@openzeppelin/contracts/access/Ownable.sol";

contract MyERC1155Token is ERC1155, Ownable {
    uint256 public constant GOLD = 0;
    uint256 public constant SILVER = 1;
    uint256 public constant BRONZE = 2;

    constructor() ERC1155("https://api.mygame.com/metadata/{id}.json") {
        _mint(msg.sender, GOLD, 10**18, "");
        _mint(msg.sender, SILVER, 10**27, "");
        _mint(msg.sender, BRONZE, 10**27, "");
    }

    function mint(address to, uint256 id, uint256 amount, bytes memory data) public onlyOwner {
        _mint(to, id, amount, data);
```

        }
}

This contract defines three token types (GOLD, SILVER, and BRONZE) and allows the owner to mint them as needed.

The primary advantage of ERC-1155 over ERC-721 is its efficiency in managing and transferring multiple tokens. For games that involve numerous types of assets, such as weapons, armor, and consumables, ERC-1155 provides a streamlined solution. It reduces the complexity and cost associated with deploying and interacting with multiple contracts.

Both ERC-721 and ERC-1155 standards support metadata, which provides additional information about the tokens. Metadata can include details like the token's name, description, and image URL, enhancing the richness and usability of NFTs. This metadata is often stored off-chain, with the token's smart contract referencing the metadata URL.

For example, an ERC-721 token might have metadata stored in a JSON file, referenced by the contract:

```
{
    "name": "Rare Sword",
    "description": "A rare and powerful sword with unique abilities.",
    "image": "https://game-assets.com/sword.png"
}
```

The contract would include a function to return the token's metadata URL:

```
function tokenURI(uint256 tokenId) public view virtual override returns (string memory) {
    return string(abi.encodePacked(baseURI, tokenId.toString(), ".json"));
}
```

Token standards like ERC-721 and ERC-1155 ensure that NFTs can be recognized and used across different platforms and applications. They provide a common framework that developers can rely on, facilitating interoperability and integration.

These standards also enable secondary markets, where NFTs can be bought, sold, and traded. Marketplaces like OpenSea, Rarible, and Mintable support ERC-721 and ERC-1155 tokens, allowing users to easily list and trade their NFTs. This secondary market adds liquidity and value to NFTs, making them more attractive to both creators and collectors.

In conclusion, ERC-721 and ERC-1155 are foundational standards for NFTs on the Ethereum blockchain. ERC-721 provides a framework for unique, non-fungible tokens, while ERC-1155 offers a versatile solution for managing multiple token types. Understanding these standards is essential for developers and users to leverage the full potential of NFTs in gaming and other applications.

2.4. The Mechanics of Minting NFTs

Minting is the process of creating new NFTs and recording them on the blockchain. This process involves deploying a smart contract, defining the properties of the NFTs, and generating unique tokens. Understanding the mechanics of minting NFTs is crucial for developers and artists looking to create and distribute their digital assets.

The first step in minting an NFT is to deploy a smart contract on a blockchain that supports NFTs, such as Ethereum. This contract defines the rules and properties of the NFTs, including their name, symbol, and metadata. For example, an ERC-721 contract might look like this:

```solidity
pragma solidity ^0.8.0;

import "@openzeppelin/contracts/token/ERC721/ERC721.sol";
import "@openzeppelin/contracts/access/Ownable.sol";

contract MyNFTCollection is ERC721, Ownable {
    uint256 public tokenCounter;

    constructor() ERC721("MyNFTCollection", "MNFT") {
        tokenCounter = 0;
    }

    function mintNFT(address to, string memory tokenURI) public onlyOwner returns (uint256) {
        uint256 newItemId = tokenCounter;
        _mint(to, newItemId);
        _setTokenURI(newItemId, tokenURI);
        tokenCounter++;
        return newItemId;
    }
}
```

This contract includes functions for minting new NFTs and setting their metadata, ensuring each token is unique and identifiable.

The mintNFT function in the contract allows the owner to create new NFTs by specifying the recipient's address and the token URI, which points to the metadata of the NFT. The tokenCounter variable ensures that each token has a unique identifier.

Metadata is an essential part of an NFT, providing additional information such as the token's name, description, and image. This metadata is typically stored off-chain in a JSON file and referenced by the token URI. For example:

```
{
    "name": "Unique Artwork",
    "description": "A one-of-a-kind digital artwork.",
    "image": "https://myartwork.com/image.png"
}
```

After deploying the smart contract, the next step is to mint the NFTs. This involves calling the `mintNFT` function and providing the necessary parameters. The smart contract then generates a new token, assigns it a unique identifier, and records it on the blockchain.

Minting NFTs incurs transaction fees, known as gas fees, which are paid in the blockchain's native cryptocurrency (e.g., ETH for Ethereum). These fees compensate the network for processing and validating the transaction. Gas fees can vary based on network congestion and the complexity of the transaction.

Once minted, the NFTs are recorded on the blockchain, ensuring their authenticity and ownership. The blockchain provides a transparent and immutable ledger of all transactions, making it easy to verify the provenance and history of each NFT.

Minting can be done through various platforms and tools that simplify the process for creators. Platforms like OpenSea, Rarible, and Mintable offer user-friendly interfaces for minting NFTs without requiring in-depth knowledge of smart contract development. These platforms handle the technical aspects, allowing creators to focus on their art and content.

For example, OpenSea provides a form for uploading metadata and minting NFTs directly from their website. The platform generates the necessary smart contract and records the NFT on the blockchain, streamlining the process for users.

In addition to the standard minting process, some platforms offer advanced features like batch minting and customizable contracts. Batch minting allows creators to generate multiple NFTs in a single transaction, reducing gas fees and increasing efficiency. Customizable contracts enable creators to define specific rules and properties for their NFTs, providing greater flexibility and control.

The minting process also includes considerations for royalties and secondary sales. Many NFT platforms allow creators to specify a royalty percentage, ensuring they receive a share of future sales. This is implemented through smart contracts that automatically distribute a portion of the sale proceeds to the original creator whenever the NFT is resold.

```solidity
pragma solidity ^0.8.0;

contract RoyaltyNFT is ERC721, Ownable {
    uint256 public tokenCounter;
    mapping(uint256 => uint256) public royalties;

    constructor() ERC721("RoyaltyNFT", "RNFT") {
        tokenCounter = 0;
    }

    function mintNFT(address to, string memory tokenURI, uint256 royalty) public onlyOwner returns (uint256) {
        uint256 newItemId = tokenCounter;
        _mint(to, newItemId);
        _setTokenURI(newItemId, tokenURI);
        royalties[newItemId] = royalty;
```

```
        tokenCounter++;
        return newItemId;
    }

    function transferFrom(address from, address to, uint256 tokenId) public override {
        super.transferFrom(from, to, tokenId);
        _payRoyalty(tokenId);
    }

    function _payRoyalty(uint256 tokenId) internal {
        uint256 salePrice = msg.value;
        uint256 royalty = (salePrice * royalties[tokenId]) / 100;
        payable(owner()).transfer(royalty);
    }
}
```

This contract ensures that the original creator receives a percentage of the sale price whenever the NFT is resold, promoting long-term benefits for artists.

In conclusion, minting NFTs involves deploying a smart contract, defining the token properties and metadata, and recording the tokens on the blockchain. This process ensures the authenticity, ownership, and traceability of digital assets. By leveraging platforms and tools, creators can easily mint NFTs and participate in the growing digital economy.

2.5. Understanding NFT Marketplaces and Exchanges

NFT marketplaces and exchanges are the platforms where NFTs are bought, sold, and traded. These platforms provide the infrastructure for creators to list their NFTs and for buyers to discover, purchase, and collect digital assets. Understanding how these marketplaces work is crucial for anyone involved in the NFT ecosystem.

NFT marketplaces can be broadly categorized into two types: centralized and decentralized. Centralized marketplaces are operated by a single entity that manages the platform, processes transactions, and enforces rules. Examples include OpenSea, Rarible, and Foundation. These platforms offer user-friendly interfaces and additional services like metadata hosting, making it easier for users to mint and trade NFTs.

Decentralized marketplaces, on the other hand, operate on blockchain networks without a central authority. They rely on smart contracts to facilitate transactions, providing greater transparency and security. Examples include AtomicMarket and Zora. Decentralized marketplaces align with the core principles of blockchain technology, promoting decentralization and trustlessness.

OpenSea is one of the largest and most popular NFT marketplaces. It supports a wide range of NFTs, including art, collectibles, virtual real estate, and in-game items. OpenSea allows users to mint NFTs directly on the platform, list them for sale, and participate in auctions. The platform charges a service fee for each transaction, which is typically a percentage of the sale price.

Rarible is another leading marketplace that combines social features with NFT trading. It allows users to create, buy, and sell NFTs, while also offering governance tokens (RARI) that enable users to participate in platform decisions. Rarible supports both fixed-price sales and auctions, providing flexibility for sellers and buyers.

Decentralized exchanges (DEXs) like AtomicMarket operate on smart contracts, ensuring that transactions are executed securely and transparently. AtomicMarket is part of the AtomicAssets standard, which supports a range of assets on the EOS blockchain. The platform allows users to create and trade NFTs without relying on a central authority, enhancing trust and decentralization.

When listing an NFT on a marketplace, creators must provide metadata that describes the asset. This metadata typically includes the name, description, image, and other relevant details. The metadata is often stored off-chain and referenced by the NFT's smart contract. For example:

```
{
    "name": "Digital Art Piece",
    "description": "A unique digital artwork by Artist X.",
    "image": "https://artstorage.com/image.png"
}
```

Marketplaces also offer features like auctions, where buyers can bid on NFTs over a specified period. Auctions can create excitement and drive higher prices for rare or sought-after assets. Sellers can set a reserve price, ensuring that the NFT is not sold below a certain value, and buyers can place bids until the auction ends.

Royalties are an important aspect of NFT marketplaces. Many platforms allow creators to set a royalty percentage, which is automatically paid to them whenever the NFT is resold. This ensures that creators continue to benefit from the increasing value of their work. Royalties are implemented through smart contracts, which enforce the payment terms without intermediaries.

Security is a critical consideration for NFT marketplaces. Centralized platforms must implement robust security measures to protect user data and assets, while decentralized platforms rely on the inherent security of blockchain technology. Users should also be aware of common scams and phishing attempts, ensuring they interact only with trusted platforms and verify the authenticity of NFTs before purchasing.

Gas fees are another factor to consider. These are transaction fees paid to the blockchain network for processing transactions. On platforms like Ethereum, gas fees can fluctuate based on network congestion and the complexity of the transaction. Some marketplaces offer solutions to reduce gas fees, such as batching transactions or using layer 2 scaling solutions.

Interoperability is a key feature of NFT marketplaces. Many platforms support multiple blockchain standards, allowing users to trade NFTs across different networks. For example, OpenSea supports both ERC-721 and ERC-1155 tokens, providing flexibility for creators and collectors. Cross-chain interoperability is also emerging, enabling NFTs to move seamlessly between different blockchains.

Community and social features are increasingly important in NFT marketplaces. Platforms like Rarible and Foundation emphasize community engagement, allowing users to follow artists, like and comment on NFTs, and participate in community governance. These features foster a sense of belonging and enhance the overall user experience.

In conclusion, NFT marketplaces and exchanges are vital components of the NFT ecosystem, providing the infrastructure for minting, trading, and discovering digital assets. By understanding how these platforms operate, creators and collectors can navigate the NFT market effectively and take advantage of the opportunities it offers. Whether using centralized or decentralized platforms, the principles of security, transparency, and community engagement remain paramount.

Chapter 3: Designing NFTs for Games

3.1. Conceptualizing NFT Assets in Gaming

The first step in integrating NFTs into a game is conceptualizing the assets that will be tokenized. These assets can range from in-game items like weapons and armor to characters, virtual real estate, and even unique player achievements. The key is to identify what types of assets will provide value to players and enhance their gaming experience.

When conceptualizing NFT assets, it's important to consider the game's genre and mechanics. For example, in a role-playing game (RPG), tokenizing characters, rare items, and spells can add depth to the game. In a strategy game, tokenizing unique units or buildings might be more appropriate. The goal is to create assets that are meaningful and desirable within the context of the game.

Scarcity and uniqueness are critical factors in the value of NFT assets. Unlike traditional in-game items that can be duplicated infinitely, NFTs are unique or part of a limited series. This scarcity can drive demand and create a sense of exclusivity among players. Developers must carefully balance the supply of NFTs to maintain their value and appeal.

Metadata plays a crucial role in defining the properties of NFT assets. This metadata includes details such as the asset's name, description, attributes, and visuals. For instance, a rare sword in an RPG might have metadata specifying its damage, special abilities, and appearance. Properly structured metadata ensures that each NFT is distinct and easily identifiable.

Here is an example of JSON metadata for an NFT sword:

```
{
    "name": "Sword of Eternity",
    "description": "A legendary sword with immense power.",
    "attributes": {
        "damage": 100,
        "durability": 500,
        "special_ability": "Fire Blast"
    },
    "image": "https://game-assets.com/sword_of_eternity.png"
}
```

Interoperability should also be considered during the conceptualization phase. Designing NFT assets that can be used across multiple games or platforms increases their utility and value. This requires adherence to standardized token protocols like ERC-721 or ERC-1155, which facilitate cross-platform compatibility.

Player ownership and customization are additional aspects to consider. Allowing players to customize their NFT assets, such as changing the appearance of a character or upgrading a weapon, can enhance the sense of ownership and investment. These customizations can be reflected in the NFT's metadata and stored on the blockchain.

Another consideration is the potential for dynamic NFTs, which can evolve based on player actions or in-game events. For example, a character NFT could gain new skills or levels as the player progresses through the game. This dynamic nature adds a layer of engagement and personalization to the gaming experience.

The economic model surrounding NFT assets is also crucial. Developers must decide how NFTs will be distributed, whether through gameplay, purchases, or events. They should also consider the secondary market, where players can trade NFTs. Implementing royalties ensures that creators continue to benefit from secondary sales, promoting a sustainable economic ecosystem.

It's essential to ensure that NFT integration aligns with the overall game design and narrative. NFT assets should feel like a natural extension of the game world rather than an external addition. This coherence enhances immersion and player satisfaction.

Finally, developers must consider the ethical implications of NFT integration. Ensuring fair access to NFT assets and avoiding pay-to-win scenarios are important to maintain a balanced and enjoyable game. Transparency in the rarity and distribution of NFTs is also vital to build trust with the player community.

In summary, conceptualizing NFT assets for a game involves careful consideration of the game's genre, mechanics, and player experience. Scarcity, metadata, interoperability, player ownership, dynamic properties, and economic models are key factors that contribute to the value and appeal of NFT assets. By thoughtfully integrating NFTs, developers can enhance gameplay and create a vibrant, player-driven economy.

3.2. Artistic and Technical Considerations

The successful integration of NFTs in games requires attention to both artistic and technical considerations. The visual and functional aspects of NFT assets play a significant role in their appeal and usability. This section explores the key artistic and technical factors that developers need to address.

From an artistic perspective, the design of NFT assets should align with the game's overall aesthetic and theme. High-quality visuals and unique designs make NFTs more attractive to players. Collaborating with skilled artists ensures that each asset is visually appealing and distinct. The art style should be consistent with the game's graphics to maintain immersion.

For example, in a fantasy RPG, NFT assets like weapons and armor should have intricate designs that reflect their magical properties and lore. In a sci-fi game, futuristic and high-tech visuals would be more appropriate. The goal is to create assets that enhance the game's world and storytelling.

Creating variations of NFT assets can also add depth and variety. Different versions of a weapon, each with unique visual elements and attributes, can make the collection more interesting. Limited-edition designs or collaborations with renowned artists can further increase the desirability and value of NFTs.

Technical considerations involve ensuring that NFT assets are seamlessly integrated into the game. This includes defining the attributes and functionalities of each asset through metadata. The metadata must be well-structured and compatible with the blockchain standards used by the game.

Developers need to choose the appropriate token standards for their NFTs. ERC-721 is suitable for unique, one-of-a-kind assets, while ERC-1155 is ideal for managing multiple types of assets within a single contract. The choice of standard impacts how NFTs are minted, transferred, and interacted with.

Here is an example of a Solidity contract for an ERC-1155 token:

```solidity
pragma solidity ^0.8.0;

import "@openzeppelin/contracts/token/ERC1155/ERC1155.sol";
import "@openzeppelin/contracts/access/Ownable.sol";

contract GameAssets is ERC1155, Ownable {
    uint256 public constant SWORD = 0;
    uint256 public constant SHIELD = 1;

    constructor() ERC1155("https://game-assets.com/metadata/{id}.json") {
        _mint(msg.sender, SWORD, 100, "");
        _mint(msg.sender, SHIELD, 50, "");
    }

    function mint(address to, uint256 id, uint256 amount) public onlyOwner {
        _mint(to, id, amount, "");
    }
}
```

This contract defines two types of assets (SWORD and SHIELD) and allows the owner to mint new tokens as needed.

Performance is another critical technical consideration. The integration of NFTs should not negatively impact the game's performance. Efficient coding practices and optimization are necessary to ensure that the game runs smoothly, even with the added complexity of blockchain interactions.

Security is paramount in NFT integration. Smart contracts must be thoroughly audited to prevent vulnerabilities that could lead to exploits or asset theft. Implementing secure coding practices and using established libraries like OpenZeppelin can help mitigate risks.

User experience (UX) design is essential for making NFT interactions intuitive and enjoyable. The process of acquiring, viewing, and trading NFTs should be straightforward and accessible. Integrating wallets, such as MetaMask, into the game interface allows players to manage their NFTs easily. Clear instructions and tutorials can help onboard players who are new to blockchain technology.

Cross-platform compatibility ensures that NFT assets can be used across different devices and platforms. Whether players are on PC, console, or mobile, their NFTs should be accessible and functional. This requires careful planning and testing to ensure consistent behavior across various environments.

Interoperability extends beyond platforms to other games and applications. Designing NFTs with interoperability in mind allows players to use their assets in multiple games, increasing their utility and value. This requires adherence to common standards and collaboration with other developers.

Scalability is a significant concern, especially for games with large player bases. The chosen blockchain must handle a high volume of transactions without causing delays or excessive fees. Layer 2 solutions and sidechains can help improve scalability and reduce costs.

In conclusion, the artistic and technical considerations of NFT integration in games are multifaceted. High-quality visuals, well-structured metadata, appropriate token standards, performance optimization, security, user experience, cross-platform compatibility, interoperability, and scalability are all crucial factors. By addressing these considerations, developers can create compelling NFT assets that enhance the game and provide value to players.

3.3. Creating Unique and Desirable NFTs

Creating unique and desirable NFTs requires a blend of creativity, technical expertise, and understanding of market dynamics. The goal is to design NFTs that not only look appealing but also offer value and utility to players. This section explores strategies and best practices for creating NFTs that stand out and attract interest.

The first step in creating unique NFTs is to focus on originality. Original designs, concepts, and functionalities set NFTs apart from the multitude of digital assets available. Collaborating with talented artists and designers can result in visually stunning and unique NFTs that capture the essence of the game.

Rarity and scarcity are powerful drivers of desirability. Limited-edition NFTs or assets that are difficult to obtain in the game can create a sense of exclusivity. By clearly communicating the rarity of each NFT, developers can enhance their perceived value. For example, a game might have only 100 copies of a legendary sword, making it a coveted item among players.

Dynamic and evolving NFTs add a layer of engagement. NFTs that change based on in-game achievements or player interactions are more interesting and valuable. For instance, a character NFT that gains new abilities or appearance changes as the player progresses through the game provides a unique and personalized experience.

Here's an example of a dynamic NFT contract in Solidity:

```solidity
pragma solidity ^0.8.0;

import "@openzeppelin/contracts/token/ERC721/ERC721.sol";
```

```solidity
import "@openzeppelin/contracts/access/Ownable.sol";

contract DynamicNFT is ERC721, Ownable {
    uint256 public tokenCounter;

    struct Attributes {
        uint256 level;
        string ability;
    }

    mapping(uint256 => Attributes) public tokenAttributes;

    constructor() ERC721("DynamicNFT", "DNFT") {
        tokenCounter = 0;
    }

    function mintNFT(address to, string memory initialAbility) public onlyOwner returns (uint256) {
        uint256 newItemId = tokenCounter;
        _mint(to, newItemId);
        tokenAttributes[newItemId] = Attributes({level: 1, ability: initialAbility});
        tokenCounter++;
        return newItemId;
    }

    function levelUp(uint256 tokenId) public {
        require(ownerOf(tokenId) == msg.sender, "Only the owner can level up");
        tokenAttributes[tokenId].level++;
    }

    function updateAbility(uint256 tokenId, string memory newAbility) public {
        require(ownerOf(tokenId) == msg.sender, "Only the owner can update ability");
        tokenAttributes[tokenId].ability = newAbility;
    }
}
```

This contract allows the owner of an NFT to level up their token and update its abilities, making it dynamic and interactive.

Interactivity and utility are key factors in making NFTs desirable. NFTs that serve a functional purpose within the game, such as granting special abilities or unlocking exclusive content, provide tangible benefits to players. These functional NFTs enhance gameplay and encourage players to invest in them.

Storytelling and lore can significantly enhance the appeal of NFTs. Embedding rich narratives and backstories into NFTs makes them more engaging and meaningful. Players are more likely to value and cherish NFTs that have a story or history attached to them. For example, an NFT representing a mythical creature could come with a detailed lore about its origins and powers.

Collaboration with influencers and communities can boost the desirability of NFTs. Influencers can promote NFTs to their followers, creating hype and interest. Engaging with the player community to gather feedback and ideas can also lead to the creation of NFTs that resonate with the audience.

Gamification and reward systems can drive interest in NFTs. Implementing challenges, quests, or events that reward players with exclusive NFTs can increase engagement and excitement. For example, completing a difficult in-game quest might reward players with a unique NFT that signifies their achievement.

Customization options enhance the personal connection players have with their NFTs. Allowing players to modify and personalize their NFTs, such as changing colors, adding accessories, or naming their assets, makes them more valuable and meaningful. These customizations can be reflected in the NFT's metadata.

The market strategy for launching NFTs is crucial. Timing, pricing, and marketing campaigns play significant roles in the success of an NFT launch. Setting a fair price that reflects the value and rarity of the NFT, coupled with effective marketing to generate buzz, can lead to successful sales and high demand.

Sustainability and ethical considerations are increasingly important to players. Ensuring that the minting and trading of NFTs are environmentally friendly and adhere to ethical standards can enhance their appeal. Adopting sustainable blockchain solutions and transparent practices builds trust and loyalty among players.

In conclusion, creating unique and desirable NFTs involves a combination of originality, rarity, dynamic properties, interactivity, storytelling, collaboration, gamification, customization, strategic marketing, and ethical considerations. By focusing on these aspects, developers can design NFTs that not only attract interest but also provide lasting value and engagement to players.

3.4. Balancing Game Economy with NFT Integration

Integrating NFTs into a game's economy requires careful planning and balance to ensure that it enhances the gaming experience without disrupting the overall economic system. This section explores strategies and best practices for achieving a balanced game economy with NFTs.

The primary goal of integrating NFTs should be to enhance player engagement and enjoyment. NFTs should add value to the game by offering unique experiences, items, and rewards that are meaningful to players. However, it's crucial to avoid creating a pay-to-win environment where players can purchase significant advantages over others.

One approach to maintaining balance is to ensure that NFTs provide cosmetic or non-gameplay advantages. For example, NFTs could represent unique skins, avatars, or decorative items that personalize the player's experience without affecting gameplay mechanics. This way, NFTs enhance the visual appeal and player identity without creating unfair advantages.

Another strategy is to implement earning mechanisms where players can acquire NFTs through gameplay achievements. This play-to-earn model rewards players for their time and skill, ensuring that NFTs are accessible to all players, not just those willing to spend money. Completing quests, winning battles, or achieving high scores can be ways to earn NFTs.

For example, a game could reward players with an NFT for completing a difficult dungeon:

```solidity
pragma solidity ^0.8.0;

import "@openzeppelin/contracts/token/ERC721/ERC721.sol";
import "@openzeppelin/contracts/access/Ownable.sol";

contract GameRewards is ERC721, Ownable {
    uint256 public tokenCounter;

    constructor() ERC721("GameRewards", "GWRD") {
        tokenCounter = 0;
    }

    function rewardNFT(address to) public onlyOwner returns (uint256) {
        uint256 newItemId = tokenCounter;
        _mint(to, newItemId);
        tokenCounter++;
        return newItemId;
    }
}
```

This contract allows the game owner to mint and reward NFTs to players for their achievements.

Balancing supply and demand is crucial for maintaining a healthy game economy. Over-minting NFTs can lead to inflation, reducing their value and appeal. Conversely, making NFTs too scarce can limit player engagement and market activity. Developers must carefully monitor and adjust the supply of NFTs based on player activity and market trends.

NFTs can also be integrated into crafting and upgrading systems. Players can collect and combine different NFTs or in-game items to create more valuable or powerful assets. This adds depth to the game's economy by encouraging players to engage in various activities to gather the necessary components.

Implementing a robust marketplace within the game allows players to buy, sell, and trade NFTs. This player-driven economy can create dynamic market conditions where supply and demand determine the value of assets. Developers should ensure that the marketplace is secure, fair, and user-friendly to facilitate smooth transactions.

Economic sinks are mechanisms that remove currency or items from the game, helping to control inflation. Introducing sinks, such as transaction fees, crafting costs, or limited-use items, can help balance the influx of NFTs and in-game currency. These mechanisms ensure that the game economy remains stable and sustainable.

Royalties and secondary sales can benefit both creators and the game economy. By implementing smart contracts that pay royalties to creators on every secondary sale, developers can ensure ongoing revenue streams for content creators. This incentivizes the creation of high-quality NFTs and maintains economic activity in the secondary market.

Here's an example of a royalty mechanism in Solidity:

```solidity
pragma solidity ^0.8.0;

contract RoyaltyNFT is ERC721, Ownable {
    uint256 public tokenCounter;
    mapping(uint256 => uint256) public royalties;

    constructor() ERC721("RoyaltyNFT", "RNFT") {
        tokenCounter = 0;
    }

    function mintNFT(address to, string memory tokenURI, uint256 royalty) public onlyOwner returns (uint256) {
        uint256 newItemId = tokenCounter;
        _mint(to, newItemId);
        _setTokenURI(newItemId, tokenURI);
        royalties[newItemId] = royalty;
        tokenCounter++;
        return newItemId;
    }

    function transferFrom(address from, address to, uint256 tokenId) public override {
        super.transferFrom(from, to, tokenId);
        _payRoyalty(tokenId);
    }

    function _payRoyalty(uint256 tokenId) internal {
        uint256 salePrice = msg.value;
        uint256 royalty = (salePrice * royalties[tokenId]) / 100;
        payable(owner()).transfer(royalty);
    }
}
```

This contract ensures that a percentage of the sale price is paid to the creator whenever the NFT is resold.

Transparency and communication with the player community are essential for maintaining trust and engagement. Developers should clearly explain how NFTs are integrated into the game, how they can be acquired, and their impact on gameplay. Regular updates and open communication help address player concerns and ensure that the NFT integration aligns with player expectations.

Finally, monitoring and analytics are vital for maintaining a balanced game economy. Developers should continuously track player activity, market trends, and economic indicators to make data-driven decisions. Adjusting the supply of NFTs, tweaking gameplay mechanics, and implementing new features based on analytics can help keep the game economy healthy and engaging.

In conclusion, balancing a game economy with NFT integration involves ensuring that NFTs enhance the player experience without creating unfair advantages, managing supply and demand, implementing earning mechanisms, crafting systems, marketplaces, economic sinks, royalties, transparency, and continuous monitoring. By carefully designing and managing these aspects, developers can create a sustainable and engaging game economy that benefits all players.

3.5. Case Studies: Successful NFT Integrations in Games

Examining successful case studies of NFT integrations in games provides valuable insights into best practices and innovative approaches. This section explores several prominent examples of games that have effectively incorporated NFTs, highlighting their strategies and outcomes.

Axie Infinity: One of the most well-known examples of NFT integration in gaming, Axie Infinity is a blockchain-based game where players collect, breed, and battle fantasy creatures called Axies. Each Axie is an NFT with unique traits and abilities. The game's play-to-earn model allows players to earn tokens by participating in battles and completing quests. Axie Infinity's success lies in its strong community, engaging gameplay, and robust economic model, which includes breeding fees and marketplace transactions.

Decentraland: This virtual world platform allows users to create, explore, and trade virtual properties and assets. Land parcels in Decentraland are NFTs, which users can develop and monetize. The platform also supports user-generated content, enabling creators to sell virtual goods and experiences. Decentraland's integration of NFTs creates a vibrant metaverse where users have true ownership and control over their digital assets.

CryptoKitties: As one of the first blockchain games to gain widespread attention, CryptoKitties allows players to collect, breed, and trade unique digital cats. Each CryptoKitty is an NFT with distinct attributes, determined by its genetic code. The game's breeding mechanics and rarity of certain traits create a dynamic market for trading CryptoKitties. This game's success demonstrated the potential of NFTs in gaming and laid the groundwork for future developments in the space.

Gods Unchained: This blockchain-based trading card game incorporates NFTs for its collectible cards. Players own their cards as NFTs, which can be traded, sold, or used in gameplay. Gods Unchained leverages the immutability and transparency of blockchain to ensure the authenticity and scarcity of its cards. The game's competitive gameplay and the value of rare cards drive player engagement and market activity.

The Sandbox: This virtual world game enables players to build, own, and monetize their gaming experiences using NFTs and the platform's native token, SAND. Players can create and sell in-game assets, such as characters, equipment, and environments, as NFTs. The Sandbox's emphasis on user-generated content and its robust marketplace have created a thriving ecosystem where creativity and ownership are rewarded.

Sorare: A fantasy football game that uses NFTs to represent player cards, Sorare allows players to buy, sell, and trade officially licensed digital cards of real-world footballers. These cards are used to participate in fantasy football leagues, with rewards based on the players' real-life performances. Sorare's integration of real-world data and licensed content has attracted a large and engaged user base.

My Crypto Heroes: This RPG allows players to collect and train historical heroes, represented as NFTs. Players can participate in quests and battles to earn rewards and improve their heroes' stats. The game's economy includes a marketplace for trading heroes and items, fostering a player-driven economy. My Crypto Heroes' engaging gameplay and integration of historical themes have contributed to its success.

Illuvium: An open-world RPG and auto-battler game that uses NFTs for its collectible creatures, called Illuvials. Players capture and train Illuvials, which can be used in battles or traded on the marketplace. Illuvium combines high-quality graphics, engaging gameplay, and a player-driven economy to create a compelling gaming experience. The game's approach to NFT integration ensures that each Illuvial has unique value and utility.

Zed Run: A digital horse racing game where each horse is an NFT with unique attributes and lineage. Players can breed, race, and trade their horses, with the potential to earn rewards from successful races. Zed Run's dynamic market for breeding and trading horses, along with its engaging racing mechanics, has attracted a dedicated community of players and collectors.

Alien Worlds: This decentralized metaverse game allows players to mine for resources, acquire land, and engage in battles using NFTs. Each land parcel and item in the game is an NFT, creating a player-driven economy. Alien Worlds leverages its native token, TLM, to facilitate transactions and rewards, fostering an active and engaged player base.

These case studies demonstrate that successful NFT integrations in games share several common factors: engaging gameplay, strong community involvement, robust economic models, and clear utility and value of NFTs. By focusing on these elements, developers can create compelling experiences that attract and retain players, while also fostering vibrant player-driven economies.

39

Chapter 4: NFTs and Game Development Platforms

4.1. Selecting the Right Blockchain Platform

Selecting the right blockchain platform is a critical decision for integrating NFTs into games. The chosen platform affects the scalability, security, cost, and overall user experience of the game. Several key factors should be considered when making this choice.

One of the primary considerations is the blockchain's transaction throughput and scalability. Popular blockchains like Ethereum, while widely used and secure, often face congestion issues that can lead to high transaction fees and slower processing times. Layer 2 solutions and alternative blockchains such as Binance Smart Chain, Polygon, and Solana offer higher throughput and lower fees, making them attractive options for games with high transaction volumes.

Security is another crucial factor. The blockchain platform must have a robust security infrastructure to protect against hacks and vulnerabilities. Ethereum, for instance, has a long track record and a large developer community that continuously audits and improves its security features. Newer blockchains may offer innovative security solutions, but they might also be more susceptible to undiscovered vulnerabilities.

Interoperability is important for ensuring that NFTs can be used across multiple games and platforms. Blockchains that support standards like ERC-721 and ERC-1155 provide greater flexibility for integrating NFTs into various applications. Some platforms also offer cross-chain compatibility, allowing NFTs to be transferred between different blockchains, enhancing their utility and value.

The choice of blockchain also impacts the development tools and resources available. Ethereum, for example, has a rich ecosystem of development tools, libraries, and frameworks, such as Truffle, Hardhat, and OpenZeppelin, which simplify smart contract development and deployment. Other blockchains might offer different sets of tools that cater to specific needs or preferences of developers.

Cost considerations are critical, especially for games with frequent transactions. High gas fees on Ethereum can be a barrier for both developers and players. Platforms like Binance Smart Chain and Polygon offer significantly lower transaction costs, making them more suitable for cost-sensitive projects. However, these platforms might trade off some decentralization and security for lower fees.

Community support and ecosystem maturity are also important. A vibrant developer community can provide valuable support, share best practices, and contribute to the platform's growth and improvement. Established platforms like Ethereum benefit from a large and active community, while newer platforms might still be building their developer ecosystems.

Environmental impact is becoming increasingly relevant as blockchain adoption grows. Proof-of-work blockchains, such as Ethereum, consume significant amounts of energy.

Proof-of-stake and other consensus mechanisms, used by platforms like Tezos and Solana, offer more environmentally friendly alternatives. Choosing a sustainable blockchain can align with the growing emphasis on corporate social responsibility and environmental stewardship.

Regulatory compliance and legal considerations should not be overlooked. Different blockchains might be subject to varying regulatory frameworks depending on their geographical presence and operational model. Developers should ensure that the chosen blockchain complies with relevant regulations to avoid legal complications.

Here is an example of deploying a simple NFT smart contract on Binance Smart Chain using Solidity:

```solidity
pragma solidity ^0.8.0;

import "@openzeppelin/contracts/token/ERC721/ERC721.sol";
import "@openzeppelin/contracts/access/Ownable.sol";

contract MyNFT is ERC721, Ownable {
    uint256 public tokenCounter;

    constructor() ERC721("MyNFT", "MNFT") {
        tokenCounter = 0;
    }

    function mintNFT(address to, string memory tokenURI) public onlyOwner returns (uint256) {
        uint256 newItemId = tokenCounter;
        _mint(to, newItemId);
        _setTokenURI(newItemId, tokenURI);
        tokenCounter++;
        return newItemId;
    }
}
```

This contract allows the owner to mint new NFTs, each with a unique identifier and metadata URI.

In summary, selecting the right blockchain platform involves evaluating factors such as transaction throughput, security, interoperability, development tools, cost, community support, environmental impact, and regulatory compliance. By carefully considering these aspects, developers can choose a platform that best meets their game's needs and ensures a successful NFT integration.

4.2. Integration of NFTs in Popular Game Engines

Integrating NFTs into popular game engines allows developers to leverage existing tools and frameworks to create immersive and engaging experiences. Game engines like Unity and Unreal Engine offer extensive support for various functionalities, including graphics, physics, and network connectivity, making them ideal for incorporating NFTs.

Unity is one of the most widely used game engines due to its versatility and ease of use. It supports a wide range of platforms, from mobile to desktop to VR. Integrating NFTs into a Unity game involves interacting with blockchain networks and smart contracts. Unity's flexible architecture and comprehensive asset store make it straightforward to implement NFT functionalities.

To integrate NFTs in Unity, developers can use SDKs and plugins that facilitate blockchain interactions. For example, Enjin provides a Unity SDK that simplifies the process of minting, transferring, and managing NFTs within the game. The SDK includes functions for connecting to blockchain wallets, interacting with smart contracts, and handling transactions.

Here's a basic example of integrating NFTs in Unity using the Enjin SDK:

```
using System.Collections;
using UnityEngine;
using Enjin.SDK.Core;
using Enjin.SDK.DataTypes;

public class NFTManager : MonoBehaviour
{
    private string walletAddress = "0xYourWalletAddress";
    private string tokenID = "1";

    void Start()
    {
        StartCoroutine(MintNFT());
    }

    IEnumerator MintNFT()
    {
        Enjin.Initialize("YOUR_ENJIN_APP_ID", "YOUR_ENJIN_SECRET");
        var transaction = Enjin.Mint(walletAddress, tokenID, 1);
        yield return transaction.WaitForResult();

        if (transaction.IsSuccess())
        {
            Debug.Log("NFT Minted Successfully!");
        }
        else
        {
            Debug.Log("Failed to Mint NFT: " + transaction.GetError());
        }
    }
}
```

This script initializes the Enjin SDK, mints an NFT, and assigns it to a specified wallet address.

Unreal Engine, known for its high-fidelity graphics and robust capabilities, is another popular choice for integrating NFTs. Unreal Engine's Blueprint visual scripting system allows developers to implement NFT functionalities without extensive coding. Additionally, Unreal Engine supports plugins that enable blockchain interactions, such as Blockchaining's Unreal Engine Blockchain SDK.

Integrating NFTs in Unreal Engine typically involves creating custom smart contracts and using plugins to interact with the blockchain. Developers can design in-game items, characters, or virtual real estate as NFTs and manage their ownership and transactions through smart contracts.

Here's an example of a Blueprint setup in Unreal Engine for integrating NFTs:

1. **Create a New Blueprint Class**: Start by creating a new Blueprint class derived from `Actor`.
2. **Add Variables**: Add variables for storing NFT-related data, such as `TokenID`, `OwnerAddress`, and `TokenURI`.
3. **Implement Functions**: Create functions for minting and transferring NFTs using blockchain SDK functions.

The visual scripting in Blueprints allows for intuitive NFT integration, enabling developers to focus on game design and user experience.

The integration process also involves setting up blockchain wallets within the game. Players need to connect their wallets to manage their NFTs, which can be done through user-friendly interfaces and wallet integration libraries like Web3.js or WalletConnect. These libraries facilitate secure connections between the game and blockchain wallets, enabling players to perform transactions seamlessly.

For mobile games, integrating NFTs involves additional considerations, such as optimizing for performance and ensuring compatibility with mobile wallets. Unity and Unreal Engine support mobile development, allowing developers to create NFT-integrated games for iOS and Android. Mobile-specific SDKs and APIs can help streamline the integration process and ensure a smooth user experience.

Security is paramount when integrating NFTs in game engines. Developers must ensure that all blockchain interactions are secure and that user data is protected. Implementing best practices for smart contract development, conducting thorough audits, and using secure libraries and SDKs are essential steps to safeguard the game and its players.

In conclusion, integrating NFTs into popular game engines like Unity and Unreal Engine provides developers with powerful tools to create immersive and engaging experiences. By leveraging SDKs, plugins, and blockchain wallets, developers can seamlessly incorporate NFTs into their games, enhancing gameplay and providing players with unique digital assets. Focusing on security and user experience ensures a successful integration that adds value to both the game and its community.

4.3. Utilizing NFT APIs and SDKs

Utilizing NFT APIs and SDKs is essential for integrating NFT functionalities into games. These tools provide pre-built functions and interfaces that simplify the interaction with blockchain networks, enabling developers to focus on game design and user experience rather than the complexities of blockchain technology.

APIs (Application Programming Interfaces) and SDKs (Software Development Kits) offer a range of functionalities, from minting and transferring NFTs to querying blockchain data and managing user wallets. By leveraging these tools, developers can streamline the integration process and ensure a smooth and secure implementation.

One popular API for interacting with NFTs is the OpenSea API. OpenSea is one of the largest NFT marketplaces, and its API allows developers to access a wide range of functionalities, including retrieving NFT metadata, listing assets, and managing auctions. The OpenSea API is RESTful, making it easy to integrate with various programming languages and platforms.

Here's an example of using the OpenSea API to retrieve NFT metadata in Python:

```python
import requests

def get_nft_metadata(token_address, token_id):
    url = f"https://api.opensea.io/api/v1/asset/{token_address}/{token_id}/"
    response = requests.get(url)

    if response.status_code == 200:
        metadata = response.json()
        return metadata
    else:
        return None

token_address = "0xYourTokenAddress"
token_id = "1"
metadata = get_nft_metadata(token_address, token_id)

if metadata:
    print(f"Name: {metadata['name']}")
    print(f"Description: {metadata['description']}")
    print(f"Image URL: {metadata['image_url']}")
else:
    print("Failed to retrieve metadata")
```

This script retrieves and prints the metadata of an NFT using the OpenSea API.

Enjin SDK is another powerful tool for integrating NFTs into games. Enjin provides SDKs for various platforms, including Unity, Java, and .NET. The Enjin SDK simplifies the process of minting, transferring, and managing NFTs, allowing developers to integrate blockchain functionalities with minimal effort.

To use the Enjin SDK in Unity, developers need to install the SDK package, configure the Enjin app, and implement the necessary functions to interact with the blockchain. Here's an example of minting an NFT using the Enjin SDK in Unity:

```csharp
using System.Collections;
using UnityEngine;
using Enjin.SDK.Core;
using Enjin.SDK.DataTypes;

public class NFTManager : MonoBehaviour
{
    private string walletAddress = "0xYourWalletAddress";
    private string tokenID = "1";

    void Start()
    {
        StartCoroutine(MintNFT());
    }

    IEnumerator MintNFT()
    {
        Enjin.Initialize("YOUR_ENJIN_APP_ID", "YOUR_ENJIN_SECRET");
        var transaction = Enjin.Mint(walletAddress, tokenID, 1);
        yield return transaction.WaitForResult();

        if (transaction.IsSuccess())
        {
            Debug.Log("NFT Minted Successfully!");
        }
        else
        {
            Debug.Log("Failed to Mint NFT: " + transaction.GetError());
        }
    }
}
```

This script demonstrates how to mint an NFT and assign it to a specified wallet address using the Enjin SDK.

Alchemy and Infura are popular blockchain infrastructure providers that offer APIs for interacting with Ethereum and other blockchain networks. These APIs provide reliable and scalable access to blockchain data, enabling developers to query transaction details, monitor events, and interact with smart contracts.

Here's an example of using Alchemy's API to get the balance of an Ethereum address in JavaScript:

```javascript
const axios = require('axios');

const apiKey = 'YOUR_ALCHEMY_API_KEY';
```

```
const address = '0xYourWalletAddress';

async function getBalance() {
    const url = `https://eth-mainnet.alchemyapi.io/v2/${apiKey}`;
    const data = {
        "jsonrpc": "2.0",
        "method": "eth_getBalance",
        "params": [address, "latest"],
        "id": 1
    };

    try {
        const response = await axios.post(url, data);
        const balance = response.data.result;
        console.log(`Balance: ${balance}`);
    } catch (error) {
        console.error(`Error: ${error.message}`);
    }
}

getBalance();
```

This script retrieves the balance of an Ethereum address using Alchemy's API.

Wallet integration is another critical aspect of utilizing NFT APIs and SDKs. Libraries like Web3.js and WalletConnect facilitate secure connections between the game and blockchain wallets, allowing players to manage their NFTs and perform transactions seamlessly. These libraries provide functions for connecting to wallets, signing transactions, and querying blockchain data.

Here's an example of connecting to a MetaMask wallet using Web3.js:

```
const Web3 = require('web3');

async function connectWallet() {
    if (window.ethereum) {
        const web3 = new Web3(window.ethereum);
        try {
            await window.ethereum.enable();
            const accounts = await web3.eth.getAccounts();
            console.log(`Connected: ${accounts[0]}`);
        } catch (error) {
            console.error(`Connection failed: ${error.message}`);
        }
    } else {
        console.error('MetaMask is not installed');
    }
}

connectWallet();
```

This script connects to a MetaMask wallet and retrieves the user's account address.

In conclusion, utilizing NFT APIs and SDKs is essential for integrating NFT functionalities into games. Tools like the OpenSea API, Enjin SDK, Alchemy, Infura, Web3.js, and WalletConnect provide pre-built functions and interfaces that simplify blockchain interactions. By leveraging these tools, developers can streamline the integration process, ensuring a smooth and secure implementation that enhances the gaming experience.

4.4. Cross-Platform Compatibility and Challenges

Cross-platform compatibility is a crucial aspect of modern game development, especially when integrating NFTs. Ensuring that NFTs can be accessed and used across various platforms, including PC, consoles, and mobile devices, enhances their utility and value. However, achieving cross-platform compatibility presents several challenges that developers must address.

One of the primary challenges is the difference in hardware capabilities and operating systems across platforms. Games need to be optimized for performance on each platform, ensuring that NFT functionalities do not degrade the gaming experience. This involves testing and fine-tuning the game for different screen sizes, input methods, and performance limitations.

For example, a game developed in Unity can be deployed to multiple platforms using its built-in support for cross-platform development. Unity provides tools and settings to optimize the game for each target platform, ensuring consistent performance and user experience. Developers need to consider the specific requirements of each platform, such as graphical settings for PC, control schemes for consoles, and touch interfaces for mobile devices.

Another challenge is ensuring secure and seamless integration of blockchain wallets across platforms. Desktop and mobile wallets have different interfaces and security measures. Integrating wallets like MetaMask for desktop and WalletConnect for mobile can provide a consistent user experience, but developers must handle the nuances of each platform's wallet integration.

Here's an example of integrating WalletConnect for a mobile game in Unity:

```csharp
using UnityEngine;
using WalletConnectSharp.Core;
using WalletConnectSharp.Unity;

public class WalletManager : MonoBehaviour
{
    private WalletConnect walletConnect;

    void Start()
    {
        walletConnect = GetComponent<WalletConnect>();
        walletConnect.Connected += OnWalletConnected;
```

```
        walletConnect.Connect();
    }

    private void OnWalletConnected(WalletConnectSession session)
    {
        Debug.Log("Wallet connected: " + session.Accounts[0]);
    }
}
```

This script demonstrates how to connect to a mobile wallet using WalletConnect in Unity.

Data synchronization across platforms is another critical aspect. Players expect their NFT assets and game progress to be consistent, regardless of the platform they use. Implementing cloud storage solutions and blockchain integration ensures that data is synchronized in real-time. Using decentralized storage solutions like IPFS (InterPlanetary File System) can also enhance the security and accessibility of NFT metadata.

Network connectivity and latency can vary significantly between platforms. Mobile devices, for instance, may have less reliable internet connections compared to desktops and consoles. Developers need to design the game and NFT interactions to handle varying network conditions gracefully, ensuring that players can still access and manage their NFTs even with intermittent connectivity.

User interface (UI) and user experience (UX) design must be tailored to each platform. The UI for managing NFTs should be intuitive and accessible, whether players are using a mouse and keyboard, a game controller, or a touchscreen. Consistent design principles and responsive layouts help provide a seamless experience across different devices.

Regulatory compliance and app store policies can also impact cross-platform NFT integration. Mobile app stores, such as the Apple App Store and Google Play, have specific guidelines regarding blockchain and NFT functionalities. Developers must ensure that their games comply with these guidelines to avoid rejection or removal from the stores.

For instance, Apple's guidelines may restrict certain blockchain transactions or require explicit user consent for wallet connections. Developers need to stay updated on these policies and design their games accordingly.

Maintaining security across platforms is paramount. Each platform may have different security vulnerabilities and attack vectors. Implementing robust security measures, such as encryption, secure communication protocols, and regular audits, helps protect player data and NFT assets.

Cross-platform development also involves dealing with different update cycles and patch management. Coordinating updates across platforms ensures that all players have access to the latest features and security patches simultaneously. Automated build and deployment pipelines can streamline this process, reducing the risk of discrepancies between platform versions.

In summary, achieving cross-platform compatibility for NFT-integrated games involves addressing challenges related to hardware capabilities, wallet integration, data synchronization, network connectivity, UI/UX design, regulatory compliance, security, and update management. By carefully considering and addressing these challenges, developers can provide a consistent and seamless experience for players across various platforms, enhancing the utility and value of NFTs.

4.5. Security Aspects in NFT-based Games

Security is a critical concern in NFT-based games, as both developers and players need to ensure the protection of digital assets, personal data, and in-game transactions. Addressing security aspects involves implementing robust practices and technologies to safeguard the game and its ecosystem.

One of the primary security considerations is the integrity of smart contracts. Smart contracts are the backbone of NFT transactions, managing the creation, transfer, and ownership of digital assets. Any vulnerabilities in these contracts can lead to exploits and significant losses. Developers must follow best practices in smart contract development, such as using well-audited libraries like OpenZeppelin and conducting thorough security audits.

Here's an example of a basic ERC-721 smart contract using OpenZeppelin:

```
pragma solidity ^0.8.0;

import "@openzeppelin/contracts/token/ERC721/ERC721.sol";
import "@openzeppelin/contracts/access/Ownable.sol";

contract SecureNFT is ERC721, Ownable {
    uint256 public tokenCounter;

    constructor() ERC721("SecureNFT", "SNFT") {
        tokenCounter = 0;
    }

    function mintNFT(address to, string memory tokenURI) public onlyOwner returns (uint256) {
        uint256 newItemId = tokenCounter;
        _mint(to, newItemId);
        _setTokenURI(newItemId, tokenURI);
        tokenCounter++;
        return newItemId;
    }
}
```

This contract leverages OpenZeppelin's security features to ensure robustness and reliability.

Securing the communication between the game and blockchain networks is essential. Using secure communication protocols, such as HTTPS and WebSocket Secure (WSS), helps protect data in transit from interception and tampering. Ensuring that all API calls and interactions with blockchain nodes are encrypted and authenticated adds an extra layer of security.

Wallet integration is another area where security is paramount. Players' wallets store valuable digital assets and must be protected against unauthorized access and phishing attacks. Implementing secure authentication methods, such as multi-factor authentication (MFA) and hardware wallets, can enhance the security of wallet interactions. Educating players on safe wallet practices, such as verifying URLs and avoiding suspicious links, also helps mitigate risks.

Preventing and mitigating denial-of-service (DoS) attacks is crucial for maintaining the availability and performance of NFT-based games. DoS attacks can overwhelm game servers and blockchain nodes, disrupting gameplay and transactions. Implementing rate limiting, load balancing, and distributed denial-of-service (DDoS) protection mechanisms helps safeguard against these attacks.

Monitoring and logging are essential for detecting and responding to security incidents. Setting up comprehensive logging for smart contract interactions, wallet transactions, and server activities allows developers to identify suspicious behavior and take appropriate action. Real-time monitoring tools and alerting systems can help quickly detect and mitigate potential security breaches.

User data privacy is another critical aspect. Compliance with data protection regulations, such as GDPR and CCPA, ensures that players' personal information is handled securely and responsibly. Implementing data encryption, anonymization, and secure storage practices helps protect user data from unauthorized access and breaches.

Here's an example of encrypting user data in a Unity game using AES encryption:

```csharp
using System;
using System.Security.Cryptography;
using System.Text;

public static class EncryptionUtility
{
    private static readonly string key = "YourEncryptionKeyHere";

    public static string Encrypt(string plainText)
    {
        using (Aes aes = Aes.Create())
        {
            aes.Key = Encoding.UTF8.GetBytes(key);
            aes.GenerateIV();
            byte[] iv = aes.IV;
            using (var encryptor = aes.CreateEncryptor(aes.Key, iv))
            {
```

```
            byte[] encrypted = PerformCryptography(plainText, encryptor);
            byte[] result = new byte[iv.Length + encrypted.Length];
            Buffer.BlockCopy(iv, 0, result, 0, iv.Length);
            Buffer.BlockCopy(encrypted, 0, result, iv.Length, encrypted.Length);
            return Convert.ToBase64String(result);
        }
    }
}

    public static string Decrypt(string encryptedText)
    {
        byte[] fullCipher = Convert.FromBase64String(encryptedText);
        using (Aes aes = Aes.Create())
        {
            aes.Key = Encoding.UTF8.GetBytes(key);
            byte[] iv = new byte[aes.BlockSize / 8];
            byte[] cipherText = new byte[fullCipher.Length - iv.Length];
            Buffer.BlockCopy(fullCipher, 0, iv, 0, iv.Length);
            Buffer.BlockCopy(fullCipher, iv.Length, cipherText, 0, cipherText.Length);
            using (var decryptor = aes.CreateDecryptor(aes.Key, iv))
            {
                return PerformCryptography(cipherText, decryptor);
            }
        }
    }

    private static string PerformCryptography(string data, ICryptoTransform cryptoTransform)
    {
        byte[] input = Encoding.UTF8.GetBytes(data);
        byte[] output = cryptoTransform.TransformFinalBlock(input, 0, input.Length);
        return Encoding.UTF8.GetString(output);
    }
}
```

This utility class provides methods for encrypting and decrypting user data using AES encryption.

Ensuring the security of the game's infrastructure involves regular updates and patch management. Keeping the game engine, libraries, and dependencies up-to-date with the latest security patches reduces the risk of exploits. Implementing automated update systems and continuous integration/continuous deployment (CI/CD) pipelines helps streamline this process.

Community engagement and bug bounty programs can also enhance security. Encouraging players and security researchers to report vulnerabilities through structured programs helps identify and address security issues proactively. Offering rewards for valid bug reports incentivizes responsible disclosure and collaboration.

In conclusion, addressing security aspects in NFT-based games involves ensuring the integrity of smart contracts, securing communication, protecting wallet interactions, preventing DoS attacks, monitoring and logging activities, safeguarding user data, maintaining infrastructure security, and engaging with the community. By implementing robust security practices and technologies, developers can protect their games and players, fostering trust and confidence in the NFT ecosystem.

Chapter 5: Programming NFTs for Gamers

5.1. Basics of Writing Smart Contracts for Gaming NFTs

Writing smart contracts for gaming NFTs involves understanding the basic principles of blockchain technology, Solidity programming, and how to implement key functionalities such as minting, transferring, and managing NFTs. This section covers the foundational aspects necessary for creating robust and secure smart contracts for gaming NFTs.

Smart contracts are self-executing contracts with the terms of the agreement directly written into code. For NFTs, these contracts are often implemented on the Ethereum blockchain using the Solidity programming language. The ERC-721 and ERC-1155 standards define the structure and functionality of NFTs on Ethereum, ensuring interoperability and consistency across different platforms and applications.

Here is a simple example of an ERC-721 smart contract for minting gaming NFTs:

```solidity
pragma solidity ^0.8.0;

import "@openzeppelin/contracts/token/ERC721/ERC721.sol";
import "@openzeppelin/contracts/access/Ownable.sol";

contract GameNFT is ERC721, Ownable {
    uint256 public tokenCounter;

    constructor() ERC721("GameNFT", "GNFT") {
        tokenCounter = 0;
    }

    function mintNFT(address to, string memory tokenURI) public onlyOwner returns (uint256) {
        uint256 newItemId = tokenCounter;
        _mint(to, newItemId);
        _setTokenURI(newItemId, tokenURI);
        tokenCounter++;
        return newItemId;
    }
}
```

This contract allows the owner to mint new NFTs, each with a unique identifier and metadata URI. The tokenCounter variable ensures that each minted NFT has a unique ID.

To deploy and interact with this contract, developers need to set up a development environment. Tools like Truffle and Hardhat provide comprehensive frameworks for compiling, deploying, and testing smart contracts. Additionally, developers need access to an Ethereum node, which can be provided by services like Infura or Alchemy.

After setting up the environment, developers can deploy the contract to a test network, such as Ropsten or Rinkeby, before deploying it to the main Ethereum network. This allows for thorough testing and debugging of the contract's functionality.

Here's an example of deploying the contract using Truffle:

1. **Install Truffle**:

   ```
   npm install -g truffle
   ```

2. **Initialize a Truffle project**:

   ```
   truffle init
   ```

3. **Create a migration script** (`migrations/2_deploy_contracts.js`):

   ```javascript
   const GameNFT = artifacts.require("GameNFT");

   module.exports = function (deployer) {
     deployer.deploy(GameNFT);
   };
   ```

4. **Deploy the contract**:

   ```
   truffle migrate --network ropsten
   ```

This process compiles the smart contract and deploys it to the specified Ethereum network.

Interacting with the deployed contract involves calling its functions from a frontend application or another smart contract. For web applications, libraries like Web3.js or Ethers.js can be used to connect to the Ethereum network and interact with the smart contract.

Here's an example of interacting with the contract using Web3.js:

```javascript
const Web3 = require('web3');
const web3 = new Web3('https://ropsten.infura.io/v3/YOUR_INFURA_PROJECT_ID');

const abi = [/* Contract ABI */];
const contractAddress = '0xYourContractAddress';
const contract = new web3.eth.Contract(abi, contractAddress);

async function mintNFT(to, tokenURI) {
    const accounts = await web3.eth.getAccounts();
    const receipt = await contract.methods.mintNFT(to, tokenURI).send({ from: accounts[0] });
    console.log('NFT Minted: ', receipt);
}

mintNFT('0xRecipientAddress', 'https://token-metadata-url.com');
```

This script connects to the Ropsten network, retrieves the user's accounts, and calls the mintNFT function to mint a new NFT.

Security is a crucial aspect of smart contract development. Developers must ensure that their contracts are free of vulnerabilities that could be exploited by malicious actors. Common security issues include reentrancy attacks, integer overflows, and unauthorized access. Using well-audited libraries like OpenZeppelin and following best practices in smart contract development can mitigate these risks.

Testing is another vital component. Writing comprehensive test cases to cover all possible scenarios and edge cases helps ensure the contract behaves as expected. Tools like Mocha and Chai, integrated with Truffle or Hardhat, can be used for automated testing.

In summary, writing smart contracts for gaming NFTs involves understanding blockchain principles, Solidity programming, and the ERC-721/1155 standards. Setting up a development environment, deploying contracts, interacting with them, ensuring security, and thorough testing are all essential steps in creating robust and secure smart contracts for gaming NFTs.

5.2. Implementing Gameplay Mechanics with NFTs

Integrating NFTs into gameplay mechanics involves designing and implementing features that leverage the unique properties of NFTs to enhance the gaming experience. This section explores how NFTs can be used to create engaging and innovative gameplay elements.

One of the primary ways NFTs can be integrated into gameplay is by using them as in-game assets. These assets can include characters, items, weapons, and equipment that players can own, trade, and upgrade. By tokenizing these assets as NFTs, players gain true ownership, enabling them to trade or sell their assets outside the game.

For example, in a role-playing game (RPG), players could own NFT-based characters with unique attributes and abilities. These characters can be upgraded and customized through gameplay, increasing their value. The following Solidity contract snippet demonstrates how to create and upgrade an NFT-based character:

```solidity
pragma solidity ^0.8.0;

import "@openzeppelin/contracts/token/ERC721/ERC721.sol";
import "@openzeppelin/contracts/access/Ownable.sol";

contract GameCharacter is ERC721, Ownable {
    struct Character {
        uint256 level;
        uint256 experience;
    }

    mapping(uint256 => Character) public characters;

    uint256 public tokenCounter;
```

```solidity
    constructor() ERC721("GameCharacter", "GCHAR") {
        tokenCounter = 0;
    }

    function mintCharacter(address to) public onlyOwner returns (uint256) {
        uint256 newCharacterId = tokenCounter;
        characters[newCharacterId] = Character({level: 1, experience: 0});
        _mint(to, newCharacterId);
        tokenCounter++;
        return newCharacterId;
    }

    function levelUp(uint256 tokenId) public {
        require(ownerOf(tokenId) == msg.sender, "Only the owner can level up"
);
        characters[tokenId].level++;
    }

    function addExperience(uint256 tokenId, uint256 amount) public {
        require(ownerOf(tokenId) == msg.sender, "Only the owner can add experience");
        characters[tokenId].experience += amount;
    }
}
```

This contract allows the game owner to mint new characters and players to level up and add experience to their characters.

Another engaging use of NFTs in gameplay is through quests and achievements. Players can earn unique NFTs as rewards for completing specific tasks, challenges, or milestones. These NFTs can represent trophies, badges, or rare items that signify the player's accomplishments. Integrating these elements encourages players to engage more deeply with the game and strive for unique rewards.

For instance, in an adventure game, completing a difficult dungeon could reward players with a rare NFT sword. The following Solidity contract snippet demonstrates how to mint an NFT as a reward for completing a quest:

```solidity
pragma solidity ^0.8.0;

import "@openzeppelin/contracts/token/ERC721/ERC721.sol";
import "@openzeppelin/contracts/access/Ownable.sol";

contract QuestReward is ERC721, Ownable {
    uint256 public tokenCounter;

    constructor() ERC721("QuestReward", "QREWARD") {
        tokenCounter = 0;
```

```
    }

    function rewardNFT(address to, string memory tokenURI) public onlyOwner r
eturns (uint256) {
        uint256 newItemId = tokenCounter;
        _mint(to, newItemId);
        _setTokenURI(newItemId, tokenURI);
        tokenCounter++;
        return newItemId;
    }
}
```

This contract allows the game owner to mint an NFT as a reward for a quest and assign it to the player.

NFTs can also be used to enable player-driven economies within games. Players can create, trade, and sell NFT-based assets, creating a vibrant marketplace. This economic activity can be facilitated through in-game marketplaces or external platforms like OpenSea. Integrating a marketplace within the game allows players to trade assets seamlessly and fosters a sense of community and collaboration.

For example, in a strategy game, players could trade NFT-based resources, buildings, or units. The following Solidity contract snippet demonstrates a simple marketplace for trading NFTs:

```
pragma solidity ^0.8.0;

import "@openzeppelin/contracts/token/ERC721/ERC721.sol";
import "@openzeppelin/contracts/access/Ownable.sol";

contract Marketplace is Ownable {
    struct Listing {
        address seller;
        uint256 price;
    }

    mapping(uint256 => Listing) public listings;

    ERC721 public nftContract;

    constructor(address _nftContract) {
        nftContract = ERC721(_nftContract);
    }

    function listNFT(uint256 tokenId, uint256 price) public {
        require(nftContract.ownerOf(tokenId) == msg.sender, "Only the owner c
an list the NFT");
        listings[tokenId] = Listing({seller: msg.sender, price: price});
    }
```

```
    function buyNFT(uint256 tokenId) public payable {
        Listing memory listing = listings[tokenId];
        require(msg.value == listing.price, "Incorrect price");
        require(listing.seller != address(0), "NFT not listed");

        nftContract.transferFrom(listing.seller, msg.sender, tokenId);
        payable(listing.seller).transfer(msg.value);
        delete listings[tokenId];
    }
}
```

This contract enables players to list and buy NFTs within the game.

NFTs can also facilitate player governance and community-driven development. By issuing governance tokens as NFTs, developers can allow players to vote on game updates, new features, and community policies. This decentralized approach empowers players and fosters a sense of ownership and involvement in the game's evolution.

In summary, implementing gameplay mechanics with NFTs involves using NFTs as in-game assets, rewards for quests and achievements, enabling player-driven economies, and facilitating player governance. By leveraging the unique properties of NFTs, developers can create engaging and innovative gameplay experiences that enhance player involvement and satisfaction.

5.3. User Authentication and Ownership Verification

User authentication and ownership verification are critical components in integrating NFTs into games. Ensuring that players can securely access their accounts and verify ownership of their NFT assets is essential for a seamless and secure gaming experience. This section explores various methods and best practices for implementing user authentication and ownership verification.

One of the most common methods for user authentication in blockchain-based games is through wallet connections. Wallets like MetaMask, WalletConnect, and Coinbase Wallet provide secure ways for players to log in to the game using their blockchain wallets. These wallets store the user's private keys and facilitate signing transactions, ensuring secure access and ownership verification.

Here's an example of using Web3.js to authenticate users with MetaMask:

```
const Web3 = require('web3');

async function connectWallet() {
    if (window.ethereum) {
        const web3 = new Web3(window.ethereum);
        try {
            await window.ethereum.enable();
            const accounts = await web3.eth.getAccounts();
            console.log(`Connected: ${accounts[0]}`);
```

```
            return accounts[0];
        } catch (error) {
            console.error(`Connection failed: ${error.message}`);
        }
    } else {
        console.error('MetaMask is not installed');
    }
}

connectWallet();
```

This script connects to MetaMask, prompts the user to log in, and retrieves the user's account address.

Once authenticated, the game needs to verify the ownership of NFTs associated with the user. This involves querying the blockchain to check if the user's wallet address owns the specified NFTs. Libraries like Web3.js or Ethers.js can be used to interact with smart contracts and retrieve ownership information.

Here's an example of verifying NFT ownership using Web3.js:

```
const contractABI = [/* Contract ABI */];
const contractAddress = '0xYourContractAddress';
const tokenId = 1;

async function verifyOwnership(userAddress) {
    const web3 = new Web3('https://mainnet.infura.io/v3/YOUR_INFURA_PROJECT_ID');
    const contract = new web3.eth.Contract(contractABI, contractAddress);
    const owner = await contract.methods.ownerOf(tokenId).call();

    if (owner.toLowerCase() === userAddress.toLowerCase()) {
        console.log('User owns the NFT');
    } else {
        console.log('User does not own the NFT');
    }
}

const userAddress = '0xUserWalletAddress';
verifyOwnership(userAddress);
```

This script verifies whether the specified user address owns the NFT with the given token ID.

Implementing session management is also important for maintaining secure and persistent user sessions. Once the user is authenticated, a session token can be generated and stored in the client's local storage or cookies. This token can be used to validate the user's session in subsequent interactions, reducing the need for repeated wallet connections.

Here's an example of generating a session token in Node.js:

```javascript
const crypto = require('crypto');

function generateSessionToken() {
    return crypto.randomBytes(64).toString('hex');
}

const sessionToken = generateSessionToken();
console.log(`Session Token: ${sessionToken}`);
```

This script generates a random session token using the crypto library.

Multi-factor authentication (MFA) adds an extra layer of security to user authentication. Combining wallet-based authentication with additional factors such as email verification, SMS codes, or authenticator apps can enhance security. Implementing MFA ensures that even if a user's wallet is compromised, the additional authentication step provides an extra layer of protection.

User-friendly interfaces and clear instructions are essential for smooth authentication and ownership verification processes. Providing intuitive UI elements for connecting wallets, clear messages for successful or failed authentication, and guidance on resolving common issues helps improve the user experience.

Ensuring data privacy and compliance with regulations such as GDPR and CCPA is critical when handling user authentication and ownership information. Implementing data encryption, secure storage practices, and transparent data handling policies helps protect user information and maintain compliance.

In summary, user authentication and ownership verification are crucial for integrating NFTs into games. Using wallet connections for secure authentication, verifying NFT ownership on the blockchain, implementing session management, adding multi-factor authentication, providing user-friendly interfaces, and ensuring data privacy are essential steps. By following these best practices, developers can create secure and seamless experiences for players, ensuring the integrity and trustworthiness of the game.

5.4. Managing NFT Transactions Within Games

Managing NFT transactions within games involves handling the minting, transferring, and trading of NFTs securely and efficiently. This section explores the various aspects of managing NFT transactions, including best practices, smart contract functions, and integration with in-game economies.

Minting NFTs is the process of creating new NFTs and assigning them to players. This can be done as rewards for achievements, purchases, or other in-game activities. Minting involves interacting with smart contracts to generate unique tokens and record them on the blockchain.

Here's an example of a Solidity function for minting NFTs:

```solidity
pragma solidity ^0.8.0;

import "@openzeppelin/contracts/token/ERC721/ERC721.sol";
import "@openzeppelin/contracts/access/Ownable.sol";

contract GameNFT is ERC721, Ownable {
    uint256 public tokenCounter;

    constructor() ERC721("GameNFT", "GNFT") {
        tokenCounter = 0;
    }

    function mintNFT(address to, string memory tokenURI) public onlyOwner returns (uint256) {
        uint256 newItemId = tokenCounter;
        _mint(to, newItemId);
        _setTokenURI(newItemId, tokenURI);
        tokenCounter++;
        return newItemId;
    }
}
```

This contract allows the game owner to mint new NFTs and assign them to players.

Transferring NFTs between players involves updating the ownership records on the blockchain. This can be done through in-game trading, gifting, or marketplace transactions. Ensuring secure and smooth transfers requires implementing functions that handle ownership changes and validate transactions.

Here's an example of a Solidity function for transferring NFTs:

```solidity
pragma solidity ^0.8.0;

import "@openzeppelin/contracts/token/ERC721/ERC721.sol";

contract TransferNFT is ERC721 {
    constructor() ERC721("TransferNFT", "TNFT") {}

    function safeTransferNFT(address from, address to, uint256 tokenId) public {
        require(ownerOf(tokenId) == from, "Sender does not own the NFT");
        _safeTransfer(from, to, tokenId, "");
    }
}
```

This contract allows players to safely transfer NFTs by verifying ownership before executing the transfer.

Implementing an in-game marketplace enables players to buy, sell, and trade NFTs. This marketplace can be integrated within the game or linked to external platforms like

OpenSea. Providing a secure and user-friendly interface for marketplace transactions ensures players can easily manage their assets.

Here's an example of a Solidity contract for an NFT marketplace:

```solidity
pragma solidity ^0.8.0;

import "@openzeppelin/contracts/token/ERC721/ERC721.sol";
import "@openzeppelin/contracts/access/Ownable.sol";

contract Marketplace is Ownable {
    struct Listing {
        address seller;
        uint256 price;
    }

    mapping(uint256 => Listing) public listings;

    ERC721 public nftContract;

    constructor(address _nftContract) {
        nftContract = ERC721(_nftContract);
    }

    function listNFT(uint256 tokenId, uint256 price) public {
        require(nftContract.ownerOf(tokenId) == msg.sender, "Only the owner can list the NFT");
        listings[tokenId] = Listing({seller: msg.sender, price: price});
    }

    function buyNFT(uint256 tokenId) public payable {
        Listing memory listing = listings[tokenId];
        require(msg.value == listing.price, "Incorrect price");
        require(listing.seller != address(0), "NFT not listed");

        nftContract.transferFrom(listing.seller, msg.sender, tokenId);
        payable(listing.seller).transfer(msg.value);
        delete listings[tokenId];
    }
}
```

This contract enables players to list and buy NFTs within the game.

Handling transaction fees and gas costs is another important aspect. NFT transactions on the Ethereum network, for example, incur gas fees paid in ETH. Developers can optimize transactions to minimize gas costs, such as batching multiple transactions or using layer 2 scaling solutions. Informing players about potential fees and providing options to manage them enhances the user experience.

Security is paramount when managing NFT transactions. Ensuring the integrity of smart contracts, implementing secure communication protocols, and regularly auditing the code are essential practices. Protecting against common vulnerabilities, such as reentrancy attacks and unauthorized access, helps safeguard transactions and player assets.

Providing transaction transparency and history is also important. Players should have access to detailed records of their NFT transactions, including minting, transfers, and sales. This transparency builds trust and allows players to track the provenance and ownership history of their assets.

Integrating with external NFT standards and platforms ensures interoperability. Adhering to standards like ERC-721 and ERC-1155 allows NFTs to be recognized and used across different games and marketplaces. Collaborating with platforms like OpenSea or Rarible can extend the reach and utility of in-game NFTs.

User education and support are vital for managing NFT transactions. Providing clear instructions, FAQs, and customer support helps players understand how to manage their NFTs and resolve any issues. Educating players about the risks and best practices for handling NFTs enhances their security and confidence.

In summary, managing NFT transactions within games involves minting, transferring, and trading NFTs securely and efficiently. Implementing robust smart contract functions, integrating with in-game marketplaces, handling transaction fees, ensuring security, providing transparency, adhering to standards, and educating players are essential steps. By following these best practices, developers can create a secure and user-friendly environment for managing NFT transactions, enhancing the overall gaming experience.

5.5. Enhancing Player Experience through NFTs

Enhancing player experience through NFTs involves leveraging the unique properties of NFTs to create more engaging, personalized, and rewarding gameplay. This section explores various strategies and best practices for using NFTs to improve player satisfaction and immersion.

One of the primary ways to enhance player experience is by providing true ownership of in-game assets. NFTs allow players to own, trade, and sell their in-game items, characters, and achievements. This sense of ownership adds value to the assets and creates a deeper connection between the player and the game.

For example, in a collectible card game, each card can be an NFT that the player owns and can trade with others. The following Solidity contract snippet demonstrates how to create an NFT-based card:

```solidity
pragma solidity ^0.8.0;

import "@openzeppelin/contracts/token/ERC721/ERC721.sol";
import "@openzeppelin/contracts/access/Ownable.sol";

contract CardGame is ERC721, Ownable {
```

```solidity
    uint256 public tokenCounter;

    constructor() ERC721("CardGame", "CGAME") {
        tokenCounter = 0;
    }

    function mintCard(address to, string memory tokenURI) public onlyOwner returns (uint256) {
        uint256 newCardId = tokenCounter;
        _mint(to, newCardId);
        _setTokenURI(newCardId, tokenURI);
        tokenCounter++;
        return newCardId;
    }
}
```

This contract allows the game owner to mint new cards and assign them to players.

Customization and personalization are key elements in enhancing player experience. NFTs can be used to create unique and customizable in-game assets that players can modify to suit their preferences. For instance, players can customize their NFT characters with different skins, accessories, and abilities, making their avatars truly unique.

Dynamic and evolving NFTs add a layer of engagement and progression. NFTs that change based on player actions, achievements, or time create a sense of growth and development. For example, an NFT character could gain new abilities or evolve into a more powerful form as the player progresses through the game.

Here's an example of a Solidity contract for a dynamic NFT character:

```solidity
pragma solidity ^0.8.0;

import "@openzeppelin/contracts/token/ERC721/ERC721.sol";
import "@openzeppelin/contracts/access/Ownable.sol";

contract DynamicCharacter is ERC721, Ownable {
    struct Character {
        uint256 level;
        string ability;
    }

    mapping(uint256 => Character) public characters;

    uint256 public tokenCounter;

    constructor() ERC721("DynamicCharacter", "DCHAR") {
        tokenCounter = 0;
    }

    function mintCharacter(address to, string memory ability) public onlyOwne
```

```
r returns (uint256) {
        uint256 newCharacterId = tokenCounter;
        characters[newCharacterId] = Character({level: 1, ability: ability});
        _mint(to, newCharacterId);
        tokenCounter++;
        return newCharacterId;
    }

    function levelUp(uint256 tokenId) public {
        require(ownerOf(tokenId) == msg.sender, "Only the owner can level up"
);
        characters[tokenId].level++;
    }

    function updateAbility(uint256 tokenId, string memory newAbility) public
{
        require(ownerOf(tokenId) == msg.sender, "Only the owner can update ab
ility");
        characters[tokenId].ability = newAbility;
    }
}
```

This contract allows the owner to mint characters and players to level up and update their abilities.

Exclusive content and limited editions can create excitement and drive player engagement. Offering rare and limited-edition NFTs as rewards for special events, achievements, or purchases creates a sense of exclusivity and urgency. Players are more likely to participate in events and challenges to obtain these unique assets.

Integrating NFTs into social and community features enhances player interaction and collaboration. Players can showcase their NFT collections, trade assets, and participate in community-driven events. Creating social spaces where players can display and interact with their NFTs fosters a sense of community and belonging.

Rewarding players with NFTs for their achievements and milestones incentivizes continued engagement. Players can earn NFTs as they complete quests, win battles, or reach specific milestones. These rewards provide tangible recognition of their efforts and encourage them to keep playing.

Implementing NFTs in player-driven economies allows for vibrant marketplaces where players can buy, sell, and trade assets. This economic activity creates additional layers of interaction and engagement, as players can profit from their in-game achievements and investments.

Cross-platform interoperability enhances the value and utility of NFTs. Allowing players to use their NFTs across different games and platforms creates a seamless and consistent experience. For example, an NFT character obtained in one game could be used in another game, retaining its attributes and value.

Providing clear and transparent information about NFTs, including their rarity, attributes, and provenance, builds trust and enhances the player experience. Players should have access to detailed metadata and transaction history for their NFTs, allowing them to understand and appreciate the value of their assets.

Ensuring the security and authenticity of NFTs is critical for maintaining player trust. Implementing robust smart contract security, secure wallet integrations, and transparent auditing practices helps protect player assets and transactions.

In summary, enhancing player experience through NFTs involves providing true ownership, customization, dynamic progression, exclusive content, social features, rewards, player-driven economies, cross-platform interoperability, transparency, and security. By leveraging these strategies, developers can create engaging and rewarding experiences that enhance player satisfaction and immersion in the game.

Chapter 6: Monetizing Games with NFTs

6.1. New Revenue Models with NFTs

Non-fungible tokens (NFTs) are revolutionizing the way games generate revenue by introducing innovative and diverse monetization models. Unlike traditional in-game purchases, NFTs offer players true ownership of digital assets, enabling new revenue streams for developers and economic opportunities for players.

One of the most significant revenue models is the sale of NFT-based in-game assets. Developers can create and sell unique items, characters, and collectibles as NFTs. These assets can be sold directly to players through in-game stores or external marketplaces. The rarity and uniqueness of NFTs drive demand, allowing developers to price these assets higher than traditional in-game items.

For example, a game could sell exclusive NFT skins for characters. Players who purchase these skins own them outright and can trade them in secondary markets. The following Solidity contract snippet demonstrates how to create and sell NFT skins:

```solidity
pragma solidity ^0.8.0;

import "@openzeppelin/contracts/token/ERC721/ERC721.sol";
import "@openzeppelin/contracts/access/Ownable.sol";

contract GameSkins is ERC721, Ownable {
    uint256 public tokenCounter;

    constructor() ERC721("GameSkins", "GSKIN") {
        tokenCounter = 0;
    }

    function mintSkin(address to, string memory tokenURI) public onlyOwner returns (uint256) {
        uint256 newSkinId = tokenCounter;
        _mint(to, newSkinId);
        _setTokenURI(newSkinId, tokenURI);
        tokenCounter++;
        return newSkinId;
    }
}
```

This contract allows the game owner to mint and sell NFT skins to players.

Another revenue model is the implementation of play-to-earn (P2E) mechanics. In P2E games, players earn NFTs or cryptocurrency by participating in gameplay activities such as completing quests, winning battles, or achieving high scores. These rewards can be sold or traded, providing players with a tangible return on their time and effort. Developers benefit from increased player engagement and retention.

Additionally, developers can earn revenue through transaction fees and royalties. Every time an NFT is sold or traded on secondary markets, a small fee or royalty can be automatically deducted and sent to the developer. This creates a continuous revenue stream long after the initial sale. The following Solidity contract snippet demonstrates how to implement royalties:

```solidity
pragma solidity ^0.8.0;

import "@openzeppelin/contracts/token/ERC721/ERC721.sol";
import "@openzeppelin/contracts/access/Ownable.sol";

contract RoyaltyNFT is ERC721, Ownable {
    uint256 public tokenCounter;
    mapping(uint256 => uint256) public royalties;

    constructor() ERC721("RoyaltyNFT", "RNFT") {
        tokenCounter = 0;
    }

    function mintNFT(address to, string memory tokenURI, uint256 royalty) public onlyOwner returns (uint256) {
        uint256 newItemId = tokenCounter;
        _mint(to, newItemId);
        _setTokenURI(newItemId, tokenURI);
        royalties[newItemId] = royalty;
        tokenCounter++;
        return newItemId;
    }

    function transferFrom(address from, address to, uint256 tokenId) public override {
        super.transferFrom(from, to, tokenId);
        uint256 salePrice = msg.value;
        uint256 royalty = (salePrice * royalties[tokenId]) / 100;
        payable(owner()).transfer(royalty);
    }
}
```

This contract ensures that a percentage of the sale price is paid to the creator whenever the NFT is resold.

Subscription-based models can also incorporate NFTs. Players can subscribe to receive exclusive NFTs periodically, such as monthly drops of rare items or characters. This model provides a steady revenue stream and maintains player interest through regular content updates.

Limited-time events and auctions are effective ways to monetize NFTs. Developers can create special events where players compete for unique NFTs or participate in auctions for rare assets. These events generate excitement and urgency, driving higher participation and spending.

Collaborations and partnerships with artists, brands, and influencers can further enhance revenue opportunities. Limited-edition NFTs created in collaboration with popular figures can attract their fanbase, expanding the game's reach and appeal. These partnerships can also provide marketing benefits, increasing visibility and player acquisition.

NFTs can also be used to create decentralized autonomous organizations (DAOs) that allow players to participate in game governance. Players who own governance tokens can vote on game updates, new features, and community policies. Developers can monetize this model by selling governance tokens or offering them as rewards for in-game achievements.

Another innovative model is the integration of NFTs with real-world assets and experiences. Players can purchase NFTs that grant them access to exclusive real-world events, merchandise, or experiences. This model bridges the digital and physical worlds, creating unique value propositions for players.

In conclusion, NFTs offer a wide range of new revenue models for games. By selling NFT-based assets, implementing play-to-earn mechanics, earning transaction fees and royalties, offering subscriptions, hosting events and auctions, collaborating with partners, creating DAOs, and integrating real-world experiences, developers can diversify their revenue streams and enhance player engagement. These models leverage the unique properties of NFTs to create value for both developers and players, driving the growth and sustainability of the gaming industry.

6.2. Pricing Strategies for In-Game NFTs

Effective pricing strategies for in-game NFTs are crucial for maximizing revenue and ensuring player satisfaction. These strategies need to balance the perceived value of NFTs, market demand, and player affordability. This section explores various pricing models and best practices for setting the right prices for in-game NFTs.

One common pricing strategy is tiered pricing, where NFTs are categorized into different tiers based on their rarity, attributes, and utility. Each tier has a distinct price range, making it easier for players to understand the value proposition of each NFT. For example, common items might be priced affordably to attract a wide audience, while rare and legendary items command higher prices due to their scarcity and unique features.

Dynamic pricing is another effective strategy. This model adjusts NFT prices based on real-time market demand and player behavior. For instance, an NFT's price could increase as more players purchase it, reflecting its growing popularity. Conversely, prices can be lowered during promotions or events to boost sales. Implementing dynamic pricing requires robust data analytics and monitoring tools to track market trends and player activity.

Auction-based pricing can be used for highly sought-after NFTs. Auctions create a competitive environment where players bid against each other, driving up the price of the

NFT. This strategy is particularly effective for limited-edition and exclusive items. Auctions can be time-limited, creating urgency and excitement among players.

Here's an example of a Solidity contract for an NFT auction:

```solidity
pragma solidity ^0.8.0;

import "@openzeppelin/contracts/token/ERC721/ERC721.sol";
import "@openzeppelin/contracts/access/Ownable.sol";

contract NFTAuction is Ownable {
    struct Auction {
        address seller;
        uint256 startingPrice;
        uint256 highestBid;
        address highestBidder;
        bool active;
    }

    mapping(uint256 => Auction) public auctions;

    ERC721 public nftContract;

    constructor(address _nftContract) {
        nftContract = ERC721(_nftContract);
    }

    function startAuction(uint256 tokenId, uint256 startingPrice) public {
        require(nftContract.ownerOf(tokenId) == msg.sender, "Only the owner can start an auction");
        auctions[tokenId] = Auction({
            seller: msg.sender,
            startingPrice: startingPrice,
            highestBid: 0,
            highestBidder: address(0),
            active: true
        });
    }

    function placeBid(uint256 tokenId) public payable {
        Auction storage auction = auctions[tokenId];
        require(auction.active, "Auction is not active");
        require(msg.value > auction.highestBid, "Bid must be higher than the current highest bid");

        if (auction.highestBid > 0) {
            payable(auction.highestBidder).transfer(auction.highestBid);
        }
```

```solidity
        auction.highestBid = msg.value;
        auction.highestBidder = msg.sender;
    }

    function endAuction(uint256 tokenId) public onlyOwner {
        Auction storage auction = auctions[tokenId];
        require(auction.active, "Auction is not active");

        auction.active = false;
        nftContract.transferFrom(auction.seller, auction.highestBidder, tokenId);
        payable(auction.seller).transfer(auction.highestBid);
    }
}
```

This contract allows the owner to start, manage, and end auctions for NFTs.

Subscription-based pricing models can offer recurring revenue streams. Players can subscribe to receive periodic drops of NFTs, such as monthly or seasonal exclusive items. Subscriptions provide consistent content updates and maintain player interest over time. Pricing for subscriptions should reflect the value of the NFTs included and the frequency of drops.

Limited-time offers and discounts are effective for driving short-term sales. Developers can create special promotions where certain NFTs are available at a discounted price for a limited period. This strategy creates urgency and encourages players to make purchases before the offer expires.

Bundle pricing involves selling multiple NFTs as a package deal at a discounted rate compared to buying each item individually. Bundles can be themed around specific events, seasons, or gameplay mechanics, providing players with a cohesive set of assets. This strategy increases the perceived value and encourages players to spend more.

Pricing based on utility is another important consideration. NFTs that provide significant gameplay advantages, such as powerful weapons or rare characters, should be priced higher than purely cosmetic items. Players are generally willing to pay more for assets that enhance their gameplay experience and provide tangible benefits.

Market segmentation can help tailor pricing strategies to different player demographics. By analyzing player behavior and preferences, developers can create pricing models that cater to various segments, such as casual players, collectors, and competitive gamers. Offering a range of price points ensures accessibility and maximizes revenue potential.

Transparency in pricing builds trust with players. Clearly communicating the factors that determine an NFT's price, such as rarity, attributes, and demand, helps players understand the value they are receiving. Providing detailed information about the NFT's characteristics and potential uses enhances the perceived value.

In conclusion, effective pricing strategies for in-game NFTs involve tiered pricing, dynamic pricing, auctions, subscriptions, limited-time offers, bundle pricing, utility-based pricing, market segmentation, and transparency. By carefully considering these strategies and tailoring them to the game's audience and market conditions, developers can maximize revenue while ensuring player satisfaction and engagement.

6.3. Auctions and Secondary Markets

Auctions and secondary markets are pivotal components of the NFT ecosystem in gaming, enabling dynamic pricing, liquidity, and ongoing revenue opportunities for developers and players alike. This section delves into the mechanics, benefits, and implementation of auctions and secondary markets for NFTs.

Auctions are a powerful mechanism for determining the market value of unique and rare NFTs. They create a competitive environment where players bid against each other, driving up the price of the asset. This is particularly effective for limited-edition items, exclusive content, and highly sought-after assets. There are several types of auctions, including English auctions, Dutch auctions, and sealed-bid auctions, each with its own dynamics and strategic implications.

English auctions, where the highest bid wins, are the most common type in the NFT space. Here's an example of a Solidity contract for an English auction:

```solidity
pragma solidity ^0.8.0;

import "@openzeppelin/contracts/token/ERC721/ERC721.sol";
import "@openzeppelin/contracts/access/Ownable.sol";

contract EnglishAuction is Ownable {
    struct Auction {
        address seller;
        uint256 startingPrice;
        uint256 highestBid;
        address highestBidder;
        bool active;
        uint256 endTime;
    }

    mapping(uint256 => Auction) public auctions;

    ERC721 public nftContract;

    constructor(address _nftContract) {
        nftContract = ERC721(_nftContract);
    }

    function startAuction(uint256 tokenId, uint256 startingPrice, uint256 duration) public {
        require(nftContract.ownerOf(tokenId) == msg.sender, "Only the owner c
```

```
an start an auction");
        auctions[tokenId] = Auction({
            seller: msg.sender,
            startingPrice: startingPrice,
            highestBid: 0,
            highestBidder: address(0),
            active: true,
            endTime: block.timestamp + duration
        });
    }

    function placeBid(uint256 tokenId) public payable {
        Auction storage auction = auctions[tokenId];
        require(auction.active, "Auction is not active");
        require(block.timestamp < auction.endTime, "Auction has ended");
        require(msg.value > auction.highestBid, "Bid must be higher than the current highest bid");

        if (auction.highestBid > 0) {
            payable(auction.highestBidder).transfer(auction.highestBid);
        }

        auction.highestBid = msg.value;
        auction.highestBidder = msg.sender;
    }

    function endAuction(uint256 tokenId) public {
        Auction storage auction = auctions[tokenId];
        require(auction.active, "Auction is not active");
        require(block.timestamp >= auction.endTime, "Auction has not ended");

        auction.active = false;
        nftContract.transferFrom(auction.seller, auction.highestBidder, tokenId);
        payable(auction.seller).transfer(auction.highestBid);
    }
}
```

This contract facilitates the auction process, allowing players to bid on NFTs and the highest bidder to win the auction.

Secondary markets provide liquidity and ongoing trading opportunities for NFTs. These markets enable players to buy, sell, and trade NFTs after the initial sale, creating a vibrant and dynamic marketplace. Developers benefit from secondary markets through transaction fees and royalties, generating continuous revenue from resales.

Platforms like OpenSea, Rarible, and Mintable are popular secondary marketplaces for NFTs. They offer user-friendly interfaces and robust trading features, making it easy for players to list and trade their assets. Integration with these platforms can extend the reach of in-game NFTs, attracting a broader audience and increasing liquidity.

Implementing royalties in secondary markets ensures that creators and developers earn a percentage of each resale. This incentivizes high-quality content creation and provides a sustainable revenue stream. The following Solidity contract snippet demonstrates how to implement royalties:

```solidity
pragma solidity ^0.8.0;

import "@openzeppelin/contracts/token/ERC721/ERC721.sol";
import "@openzeppelin/contracts/access/Ownable.sol";

contract RoyaltyNFT is ERC721, Ownable {
    uint256 public tokenCounter;
    mapping(uint256 => uint256) public royalties;

    constructor() ERC721("RoyaltyNFT", "RNFT") {
        tokenCounter = 0;
    }

    function mintNFT(address to, string memory tokenURI, uint256 royalty) public onlyOwner returns (uint256) {
        uint256 newItemId = tokenCounter;
        _mint(to, newItemId);
        _setTokenURI(newItemId, tokenURI);
        royalties[newItemId] = royalty;
        tokenCounter++;
        return newItemId;
    }

    function transferFrom(address from, address to, uint256 tokenId) public override {
        super.transferFrom(from, to, tokenId);
        uint256 salePrice = msg.value;
        uint256 royalty = (salePrice * royalties[tokenId]) / 100;
        payable(owner()).transfer(royalty);
    }
}
```

This contract ensures that a percentage of the sale price is paid to the creator whenever the NFT is resold.

Creating in-game marketplaces where players can trade NFTs directly within the game environment enhances player engagement and convenience. These marketplaces can be integrated into the game's interface, allowing players to browse, list, and purchase NFTs without leaving the game. Providing features like search filters, categories, and user reviews enhances the trading experience.

Ensuring security and authenticity in auctions and secondary markets is paramount. Smart contracts must be thoroughly audited to prevent vulnerabilities and exploits. Implementing secure communication protocols and user authentication measures helps protect transactions and user data. Transparency in auction processes and transaction histories builds trust among players.

Promoting auctions and secondary markets through in-game events, social media, and partnerships can drive traffic and participation. Highlighting rare and exclusive items, featuring popular auctions, and collaborating with influencers can create buzz and attract new players.

In conclusion, auctions and secondary markets are integral to the NFT ecosystem in gaming, providing dynamic pricing, liquidity, and continuous revenue opportunities. By implementing robust auction mechanisms, integrating with secondary marketplaces, ensuring security, promoting trading activities, and leveraging royalties, developers can create vibrant and sustainable NFT economies that benefit both players and creators.

6.4. Royalties and Continuous Earning Models

Royalties and continuous earning models are essential components for sustainable revenue generation in the NFT ecosystem. These mechanisms ensure that creators and developers receive ongoing compensation from secondary sales and long-term engagement. This section explores the implementation and benefits of royalties and continuous earning models in gaming NFTs.

Royalties are a percentage of the sale price paid to the original creator whenever an NFT is resold on secondary markets. This model provides a continuous revenue stream and incentivizes high-quality content creation. Implementing royalties requires smart contract functions that automatically calculate and distribute the royalty payments.

Here's an example of a Solidity contract implementing royalties for NFTs:

```solidity
pragma solidity ^0.8.0;

import "@openzeppelin/contracts/token/ERC721/ERC721.sol";
import "@openzeppelin/contracts/access/Ownable.sol";

contract RoyaltyNFT is ERC721, Ownable {
    uint256 public tokenCounter;
    mapping(uint256 => uint256) public royalties;

    constructor() ERC721("RoyaltyNFT", "RNFT") {
        tokenCounter = 0;
    }

    function mintNFT(address to, string memory tokenURI, uint256 royalty) public onlyOwner returns (uint256) {
        uint256 newItemId = tokenCounter;
        _mint(to, newItemId);
```

```
        _setTokenURI(newItemId, tokenURI);
        royalties[newItemId] = royalty;
        tokenCounter++;
        return newItemId;
    }

    function transferFrom(address from, address to, uint256 tokenId) public o
verride {
        super.transferFrom(from, to, tokenId);
        uint256 salePrice = msg.value;
        uint256 royalty = (salePrice * royalties[tokenId]) / 100;
        payable(owner()).transfer(royalty);
    }
}
```

This contract ensures that a percentage of the sale price is paid to the creator whenever the NFT is resold.

Continuous earning models can extend beyond royalties. Subscription-based models offer recurring revenue streams by providing players with regular drops of exclusive NFTs, in-game items, or premium content. Subscriptions can be monthly, seasonal, or event-based, keeping players engaged with fresh content and generating consistent income for developers.

Implementing a subscription model requires setting up smart contracts that manage subscription payments and content delivery. The following Solidity contract snippet demonstrates a basic subscription model:

```
pragma solidity ^0.8.0;

import "@openzeppelin/contracts/access/Ownable.sol";

contract NFTSubscription is Ownable {
    uint256 public subscriptionPrice;
    mapping(address => uint256) public subscriptions;

    constructor(uint256 _subscriptionPrice) {
        subscriptionPrice = _subscriptionPrice;
    }

    function subscribe() public payable {
        require(msg.value == subscriptionPrice, "Incorrect subscription price
");
        subscriptions[msg.sender] = block.timestamp + 30 days;
    }

    function isSubscribed(address user) public view returns (bool) {
        return subscriptions[user] > block.timestamp;
    }
```

```solidity
    function setSubscriptionPrice(uint256 newPrice) public onlyOwner {
        subscriptionPrice = newPrice;
    }
}
```

This contract allows users to subscribe and checks if their subscription is active.

Play-to-earn (P2E) models offer continuous earning opportunities by rewarding players with NFTs or cryptocurrency for their in-game achievements. This model enhances player engagement and retention, as players can monetize their time and skills. Implementing P2E mechanics involves setting up reward systems and ensuring a fair distribution of rewards.

For example, a game could reward players with NFTs for completing quests or winning battles. The following Solidity contract snippet demonstrates how to distribute rewards:

```solidity
pragma solidity ^0.8.0;

import "@openzeppelin/contracts/token/ERC721/ERC721.sol";
import "@openzeppelin/contracts/access/Ownable.sol";

contract GameRewards is ERC721, Ownable {
    uint256 public tokenCounter;

    constructor() ERC721("GameRewards", "GREWARD") {
        tokenCounter = 0;
    }

    function rewardNFT(address to, string memory tokenURI) public onlyOwner returns (uint256) {
        uint256 newItemId = tokenCounter;
        _mint(to, newItemId);
        _setTokenURI(newItemId, tokenURI);
        tokenCounter++;
        return newItemId;
    }
}
```

This contract allows the game owner to mint and distribute NFTs as rewards.

In-game staking is another continuous earning model where players lock up their NFTs or in-game assets to earn rewards over time. Staking incentivizes players to hold onto their assets, reducing market supply and increasing demand. Implementing staking requires smart contracts that manage the staking process and reward distribution.

The following Solidity contract snippet demonstrates an NFT staking mechanism:

```solidity
pragma solidity ^0.8.0;

import "@openzeppelin/contracts/token/ERC721/ERC721.sol";
```

```solidity
import "@openzeppelin/contracts/access/Ownable.sol";

contract NFTStaking is Ownable {
    struct Stake {
        uint256 tokenId;
        uint256 startTime;
    }

    mapping(address => Stake[]) public stakes;
    ERC721 public nftContract;

    constructor(address _nftContract) {
        nftContract = ERC721(_nftContract);
    }

    function stakeNFT(uint256 tokenId) public {
        nftContract.transferFrom(msg.sender, address(this), tokenId);
        stakes[msg.sender].push(Stake({tokenId: tokenId, startTime: block.timestamp}));
    }

    function unstakeNFT(uint256 tokenId) public {
        Stake[] storage userStakes = stakes[msg.sender];
        for (uint256 i = 0; i < userStakes.length; i++) {
            if (userStakes[i].tokenId == tokenId) {
                nftContract.transferFrom(address(this), msg.sender, tokenId);
                userStakes[i] = userStakes[userStakes.length - 1];
                userStakes.pop();
                break;
            }
        }
    }

    function calculateRewards(address user, uint256 tokenId) public view returns (uint256) {
        Stake[] storage userStakes = stakes[user];
        for (uint256 i = 0; i < userStakes.length; i++) {
            if (userStakes[i].tokenId == tokenId) {
                uint256 stakingDuration = block.timestamp - userStakes[i].startTime;
                return stakingDuration * 1e18; // Example reward calculation
            }
        }
        return 0;
    }
}
```

This contract allows users to stake their NFTs and calculates rewards based on the staking duration.

Transparency and fairness in continuous earning models build trust with players. Clearly communicating how rewards are calculated, distributed, and managed ensures players understand the value they are receiving. Regular updates and transparent reporting of earnings and distributions enhance player confidence.

In conclusion, royalties and continuous earning models are crucial for sustainable revenue generation in the NFT ecosystem. By implementing royalties, subscription-based models, play-to-earn mechanics, staking, and ensuring transparency, developers can create ongoing revenue streams and incentivize high-quality content creation. These models enhance player engagement and provide long-term value for both developers and players.

6.5. Case Studies of Monetization Success

Examining case studies of successful NFT monetization provides valuable insights into effective strategies and best practices. This section explores several games and platforms that have successfully integrated NFTs to generate substantial revenue and enhance player engagement.

Axie Infinity: Axie Infinity is a pioneering play-to-earn game that allows players to collect, breed, and battle fantasy creatures called Axies, which are represented as NFTs. The game's success is attributed to its robust play-to-earn mechanics, vibrant marketplace, and strong community engagement. Players earn cryptocurrency (AXS and SLP) by participating in battles and completing quests, which they can trade on secondary markets. Axie Infinity's economic model incentivizes player retention and spending, resulting in significant revenue for the developers and substantial earnings for players.

Decentraland: Decentraland is a decentralized virtual world where users can buy, sell, and build on virtual land parcels represented as NFTs. The platform's success stems from its open-ended nature, allowing users to create and monetize their content. Developers and creators earn revenue by selling land, building experiences, and offering virtual goods and services. Decentraland's marketplace enables continuous trading and revenue generation, supported by a strong community and active user base.

CryptoKitties: As one of the first NFT-based games, CryptoKitties introduced the concept of collectible digital cats represented as NFTs. Players can breed, trade, and sell CryptoKitties, each with unique attributes and rarity. The game's initial success highlighted the potential of NFTs for generating revenue through scarcity and desirability. CryptoKitties' marketplace facilitated high-value sales and continuous trading, demonstrating the viability of NFT-based economies.

The Sandbox: The Sandbox is a virtual world where players can create, own, and monetize gaming experiences using NFTs and the platform's native token, SAND. The game's success lies in its user-generated content model, enabling creators to build and sell assets, games, and experiences. The Sandbox's marketplace supports continuous trading and revenue generation, incentivizing creativity and collaboration. The platform's partnerships with popular brands and artists further enhance its appeal and revenue potential.

Sorare: Sorare is a fantasy football game that uses blockchain technology to create and trade officially licensed digital player cards as NFTs. Players build teams and compete in fantasy leagues, earning rewards based on real-world player performances. Sorare's monetization success is driven by its collectible cards, real-world integration, and competitive gameplay. The platform's secondary market for trading cards generates ongoing revenue for both developers and players.

Zed Run: Zed Run is a digital horse racing game where players can buy, breed, and race digital horses represented as NFTs. The game's success is attributed to its innovative use of blockchain technology, dynamic gameplay, and active community. Players earn revenue through racing winnings, breeding fees, and trading horses on the secondary market. Zed Run's marketplace supports continuous trading and revenue generation, attracting a dedicated player base.

Alien Worlds: Alien Worlds is a decentralized metaverse game that allows players to mine for resources, acquire land, and engage in battles using NFTs. The game's economic model revolves around its native token, TLM, and NFT-based assets, creating a vibrant player-driven economy. Players earn revenue through mining, trading NFTs, and participating in governance. Alien Worlds' success is driven by its engaging gameplay, active community, and continuous earning opportunities.

NBA Top Shot: NBA Top Shot is a blockchain-based platform that allows users to buy, sell, and trade officially licensed NBA collectible highlights as NFTs. The platform's success is due to its strong brand partnership, engaging content, and user-friendly marketplace. NBA Top Shot's revenue model includes primary sales, transaction fees, and royalties from secondary market trades. The platform's continuous release of new collectible moments keeps players engaged and drives ongoing revenue.

Gods Unchained: Gods Unchained is a blockchain-based trading card game where players own their cards as NFTs. The game's success stems from its competitive gameplay, high-quality graphics, and robust marketplace. Players can buy, sell, and trade cards, earning revenue from both primary sales and secondary market transactions. Gods Unchained's play-to-earn mechanics and tournaments provide continuous earning opportunities, enhancing player engagement and retention.

These case studies highlight several key strategies for successful NFT monetization:

1. **Play-to-Earn Mechanics**: Games like Axie Infinity and Alien Worlds incentivize player engagement and spending by rewarding players with valuable NFTs and cryptocurrency for their in-game activities.

2. **User-Generated Content**: Platforms like Decentraland and The Sandbox empower users to create and monetize their content, driving continuous revenue through sales and trading.

3. **Scarcity and Collectibility**: Games like CryptoKitties and Sorare leverage the scarcity and uniqueness of NFTs to drive demand and high-value sales.

4. **Secondary Markets**: Successful platforms integrate robust marketplaces that facilitate continuous trading and revenue generation through transaction fees and royalties.

5. **Brand Partnerships**: Platforms like NBA Top Shot benefit from strong brand partnerships, attracting a broad audience and enhancing the perceived value of NFTs.

6. **Engaging Gameplay**: Games like Gods Unchained and Zed Run combine engaging gameplay with NFT ownership, creating a compelling experience that retains players and drives spending.

In conclusion, these case studies demonstrate that effective NFT monetization strategies involve leveraging play-to-earn mechanics, user-generated content, scarcity, secondary markets, brand partnerships, and engaging gameplay. By adopting these strategies, developers can create successful and sustainable NFT-based economies that generate significant revenue and enhance player engagement.

Chapter 7: Building NFT Game Communities

7.1. Engaging Players with NFT Collectibles

Engaging players with NFT collectibles involves creating desirable, valuable, and interactive digital assets that enhance the gaming experience and foster community involvement. This section explores various strategies and best practices for designing and implementing NFT collectibles to maximize player engagement.

One effective strategy is to create NFT collectibles with unique and appealing designs. Collaborating with talented artists to produce high-quality visuals ensures that NFTs stand out and attract players. Limited edition and exclusive designs add value and scarcity, making them more desirable. Providing detailed backstories and lore for these collectibles can further enhance their appeal.

Dynamic and evolving NFTs are another way to engage players. NFTs that change based on player actions or in-game events add an interactive element. For example, an NFT character that gains new abilities or changes appearance as the player progresses through the game creates a sense of growth and personalization. Here's an example of a Solidity contract for a dynamic NFT character:

```solidity
pragma solidity ^0.8.0;

import "@openzeppelin/contracts/token/ERC721/ERC721.sol";
import "@openzeppelin/contracts/access/Ownable.sol";

contract DynamicCharacter is ERC721, Ownable {
    struct Character {
        uint256 level;
        string ability;
    }

    mapping(uint256 => Character) public characters;

    uint256 public tokenCounter;

    constructor() ERC721("DynamicCharacter", "DCHAR") {
        tokenCounter = 0;
    }

    function mintCharacter(address to, string memory ability) public onlyOwner returns (uint256) {
        uint256 newCharacterId = tokenCounter;
        characters[newCharacterId] = Character({level: 1, ability: ability});
        _mint(to, newCharacterId);
        tokenCounter++;
        return newCharacterId;
```

```
    }

    function levelUp(uint256 tokenId) public {
        require(ownerOf(tokenId) == msg.sender, "Only the owner can level up"
);
        characters[tokenId].level++;
    }

    function updateAbility(uint256 tokenId, string memory newAbility) public
{
        require(ownerOf(tokenId) == msg.sender, "Only the owner can update ab
ility");
        characters[tokenId].ability = newAbility;
    }
}
```

This contract allows the owner to mint characters and players to level up and update their abilities, creating a dynamic and interactive experience.

Integrating NFT collectibles into the core gameplay loop can significantly boost engagement. Players can earn NFTs as rewards for completing quests, winning battles, or achieving milestones. These rewards provide tangible recognition of player achievements and encourage continued participation. Implementing leaderboards and achievements tied to NFT rewards adds a competitive element that further motivates players.

Community-driven content creation and customization are powerful tools for engagement. Allowing players to create, modify, and trade their own NFT collectibles fosters a sense of ownership and creativity. Providing tools and platforms for players to showcase and sell their creations can build a thriving community. For example, a game could implement a marketplace where players can list their custom NFTs for sale.

Hosting events and challenges that revolve around NFT collectibles can also drive engagement. Special events, tournaments, and seasonal activities that offer exclusive NFT rewards generate excitement and encourage players to participate. These events can be time-limited to create urgency and increase player involvement.

Collaboration with influencers and content creators can amplify the reach and impact of NFT collectibles. Partnering with popular figures in the gaming community to create and promote exclusive NFTs can attract their followers and generate buzz. Influencers can also engage with the community through live streams, social media, and events, showcasing the unique features and value of the NFTs.

Storytelling and narrative integration enhance the emotional connection players have with NFT collectibles. Embedding rich narratives and lore into NFTs makes them more meaningful and memorable. Players are more likely to value and cherish NFTs that have a compelling story or history attached to them.

Transparency and fairness in the distribution of NFT collectibles build trust within the community. Clearly communicating how NFTs are minted, distributed, and traded ensures that players understand the value and rarity of their assets. Implementing fair and transparent mechanics for obtaining NFTs, such as random drops or guaranteed rewards for specific achievements, prevents frustration and fosters a positive player experience.

Leveraging social features to showcase NFT collections enhances community interaction. Allowing players to display their NFT collections in their profiles, share them on social media, and compare them with others fosters a sense of pride and competition. Implementing social features such as likes, comments, and sharing further enhances community engagement.

In conclusion, engaging players with NFT collectibles involves creating unique and appealing designs, integrating dynamic and evolving elements, embedding them into core gameplay, enabling community-driven content creation, hosting events, collaborating with influencers, integrating storytelling, ensuring transparency, and leveraging social features. By implementing these strategies, developers can create a vibrant and engaged community around their NFT collectibles, enhancing the overall gaming experience.

7.2. Community Building on Blockchain

Building a strong community on blockchain involves leveraging the decentralized nature of blockchain technology to foster engagement, trust, and collaboration among players. This section explores various strategies and best practices for community building in blockchain-based games.

One of the key elements of community building on blockchain is transparency. Blockchain's immutable and transparent nature allows developers to provide verifiable proof of ownership, transaction history, and game mechanics. This transparency builds trust among players, as they can independently verify the integrity and fairness of the game. Regularly communicating with the community about updates, changes, and events further enhances transparency.

Decentralized governance is another powerful tool for community building. Implementing decentralized autonomous organizations (DAOs) allows players to participate in decision-making processes, such as voting on game updates, new features, and community policies. This empowers players and fosters a sense of ownership and involvement in the game's development. Here's an example of a Solidity contract for a simple DAO:

```solidity
pragma solidity ^0.8.0;

contract SimpleDAO {
    struct Proposal {
        string description;
        uint256 voteCount;
    }

    Proposal[] public proposals;
    mapping(address => bool) public voters;

    function createProposal(string memory description) public {
```

```
        proposals.push(Proposal({description: description, voteCount: 0}));
    }

    function vote(uint256 proposalIndex) public {
        require(!voters[msg.sender], "Already voted");
        proposals[proposalIndex].voteCount++;
        voters[msg.sender] = true;
    }

    function getProposal(uint256 proposalIndex) public view returns (string memory, uint256) {
        Proposal memory proposal = proposals[proposalIndex];
        return (proposal.description, proposal.voteCount);
    }
}
```

This contract allows players to create proposals and vote on them, enabling decentralized governance.

Incentivizing community participation through rewards and recognition can drive engagement. Players can earn tokens, NFTs, or other rewards for contributing to the community, such as providing feedback, creating content, or participating in events. Recognizing top contributors and highlighting their achievements fosters a positive and active community.

Creating social spaces and platforms for community interaction is essential. Dedicated forums, Discord channels, and social media groups provide players with places to discuss the game, share experiences, and collaborate on projects. These platforms facilitate communication between developers and players, enabling direct feedback and engagement.

Regularly hosting community events, such as tournaments, challenges, and Q&A sessions, can keep the community active and engaged. Events that offer exclusive rewards and recognition create excitement and encourage participation. Live streaming events and involving influencers can amplify their reach and impact.

Collaborating with other blockchain projects and communities can expand the reach and visibility of the game. Cross-promotions, joint events, and shared initiatives with other blockchain games or platforms can attract new players and foster collaboration. These partnerships can also provide additional value and utility to players by enabling cross-game interactions and asset interoperability.

Educational initiatives can help onboard new players and increase community involvement. Providing resources, tutorials, and guides about blockchain technology, game mechanics, and community participation empowers players to understand and engage with the game. Hosting webinars, workshops, and AMA (Ask Me Anything) sessions with developers and experts can further enhance player knowledge and involvement.

Implementing fair and inclusive practices ensures that all players feel welcome and valued. Establishing clear community guidelines, addressing toxic behavior, and promoting diversity and inclusion foster a positive and respectful environment. Ensuring that the game and community platforms are accessible to players with different backgrounds and abilities is also crucial.

Leveraging feedback loops allows developers to continuously improve the game based on player input. Regularly soliciting feedback through surveys, polls, and discussions helps identify areas for improvement and new features that players want. Acting on this feedback and communicating the changes made based on player suggestions builds trust and demonstrates a commitment to the community.

Finally, fostering a culture of collaboration and co-creation empowers players to contribute to the game's development. Providing tools and platforms for players to create and share content, such as mods, levels, and assets, encourages creativity and collaboration. Recognizing and rewarding player contributions further incentivizes active participation.

In conclusion, building a strong community on blockchain involves leveraging transparency, decentralized governance, incentivizing participation, creating social spaces, hosting events, collaborating with other projects, providing educational initiatives, ensuring inclusivity, leveraging feedback loops, and fostering a culture of collaboration. By implementing these strategies, developers can create a vibrant and engaged community that enhances the overall gaming experience.

7.3. Leveraging Social Media for NFT Gaming Promotion

Leveraging social media for NFT gaming promotion is essential for building awareness, engaging the community, and driving player acquisition. This section explores various strategies and best practices for effectively using social media to promote NFT games.

One of the key strategies is to create and maintain active social media profiles on major platforms such as Twitter, Facebook, Instagram, and LinkedIn. Regularly posting updates, news, and engaging content keeps the community informed and interested. Visual content, such as images, videos, and GIFs, tends to perform well on social media and can highlight the game's unique features and NFT assets.

Collaborating with influencers and content creators can significantly amplify the reach of social media campaigns. Partnering with popular figures in the gaming and blockchain communities to promote the game and its NFTs can attract their followers and generate buzz. Influencers can create content such as live streams, reviews, and tutorials, showcasing the game and its features to a wider audience.

Hosting social media contests and giveaways can drive engagement and increase visibility. Encouraging followers to participate in challenges, share content, and use specific hashtags can create viral campaigns. Offering exclusive NFTs or in-game rewards as prizes incentivizes participation and spreads awareness about the game.

Here's an example of a simple social media contest announcement:

🎉 Giveaway Alert! 🎉

We're giving away 10 exclusive NFTs to celebrate our game launch! 🎮

To enter:
1️⃣ Follow us @GameProfile
2️⃣ Like and retweet this post
3️⃣ Tag 3 friends in the comments

Winners will be announced on [date]. Good luck! 🍀 #GameNFTGiveaway #NFTGaming

This announcement encourages followers to engage with the post and spread it to their networks.

Creating a content calendar helps plan and organize social media activities. Scheduling regular posts, updates, and promotions ensures consistent engagement and keeps the community informed. A content calendar can also help coordinate campaigns across different platforms, maximizing their impact.

Engaging with the community through comments, messages, and replies builds a positive and interactive social media presence. Responding to questions, acknowledging feedback, and participating in discussions show that the developers value the community's input. This engagement fosters a sense of connection and loyalty among players.

Utilizing hashtags effectively can increase the visibility of social media posts. Using popular and relevant hashtags, such as #NFT, #BlockchainGaming, and #PlayToEarn, helps reach a broader audience. Creating branded hashtags for specific campaigns or events can also generate a cohesive and recognizable social media presence.

Sharing user-generated content (UGC) highlights the community's involvement and creativity. Encouraging players to share their experiences, creations, and achievements with the game, and then featuring their content on the game's social media profiles, builds a sense of community and recognition. UGC campaigns can include fan art, gameplay clips, and testimonials.

Running targeted social media ads can effectively reach potential players. Platforms like Facebook, Twitter, and Instagram offer advanced targeting options based on demographics, interests, and behaviors. Crafting compelling ad creatives and copy that highlight the game's unique features and benefits can attract new players and drive conversions.

Creating and sharing engaging video content can capture the audience's attention and convey the game's value proposition effectively. Videos such as trailers, gameplay demos, behind-the-scenes footage, and developer interviews provide an immersive glimpse into the game. Live streaming events and updates also create real-time engagement with the community.

Analytics and metrics tracking are crucial for evaluating the effectiveness of social media campaigns. Monitoring key performance indicators (KPIs) such as reach, engagement, click-through rates, and conversion rates helps identify what works and what doesn't.

Analyzing this data enables continuous improvement and optimization of social media strategies.

Collaborating with other blockchain projects and communities on social media can expand the reach and impact of promotional efforts. Cross-promotions, joint events, and shared initiatives with other games or platforms can attract new players and foster collaboration. These partnerships can also provide additional value and utility to players by enabling cross-game interactions and asset interoperability.

In conclusion, leveraging social media for NFT gaming promotion involves creating active profiles, collaborating with influencers, hosting contests, planning content, engaging with the community, utilizing hashtags, sharing user-generated content, running targeted ads, creating engaging videos, tracking analytics, and collaborating with other projects. By implementing these strategies, developers can effectively promote their NFT games, attract new players, and build a strong and engaged community.

7.4. Organizing Online Events and Tournaments

Organizing online events and tournaments is an effective way to engage the community, showcase the game, and attract new players. This section explores various strategies and best practices for planning and executing successful online events and tournaments for NFT games.

One of the key strategies is to create events that offer exclusive rewards and recognition. Players are more likely to participate if they have the opportunity to earn rare NFTs, in-game items, or other valuable rewards. Limited-time events create urgency and excitement, encouraging players to join and compete.

Structuring tournaments with clear rules, brackets, and schedules ensures a smooth and organized experience for participants. Providing detailed information about the tournament format, eligibility criteria, and prize distribution helps set expectations and reduces confusion. Platforms like Discord, Battlefy, and Toornament offer tools for managing and organizing online tournaments.

Here's an example of a tournament announcement:

□ Get Ready for the Ultimate Battle! □

Join our [Game Name] Tournament for a chance to win exclusive NFTs and in-game rewards! □

□ Date: [Event Date]
□ Time: [Event Time]
□ Rules: [Link to Rules]
□ Prizes: [List of Prizes]

Register now at [Registration Link] and show your skills! □□#GameTournament #NFTGaming

This announcement provides essential details and a call to action for players to register.

Leveraging live streaming platforms such as Twitch and YouTube enhances the visibility and excitement of events. Live streaming the tournaments allows a broader audience to watch the action, cheer for their favorite players, and engage with the community in real-time. Incorporating live commentary, player interviews, and interactive elements like chat and polls adds to the immersive experience.

Collaborating with influencers and content creators to participate in or promote the events can significantly boost their reach and impact. Influencers can help generate buzz, attract their followers, and provide commentary or analysis during the live stream. Their involvement adds credibility and excitement to the events.

Hosting pre-event activities and challenges can build anticipation and engagement. For example, running mini-competitions, trivia quizzes, or social media contests leading up to the main event keeps the community active and excited. These activities can offer smaller rewards or exclusive entries to the main tournament.

Creating dedicated spaces for event discussions and updates ensures that participants and the community stay informed. Setting up event-specific channels on platforms like Discord or Reddit allows players to discuss strategies, share experiences, and receive timely updates from the organizers. Regularly posting announcements, schedules, and results keeps the community engaged.

Ensuring fair play and integrity during events is crucial for maintaining trust and credibility. Implementing robust anti-cheat measures, monitoring gameplay, and having clear rules and enforcement procedures helps prevent cheating and disputes. Providing a transparent and fair environment encourages more players to participate.

Offering multiple formats and difficulty levels caters to a broader range of players. Hosting events for different skill levels, such as beginner, intermediate, and advanced, ensures that players of all abilities have a chance to compete and win. Special formats like team-based tournaments, speedruns, or themed challenges add variety and appeal.

Post-event engagement is essential for maintaining momentum and community involvement. Sharing highlights, results, and player achievements on social media and community platforms keeps the conversation going. Recognizing and rewarding top performers, sharing event feedback, and announcing future events fosters a sense of continuity and anticipation.

Leveraging analytics and feedback helps improve future events. Collecting data on participation rates, viewer engagement, and player feedback provides valuable insights into what worked well and what can be improved. Using this information to refine event formats, schedules, and rewards ensures continuous improvement and better experiences for participants.

In conclusion, organizing online events and tournaments for NFT games involves offering exclusive rewards, structuring tournaments clearly, leveraging live streaming, collaborating with influencers, hosting pre-event activities, creating dedicated discussion spaces, ensuring fair play, offering multiple formats, engaging post-event, and leveraging analytics and feedback. By implementing these strategies, developers can create exciting and engaging events that attract and retain players, showcase the game, and build a strong community.

7.5. The Role of Influencers and Streamers

Influencers and streamers play a pivotal role in promoting NFT games, building communities, and driving player engagement. This section explores the strategies and best practices for effectively leveraging influencers and streamers to enhance the visibility and success of NFT games.

One of the key strategies is to identify and collaborate with influencers and streamers who align with the game's target audience and values. Choosing influencers who are passionate about gaming, blockchain technology, and NFTs ensures that their promotion is authentic and resonates with their followers. Researching and selecting influencers based on their content, engagement rates, and audience demographics is crucial for effective collaboration.

Offering influencers exclusive access to the game, early previews, and unique NFTs can generate excitement and anticipation. Providing them with special content or assets that they can showcase to their followers creates a sense of exclusivity and adds value to their promotion. For example, giving influencers rare in-game items or characters to use during their streams can attract viewers and generate buzz.

Here's an example of an influencer collaboration announcement:

□ Exciting News! □

We've partnered with [Influencer Name] to bring you an exclusive sneak peek of [Game Name] and a chance to win unique NFTs! □

Join the live stream on [Date] at [Time] and see [Influencer Name] explore the game, battle epic foes, and unlock rare items! Don't miss out on this special event! □ #GameCollab #NFTGaming #ExclusiveSneakPeek

This announcement highlights the collaboration and invites the community to join the event.

Running co-branded campaigns and events with influencers can significantly boost visibility and engagement. Collaborating on special challenges, tournaments, or in-game events where influencers participate or compete can attract their followers and create a shared experience. These co-branded initiatives can be promoted across both the game's and the influencer's social media channels for maximum reach.

Leveraging influencers for content creation helps generate diverse and engaging promotional material. Encouraging influencers to create videos, reviews, tutorials, and live streams showcasing the game and its NFTs provides valuable content that can be shared across platforms. Influencers' unique perspectives and creativity add authenticity and variety to the promotional efforts.

Engaging influencers for community interaction and engagement can enhance the player experience. Hosting Q&A sessions, live streams, and community events where influencers interact with players, answer questions, and share their experiences fosters a sense of connection and involvement. These interactions build trust and loyalty among players.

Incentivizing influencers with revenue-sharing models, affiliate programs, or exclusive rewards can motivate them to promote the game more actively. Providing influencers with unique referral codes, affiliate links, or commission on sales generated through their promotion creates a mutually beneficial partnership. This incentivization encourages influencers to invest time and effort into their promotion.

Measuring and analyzing the impact of influencer collaborations is essential for optimizing future efforts. Tracking key metrics such as reach, engagement, conversions, and player acquisition provides insights into the effectiveness of the campaigns. Using tools and platforms that offer detailed analytics and reporting helps assess the ROI of influencer partnerships.

Creating long-term relationships with influencers can lead to sustained promotion and community building. Engaging influencers as brand ambassadors or ongoing collaborators ensures continuous visibility and support. Building these long-term partnerships fosters loyalty and consistency in the game's promotion.

Leveraging micro-influencers, in addition to high-profile influencers, can expand the reach and impact of promotional efforts. Micro-influencers often have highly engaged and niche audiences, making their promotion more targeted and effective. Collaborating with multiple micro-influencers can create a broad and diverse promotional network.

Involving influencers in the game's development and feedback processes can provide valuable insights and enhance the game's appeal. Seeking input from influencers on game features, mechanics, and community initiatives ensures that the game resonates with its audience. Influencers' feedback and suggestions can help refine the game and improve player satisfaction.

In conclusion, influencers and streamers play a crucial role in promoting NFT games, building communities, and driving engagement. By identifying the right influencers, offering exclusive access, running co-branded campaigns, leveraging content creation, engaging for community interaction, incentivizing partnerships, measuring impact, building long-term relationships, leveraging micro-influencers, and involving influencers in development, developers can effectively harness the power of influencers and streamers to enhance the visibility and success of their NFT games.

Chapter 8: NFTs in Multiplayer and Online Games

8.1. NFTs in Massively Multiplayer Online Games (MMOGs)

Massively Multiplayer Online Games (MMOGs) are a natural fit for integrating NFTs, as they provide expansive virtual worlds where players can interact, trade, and compete. NFTs can enhance these environments by introducing true ownership, rarity, and interoperability of in-game assets.

In MMOGs, NFTs can represent a wide range of assets, including characters, equipment, land, and collectibles. Each asset can have unique attributes and history, providing players with a sense of ownership and investment in the game. For example, an NFT-based character might have unique abilities, appearance, and a record of its achievements and upgrades.

Here's an example of a Solidity contract for an NFT-based character in an MMOG:

```solidity
pragma solidity ^0.8.0;

import "@openzeppelin/contracts/token/ERC721/ERC721.sol";
import "@openzeppelin/contracts/access/Ownable.sol";

contract MMOGCharacter is ERC721, Ownable {
    struct Character {
        uint256 level;
        string abilities;
    }

    mapping(uint256 => Character) public characters;

    uint256 public tokenCounter;

    constructor() ERC721("MMOGCharacter", "MMOGC") {
        tokenCounter = 0;
    }

    function mintCharacter(address to, string memory abilities) public onlyOwner returns (uint256) {
        uint256 newCharacterId = tokenCounter;
        characters[newCharacterId] = Character({level: 1, abilities: abilities});
        _mint(to, newCharacterId);
        tokenCounter++;
        return newCharacterId;
    }

    function levelUp(uint256 tokenId) public {
        require(ownerOf(tokenId) == msg.sender, "Only the owner can level up"
```

```
    );
        characters[tokenId].level++;
    }

    function updateAbilities(uint256 tokenId, string memory newAbilities) public {
        require(ownerOf(tokenId) == msg.sender, "Only the owner can update abilities");
        characters[tokenId].abilities = newAbilities;
    }
}
```

This contract allows the owner to mint characters and players to level up and update their abilities, creating a dynamic and interactive experience.

NFTs enable players to trade in-game assets on secondary markets, providing a new dimension of economic activity. Players can buy, sell, and trade their NFTs, creating a player-driven economy. This adds value to in-game achievements and investments, as players can monetize their assets outside the game.

Interoperability is another significant advantage of NFTs in MMOGs. NFTs can be designed to work across different games and platforms, allowing players to use their assets in multiple virtual worlds. This enhances the utility and value of NFTs, as players are not confined to a single game. For example, a rare sword obtained in one game could be used in another game that supports the same NFT standard.

Decentralized governance can also play a crucial role in MMOGs with NFTs. Players who own governance tokens can participate in decision-making processes, such as voting on game updates, new features, and community policies. This empowers players and fosters a sense of ownership and involvement in the game's development.

Here's an example of a simple DAO contract for an MMOG:

```
pragma solidity ^0.8.0;

contract MMOGDAO {
    struct Proposal {
        string description;
        uint256 voteCount;
    }

    Proposal[] public proposals;
    mapping(address => bool) public voters;

    function createProposal(string memory description) public {
        proposals.push(Proposal({description: description, voteCount: 0}));
    }

    function vote(uint256 proposalIndex) public {
        require(!voters[msg.sender], "Already voted");
```

```
        proposals[proposalIndex].voteCount++;
        voters[msg.sender] = true;
    }

    function getProposal(uint256 proposalIndex) public view returns (string memory, uint256) {
        Proposal memory proposal = proposals[proposalIndex];
        return (proposal.description, proposal.voteCount);
    }
}
```

This contract allows players to create proposals and vote on them, enabling decentralized governance.

Incorporating NFTs into MMOGs can also enhance the social and community aspects of the game. Players can showcase their NFT collections, achievements, and creations, fostering a sense of pride and competition. Social features such as guilds, clans, and alliances can be enhanced with NFTs, providing unique rewards and recognition for group activities and accomplishments.

Special events and tournaments that offer exclusive NFTs as rewards can drive engagement and excitement. Limited-time events create urgency and encourage players to participate, while tournaments provide a competitive environment where players can earn valuable rewards. These events can be live-streamed and promoted on social media to attract a broader audience.

Ensuring the security and integrity of NFTs in MMOGs is crucial. Implementing robust smart contract security, secure wallet integrations, and transparent auditing practices helps protect player assets and transactions. Regularly updating and maintaining the game's infrastructure ensures a safe and reliable environment for players.

In conclusion, integrating NFTs into Massively Multiplayer Online Games (MMOGs) offers numerous benefits, including true ownership, economic activity, interoperability, decentralized governance, enhanced social features, and increased engagement through events and tournaments. By leveraging these advantages, developers can create immersive and engaging virtual worlds that attract and retain players, while also providing new opportunities for monetization and community building.

8.2. Creating Shared Economies in Online Worlds

Creating shared economies in online worlds with NFTs involves designing systems where players can trade, sell, and monetize their in-game assets. This section explores the strategies and best practices for building vibrant, player-driven economies in virtual environments.

A shared economy in an online world relies on the tokenization of in-game assets as NFTs. These assets can include anything from virtual land and buildings to items, characters, and collectibles. Tokenizing these assets gives players true ownership and the ability to trade them freely on secondary markets, both within and outside the game.

One of the key components of a shared economy is a robust marketplace where players can buy, sell, and trade NFTs. This marketplace should be user-friendly, secure, and integrated into the game's interface. Providing features such as search filters, categories, and detailed asset information enhances the trading experience.

Here's an example of a Solidity contract for a simple NFT marketplace:

```solidity
pragma solidity ^0.8.0;

import "@openzeppelin/contracts/token/ERC721/IERC721.sol";
import "@openzeppelin/contracts/access/Ownable.sol";

contract NFTMarketplace is Ownable {
    struct Listing {
        address seller;
        uint256 price;
    }

    mapping(uint256 => Listing) public listings;
    IERC721 public nftContract;

    constructor(address _nftContract) {
        nftContract = IERC721(_nftContract);
    }

    function listNFT(uint256 tokenId, uint256 price) public {
        require(nftContract.ownerOf(tokenId) == msg.sender, "Only the owner can list the NFT");
        listings[tokenId] = Listing({seller: msg.sender, price: price});
    }

    function buyNFT(uint256 tokenId) public payable {
        Listing memory listing = listings[tokenId];
        require(msg.value == listing.price, "Incorrect price");
        require(listing.seller != address(0), "NFT not listed");

        nftContract.safeTransferFrom(listing.seller, msg.sender, tokenId);
        payable(listing.seller).transfer(msg.value);
        delete listings[tokenId];
    }
}
```

This contract facilitates the listing and buying of NFTs, creating a basic marketplace for player-driven trading.

Economic incentives drive player engagement and participation in shared economies. Implementing play-to-earn (P2E) mechanics allows players to earn NFTs or cryptocurrency through their in-game activities. This model not only incentivizes gameplay but also provides players with tangible returns on their time and effort.

Virtual land ownership is a compelling aspect of shared economies. Players can buy, sell, and develop virtual land, creating businesses, attractions, and experiences that generate revenue. Virtual real estate can become valuable as more players invest and develop the virtual world, driving demand and prices.

Interoperability of NFTs across different games and platforms enhances their value and utility. Designing NFTs to be compatible with multiple virtual worlds allows players to use their assets in various contexts, increasing their desirability. Cross-game collaborations and partnerships can facilitate this interoperability, creating a broader ecosystem for shared economies.

Decentralized finance (DeFi) integrations can further enhance shared economies. Players can use their NFTs as collateral for loans, stake them for rewards, or participate in yield farming. These DeFi applications add layers of financial utility to in-game assets, attracting more players and investors.

Here's an example of a Solidity contract for staking NFTs:

```solidity
pragma solidity ^0.8.0;

import "@openzeppelin/contracts/token/ERC721/IERC721.sol";
import "@openzeppelin/contracts/access/Ownable.sol";

contract NFTStaking is Ownable {
    struct Stake {
        address owner;
        uint256 startTime;
    }

    mapping(uint256 => Stake) public stakes;
    IERC721 public nftContract;

    constructor(address _nftContract) {
        nftContract = IERC721(_nftContract);
    }

    function stakeNFT(uint256 tokenId) public {
        require(nftContract.ownerOf(tokenId) == msg.sender, "Only the owner can stake the NFT");
        nftContract.transferFrom(msg.sender, address(this), tokenId);
        stakes[tokenId] = Stake({owner: msg.sender, startTime: block.timestamp});
    }

    function unstakeNFT(uint256 tokenId) public {
        Stake memory stakeInfo = stakes[tokenId];
        require(stakeInfo.owner == msg.sender, "Only the owner can unstake the NFT");
```

```
        nftContract.transferFrom(address(this), msg.sender, tokenId);
        delete stakes[tokenId];
    }

    function calculateRewards(uint256 tokenId) public view returns (uint256)
{
        Stake memory stakeInfo = stakes[tokenId];
        uint256 stakingDuration = block.timestamp - stakeInfo.startTime;
        return stakingDuration * 1e18; // Example reward calculation
    }
}
```

This contract allows players to stake their NFTs and earn rewards based on the staking duration.

Transparency and fairness are crucial in shared economies. Ensuring that the rules and mechanics governing the economy are transparent and verifiable builds trust among players. Implementing decentralized governance models where players can vote on economic policies and changes fosters a sense of ownership and involvement.

Community engagement and education are essential for a thriving shared economy. Providing resources, tutorials, and support for players to understand and participate in the economy enhances their experience. Hosting events, discussions, and workshops can also drive engagement and collaboration.

Security is paramount in shared economies to protect player assets and transactions. Implementing robust smart contract security, secure wallet integrations, and regular audits helps safeguard the economy. Ensuring that the game's infrastructure is resilient and reliable is also critical.

In conclusion, creating shared economies in online worlds with NFTs involves building robust marketplaces, implementing economic incentives, enabling virtual land ownership, ensuring interoperability, integrating DeFi applications, promoting transparency and fairness, engaging the community, and ensuring security. By leveraging these strategies, developers can build vibrant, player-driven economies that enhance engagement, value, and sustainability in virtual worlds.

8.3. Player-to-Player Trade and NFT Market Dynamics

Player-to-player trade and NFT market dynamics are essential components of a thriving virtual economy. This section explores the strategies and best practices for facilitating trade between players and understanding the factors that influence NFT market dynamics in online games.

One of the foundational elements of player-to-player trade is a secure and user-friendly marketplace. This marketplace should allow players to list, buy, sell, and trade NFTs seamlessly. Integrating the marketplace into the game's interface ensures easy access and usability. Providing features like search filters, categories, detailed asset information, and transaction histories enhances the trading experience.

Here's an example of a Solidity contract for a player-to-player NFT marketplace:

```solidity
pragma solidity ^0.8.0;

import "@openzeppelin/contracts/token/ERC721/IERC721.sol";
import "@openzeppelin/contracts/access/Ownable.sol";

contract PlayerMarketplace is Ownable {
    struct Listing {
        address seller;
        uint256 price;
    }

    mapping(uint256 => Listing) public listings;
    IERC721 public nftContract;

    constructor(address _nftContract) {
        nftContract = IERC721(_nftContract);
    }

    function listNFT(uint256 tokenId, uint256 price) public {
        require(nftContract.ownerOf(tokenId) == msg.sender, "Only the owner can list the NFT");
        listings[tokenId] = Listing({seller: msg.sender, price: price});
    }

    function buyNFT(uint256 tokenId) public payable {
        Listing memory listing = listings[tokenId];
        require(msg.value == listing.price, "Incorrect price");
        require(listing.seller != address(0), "NFT not listed");

        nftContract.safeTransferFrom(listing.seller, msg.sender, tokenId);
        payable(listing.seller).transfer(msg.value);
        delete listings[tokenId];
    }
}
```

This contract facilitates the listing and buying of NFTs, creating a basic marketplace for player-driven trading.

Economic incentives play a crucial role in player-to-player trade. Implementing play-to-earn (P2E) mechanics allows players to earn NFTs or cryptocurrency through their in-game activities. This model incentivizes gameplay and provides players with valuable assets they can trade. Additionally, offering exclusive or limited-time NFTs can drive demand and trading activity.

Supply and demand dynamics significantly influence NFT market prices. Scarcity and rarity of NFTs create value, driving higher prices. Limited editions, special events, and unique attributes contribute to the perceived value of NFTs. Monitoring market trends and player behavior helps understand and anticipate these dynamics.

Interoperability enhances the value of NFTs by allowing them to be used across multiple games and platforms. Designing NFTs to be compatible with different virtual worlds increases their utility and desirability. Cross-game collaborations and partnerships can facilitate this interoperability, creating a broader ecosystem for player-to-player trade.

Player reputation and trust are critical in peer-to-peer trading. Implementing rating systems, reviews, and verified seller badges helps build trust within the community. Ensuring transparency in transactions and providing detailed information about NFTs, including their history and attributes, further enhances trust.

Decentralized finance (DeFi) integrations can add financial utility to NFTs. Players can use their NFTs as collateral for loans, stake them for rewards, or participate in yield farming. These DeFi applications create additional value and trading opportunities, attracting more players and investors.

Here's an example of a Solidity contract for staking NFTs:

```solidity
pragma solidity ^0.8.0;

import "@openzeppelin/contracts/token/ERC721/IERC721.sol";
import "@openzeppelin/contracts/access/Ownable.sol";

contract NFTStaking is Ownable {
    struct Stake {
        address owner;
        uint256 startTime;
    }

    mapping(uint256 => Stake) public stakes;
    IERC721 public nftContract;

    constructor(address _nftContract) {
        nftContract = IERC721(_nftContract);
    }

    function stakeNFT(uint256 tokenId) public {
        require(nftContract.ownerOf(tokenId) == msg.sender, "Only the owner can stake the NFT");
        nftContract.transferFrom(msg.sender, address(this), tokenId);
        stakes[tokenId] = Stake({owner: msg.sender, startTime: block.timestamp});
    }

    function unstakeNFT(uint256 tokenId) public {
        Stake memory stakeInfo = stakes[tokenId];
        require(stakeInfo.owner == msg.sender, "Only the owner can unstake th
```

```
e NFT");

        nftContract.transferFrom(address(this), msg.sender, tokenId);
        delete stakes[tokenId];
    }

    function calculateRewards(uint256 tokenId) public view returns (uint256)
{
        Stake memory stakeInfo = stakes[tokenId];
        uint256 stakingDuration = block.timestamp - stakeInfo.startTime;
        return stakingDuration * 1e18; // Example reward calculation
    }
}
```

This contract allows players to stake their NFTs and earn rewards based on the staking duration.

Transparency and fairness are essential in player-to-player trade. Ensuring that the rules and mechanics governing the marketplace are transparent and verifiable builds trust among players. Implementing decentralized governance models where players can vote on market policies and changes fosters a sense of ownership and involvement.

Community engagement and education are crucial for a thriving trading ecosystem. Providing resources, tutorials, and support for players to understand and participate in the marketplace enhances their experience. Hosting events, discussions, and workshops can also drive engagement and collaboration.

Security is paramount in player-to-player trade to protect player assets and transactions. Implementing robust smart contract security, secure wallet integrations, and regular audits helps safeguard the marketplace. Ensuring that the game's infrastructure is resilient and reliable is also critical.

In conclusion, player-to-player trade and NFT market dynamics are essential for a thriving virtual economy. By building robust marketplaces, implementing economic incentives, ensuring interoperability, fostering trust, integrating DeFi applications, promoting transparency, engaging the community, and ensuring security, developers can create vibrant, player-driven trading ecosystems that enhance engagement, value, and sustainability in online games.

8.4. Building Persistent Worlds with NFTs

Building persistent worlds with NFTs involves creating virtual environments where assets and progress are permanently stored on the blockchain, providing players with true ownership and continuity. This section explores the strategies and best practices for developing persistent virtual worlds using NFTs.

A persistent world is one where the game environment and player progress continue to exist and evolve even when players are offline. NFTs play a crucial role in these worlds by representing in-game assets, achievements, and even the game world itself. This ensures that player investments in time and resources are preserved and can be built upon over time.

One of the foundational elements of a persistent world is the tokenization of in-game assets as NFTs. These assets can include land, buildings, characters, items, and more. Each NFT can have unique attributes, history, and metadata, providing players with a sense of ownership and investment.

Here's an example of a Solidity contract for an NFT-based virtual land system:

```solidity
pragma solidity ^0.8.0;

import "@openzeppelin/contracts/token/ERC721/ERC721.sol";
import "@openzeppelin/contracts/access/Ownable.sol";

contract VirtualLand is ERC721, Ownable {
    struct Land {
        uint256 x;
        uint256 y;
        string terrain;
    }

    mapping(uint256 => Land) public lands;

    uint256 public landCounter;

    constructor() ERC721("VirtualLand", "VLAND") {
        landCounter = 0;
    }

    function mintLand(address to, uint256 x, uint256 y, string memory terrain
) public onlyOwner returns (uint256) {
        uint256 newLandId = landCounter;
        lands[newLandId] = Land({x: x, y: y, terrain: terrain});
        _mint(to, newLandId);
        landCounter++;
        return newLandId;
    }
}
```

This contract allows the owner to mint virtual land parcels with specific coordinates and terrain types, creating a persistent and unique virtual world.

Economic incentives drive player engagement and participation in persistent worlds. Implementing play-to-earn (P2E) mechanics allows players to earn NFTs or cryptocurrency through their in-game activities. This model not only incentivizes gameplay but also provides players with tangible returns on their time and effort.

Interoperability enhances the value of NFTs in persistent worlds by allowing them to be used across multiple games and platforms. Designing NFTs to be compatible with different virtual worlds increases their utility and desirability. Cross-game collaborations and partnerships can facilitate this interoperability, creating a broader ecosystem for persistent worlds.

Decentralized governance can play a crucial role in persistent worlds. Players who own governance tokens can participate in decision-making processes, such as voting on game updates, new features, and community policies. This empowers players and fosters a sense of ownership and involvement in the game's development.

Here's an example of a simple DAO contract for a persistent world:

```solidity
pragma solidity ^0.8.0;

contract WorldDAO {
    struct Proposal {
        string description;
        uint256 voteCount;
    }

    Proposal[] public proposals;
    mapping(address => bool) public voters;

    function createProposal(string memory description) public {
        proposals.push(Proposal({description: description, voteCount: 0}));
    }

    function vote(uint256 proposalIndex) public {
        require(!voters[msg.sender], "Already voted");
        proposals[proposalIndex].voteCount++;
        voters[msg.sender] = true;
    }

    function getProposal(uint256 proposalIndex) public view returns (string memory, uint256) {
        Proposal memory proposal = proposals[proposalIndex];
        return (proposal.description, proposal.voteCount);
    }
}
```

This contract allows players to create proposals and vote on them, enabling decentralized governance in the virtual world.

Persistent worlds can also benefit from integrating decentralized finance (DeFi) applications. Players can use their NFTs as collateral for loans, stake them for rewards, or participate in yield farming. These DeFi applications add layers of financial utility to in-game assets, attracting more players and investors.

Here's an example of a Solidity contract for staking NFTs in a persistent world:

```solidity
pragma solidity ^0.8.0;

import "@openzeppelin/contracts/token/ERC721/IERC721.sol";
import "@openzeppelin/contracts/access/Ownable.sol";

contract NFTStaking is Ownable {
    struct Stake {
        address owner;
        uint256 startTime;
    }

    mapping(uint256 => Stake) public stakes;
    IERC721 public nftContract;

    constructor(address _nftContract) {
        nftContract = IERC721(_nftContract);
    }

    function stakeNFT(uint256 tokenId) public {
        require(nftContract.ownerOf(tokenId) == msg.sender, "Only the owner can stake the NFT");
        nftContract.transferFrom(msg.sender, address(this), tokenId);
        stakes[tokenId] = Stake({owner: msg.sender, startTime: block.timestamp});
    }

    function unstakeNFT(uint256 tokenId) public {
        Stake memory stakeInfo = stakes[tokenId];
        require(stakeInfo.owner == msg.sender, "Only the owner can unstake the NFT");

        nftContract.transferFrom(address(this), msg.sender, tokenId);
        delete stakes[tokenId];
    }

    function calculateRewards(uint256 tokenId) public view returns (uint256) {
        Stake memory stakeInfo = stakes[tokenId];
        uint256 stakingDuration = block.timestamp - stakeInfo.startTime;
        return stakingDuration * 1e18; // Example reward calculation
    }
}
```

This contract allows players to stake their NFTs and earn rewards based on the staking duration.

Ensuring the security and integrity of NFTs in persistent worlds is crucial. Implementing robust smart contract security, secure wallet integrations, and transparent auditing practices helps protect player assets and transactions. Regularly updating and maintaining the game's infrastructure ensures a safe and reliable environment for players.

Community engagement and education are essential for a thriving persistent world. Providing resources, tutorials, and support for players to understand and participate in the world enhances their experience. Hosting events, discussions, and workshops can also drive engagement and collaboration.

In conclusion, building persistent worlds with NFTs involves creating tokenized assets, implementing economic incentives, ensuring interoperability, fostering decentralized governance, integrating DeFi applications, promoting transparency and security, engaging the community, and providing continuous updates and support. By leveraging these strategies, developers can create immersive and engaging virtual environments that attract and retain players, while also providing new opportunities for monetization and community building.

8.5. Case Study: NFT Integration in an MMOG

Analyzing real-world examples of NFT integration in Massively Multiplayer Online Games (MMOGs) provides valuable insights into effective strategies and best practices. This section presents a case study of a successful MMOG that has integrated NFTs to enhance gameplay, engagement, and monetization.

Case Study: "CryptoWorlds"

Overview: "CryptoWorlds" is a blockchain-based MMOG that combines traditional MMORPG elements with the unique properties of NFTs. The game features a vast open world where players can explore, complete quests, battle monsters, and interact with other players. NFTs play a central role in the game, representing characters, items, land, and collectibles.

NFT Integration:

1. **Character Customization:**
    - Players can mint unique NFT characters with customizable appearances, abilities, and attributes. Each character has a distinct set of traits, making them valuable and desirable.
    - Characters can level up, gain experience, and acquire new abilities, which are recorded on the blockchain. This ensures that player progress is permanent and verifiable.

    Example Solidity contract for minting characters:

```
pragma solidity ^0.8.0;

import "@openzeppelin/contracts/token/ERC721/ERC721.sol";
import "@openzeppelin/contracts/access/Ownable.sol";

contract CryptoWorldsCharacter is ERC721, Ownable {
```

```solidity
    struct Character {
        uint256 level;
        string abilities;
    }

    mapping(uint256 => Character) public characters;

    uint256 public tokenCounter;

    constructor() ERC721("CryptoWorldsCharacter", "CWC") {
        tokenCounter = 0;
    }

    function mintCharacter(address to, string memory abilities) public onlyOwner returns (uint256) {
        uint256 newCharacterId = tokenCounter;
        characters[newCharacterId] = Character({level: 1, abilities: abilities});
        _mint(to, newCharacterId);
        tokenCounter++;
        return newCharacterId;
    }

    function levelUp(uint256 tokenId) public {
        require(ownerOf(tokenId) == msg.sender, "Only the owner can level up");
        characters[tokenId].level++;
    }

    function updateAbilities(uint256 tokenId, string memory newAbilities) public {
        require(ownerOf(tokenId) == msg.sender, "Only the owner can update abilities");
        characters[tokenId].abilities = newAbilities;
    }
}
```

2. **Item Ownership and Trading:**

    - In-game items such as weapons, armor, and accessories are represented as NFTs. Players can trade these items on the in-game marketplace or external NFT platforms.
    - The rarity and attributes of items are recorded on the blockchain, ensuring transparency and verifiability.

Example Solidity contract for item trading:

```solidity
pragma solidity ^0.8.0;

import "@openzeppelin/contracts/token/ERC721/IERC721.sol";
```

```solidity
import "@openzeppelin/contracts/access/Ownable.sol";

contract CryptoWorldsMarketplace is Ownable {
    struct Listing {
        address seller;
        uint256 price;
    }

    mapping(uint256 => Listing) public listings;
    IERC721 public nftContract;

    constructor(address _nftContract) {
        nftContract = IERC721(_nftContract);
    }

    function listItem(uint256 tokenId, uint256 price) public {
        require(nftContract.ownerOf(tokenId) == msg.sender, "Only the owner can list the item");
        listings[tokenId] = Listing({seller: msg.sender, price: price});
    }

    function buyItem(uint256 tokenId) public payable {
        Listing memory listing = listings[tokenId];
        require(msg.value == listing.price, "Incorrect price");
        require(listing.seller != address(0), "Item not listed");

        nftContract.safeTransferFrom(listing.seller, msg.sender, tokenId);
        payable(listing.seller).transfer(msg.value);
        delete listings[tokenId];
    }
}
```

3. **Virtual Land Ownership:**

    - Players can purchase, develop, and trade virtual land parcels represented as NFTs. Land can be used to build structures, create businesses, and host events.
    - The value of land increases as the virtual world grows and more players invest in it.

Example Solidity contract for minting land parcels:

```solidity
pragma solidity ^0.8.0;

import "@openzeppelin/contracts/token/ERC721/ERC721.sol";
import "@openzeppelin/contracts/access/Ownable.sol";

contract CryptoWorldsLand is ERC721, Ownable {
```

```solidity
    struct Land {
        uint256 x;
        uint256 y;
        string terrain;
    }

    mapping(uint256 => Land) public lands;

    uint256 public landCounter;

    constructor() ERC721("CryptoWorldsLand", "CWL") {
        landCounter = 0;
    }

    function mintLand(address to, uint256 x, uint256 y, string memory t
errain) public onlyOwner returns (uint256) {
        uint256 newLandId = landCounter;
        lands[newLandId] = Land({x: x, y: y, terrain: terrain});
        _mint(to, newLandId);
        landCounter++;
        return newLandId;
    }
}
```

4. **Play-to-Earn Mechanics:**
   - Players can earn NFTs and cryptocurrency by completing quests, defeating monsters, and participating in events. These rewards incentivize gameplay and provide tangible returns on player investment.

5. **Community Governance:**
   - The game incorporates a decentralized governance model where players can vote on game updates, new features, and community policies. Governance tokens are distributed based on player participation and achievements.

Example Solidity contract for community governance:

```solidity
pragma solidity ^0.8.0;

contract CryptoWorldsDAO {
    struct Proposal {
        string description;
        uint256 voteCount;
    }

    Proposal[] public proposals;
    mapping(address => bool) public voters;

    function createProposal(string memory description) public {
        proposals.push(Proposal({description: description, voteCount: 0
```

```
        }));
    }

    function vote(uint256 proposalIndex) public {
        require(!voters[msg.sender], "Already voted");
        proposals[proposalIndex].voteCount++;
        voters[msg.sender] = true;
    }

    function getProposal(uint256 proposalIndex) public view returns (st
ring memory, uint256) {
        Proposal memory proposal = proposals[proposalIndex];
        return (proposal.description, proposal.voteCount);
    }
}
```

Results and Impact: "CryptoWorlds" has successfully integrated NFTs to create a dynamic and engaging virtual world. The use of NFTs for characters, items, land, and governance has provided players with true ownership and economic opportunities. The play-to-earn mechanics have incentivized participation, leading to a vibrant and active player community.

The game's decentralized governance model has empowered players and fostered a sense of ownership and involvement. The ability to trade and monetize in-game assets has attracted both gamers and investors, driving the game's growth and sustainability.

In conclusion, the case study of "CryptoWorlds" demonstrates the successful integration of NFTs in an MMOG. By leveraging NFTs for character customization, item ownership, virtual land, play-to-earn mechanics, and community governance, "CryptoWorlds" has created a compelling and engaging virtual world that attracts and retains players while providing new opportunities for monetization and community building.

Chapter 9: NFTs in Mobile Gaming

9.1. Opportunities and Challenges of NFTs in Mobile Games

The integration of NFTs in mobile games presents a unique set of opportunities and challenges. Mobile gaming is a rapidly growing segment of the gaming industry, and the addition of NFTs can enhance player engagement, create new revenue streams, and offer players true ownership of in-game assets. However, there are technical, financial, and regulatory challenges that developers must navigate to successfully implement NFTs in mobile games.

One of the primary opportunities of NFTs in mobile games is the ability to provide players with true ownership of their in-game assets. Unlike traditional mobile games where items and achievements are confined within the game, NFTs allow players to own, trade, and sell their assets outside the game environment. This adds value to the player's investment of time and money in the game.

Another significant opportunity is the creation of new revenue streams. Developers can generate income through the sale of NFTs, transaction fees on secondary markets, and royalties from resales. This can be particularly lucrative in mobile games with large and active player bases. For example, rare and limited-edition NFTs can be sold at premium prices, and developers can earn a percentage of each subsequent sale.

Play-to-earn (P2E) mechanics are also well-suited to mobile games. By allowing players to earn NFTs or cryptocurrency through gameplay, developers can incentivize engagement and retention. This model has proven successful in desktop and console games and can be adapted to the mobile platform to attract a broader audience.

However, integrating NFTs into mobile games also presents several challenges. One of the primary technical challenges is ensuring compatibility with existing mobile platforms. Both Apple and Google have stringent guidelines for apps available on their respective app stores, and developers must ensure that their NFT integrations comply with these guidelines. This may include restrictions on in-app purchases, transactions, and the use of external wallets.

Here's an example of how to integrate an NFT marketplace within a mobile game while adhering to app store guidelines:

```
import { ethers } from 'ethers';
import { Contract } from '@ethersproject/contracts';
import marketplaceABI from './MarketplaceABI.json';

const provider = new ethers.providers.JsonRpcProvider('https://mainnet.infura.io/v3/YOUR_INFURA_PROJECT_ID');
const signer = provider.getSigner();
const marketplaceAddress = '0xYourMarketplaceContractAddress';
const marketplaceContract = new Contract(marketplaceAddress, marketplaceABI,
```

```
signer);

async function listNFT(tokenId, price) {
    try {
        const tx = await marketplaceContract.listNFT(tokenId, ethers.utils.pa
rseUnits(price, 'ether'));
        await tx.wait();
        console.log('NFT listed successfully');
    } catch (error) {
        console.error('Error listing NFT:', error);
    }
}

async function buyNFT(tokenId) {
    try {
        const tx = await marketplaceContract.buyNFT(tokenId, { value: ethers.
utils.parseUnits(price, 'ether') });
        await tx.wait();
        console.log('NFT purchased successfully');
    } catch (error) {
        console.error('Error purchasing NFT:', error);
    }
}

// Example usage
listNFT(1, '0.5');
buyNFT(1);
```

This code snippet demonstrates listing and buying NFTs within a mobile game, ensuring that transactions are handled securely and efficiently.

Another challenge is the user experience. Mobile devices have limited screen real estate and processing power compared to desktops and consoles. Developers must design intuitive and user-friendly interfaces for interacting with NFTs, including browsing, purchasing, and managing digital assets. Ensuring that these interactions are smooth and seamless is critical for maintaining player engagement.

Security is also a major concern. Mobile devices are susceptible to hacking, phishing, and other security threats. Developers must implement robust security measures to protect users' NFTs and personal information. This includes secure authentication methods, encryption, and regular security audits.

Regulatory compliance is another important consideration. The legal landscape surrounding NFTs is still evolving, and developers must stay informed about the regulations in different jurisdictions. This includes compliance with anti-money laundering (AML) and know your customer (KYC) regulations, as well as data protection laws such as GDPR.

Here's an example of how to implement basic KYC checks using a third-party service:

```
import axios from 'axios';

async function performKYC(userId, userData) {
    try {
        const response = await axios.post('https://api.kyc-service.com/verify', {
            userId: userId,
            data: userData
        });
        if (response.data.verified) {
            console.log('KYC verification successful');
        } else {
            console.error('KYC verification failed');
        }
    } catch (error) {
        console.error('Error performing KYC:', error);
    }
}

// Example usage
const userId = '12345';
const userData = {
    name: 'John Doe',
    address: '123 Main St',
    dateOfBirth: '1990-01-01'
};
performKYC(userId, userData);
```

This code snippet demonstrates performing basic KYC checks to ensure regulatory compliance.

In conclusion, while the integration of NFTs in mobile games offers numerous opportunities, developers must carefully navigate the associated challenges. By addressing technical, user experience, security, and regulatory considerations, developers can successfully implement NFTs in mobile games and create engaging, valuable experiences for players.

9.2. User Experience Considerations for Mobile

User experience (UX) is a critical factor in the success of mobile games that integrate NFTs. Ensuring that players can easily interact with and manage their NFTs is essential for maintaining engagement and satisfaction. This section explores various UX considerations and best practices for integrating NFTs into mobile games.

One of the primary UX considerations is the design of intuitive and user-friendly interfaces. Mobile devices have limited screen real estate, so it is important to create clear and concise interfaces that allow players to easily browse, purchase, and manage their NFTs. This includes designing simple navigation, clear calls-to-action, and minimalistic layouts that prevent clutter and confusion.

Here's an example of a basic interface design for an NFT marketplace in a mobile game:

```jsx
import React from 'react';
import { View, Text, Button, FlatList } from 'react-native';

const NFTMarketplace = ({ nfts, onBuy }) => {
    return (
        <View style={{ padding: 20 }}>
            <Text style={{ fontSize: 24, fontWeight: 'bold', marginBottom: 10 }}>NFT Marketplace</Text>
            <FlatList
                data={nfts}
                keyExtractor={(item) => item.id.toString()}
                renderItem={({ item }) => (
                    <View style={{ marginBottom: 10 }}>
                        <Text>{item.name}</Text>
                        <Text>{item.price} ETH</Text>
                        <Button title="Buy" onPress={() => onBuy(item.id)} />
                    </View>
                )}
            />
        </View>
    );
};

export default NFTMarketplace;
```

This code snippet demonstrates a simple React Native component for an NFT marketplace, providing a clean and straightforward interface for browsing and buying NFTs.

Loading times and performance are crucial UX factors for mobile games. Slow loading times and laggy performance can frustrate players and lead to disengagement. Optimizing the performance of NFT interactions, such as loading and displaying assets, is essential. This can be achieved by using efficient data structures, minimizing network requests, and leveraging caching mechanisms.

Security and trust are paramount in the UX of mobile games with NFTs. Players need to feel confident that their assets are secure and that their transactions are safe. Implementing secure authentication methods, such as biometric authentication (fingerprint or facial recognition), can enhance security and convenience. Additionally, providing clear and transparent information about transactions and ownership helps build trust.

Here's an example of implementing biometric authentication using React Native:

```jsx
import React from 'react';
import { View, Text, Button, Alert } from 'react-native';
import * as LocalAuthentication from 'expo-local-authentication';

const BiometricAuth = ({ onAuthenticated }) => {
    const handleBiometricAuth = async () => {
```

```
        const hasHardware = await LocalAuthentication.hasHardwareAsync();
        const isEnrolled = await LocalAuthentication.isEnrolledAsync();

        if (hasHardware && isEnrolled) {
            const result = await LocalAuthentication.authenticateAsync();
            if (result.success) {
                onAuthenticated();
            } else {
                Alert.alert('Authentication failed', 'Please try again.');
            }
        } else {
            Alert.alert('Biometric authentication not available', 'Please set up biometric authentication on your device.');
        }
    };

    return (
        <View style={{ padding: 20 }}>
            <Text style={{ fontSize: 24, fontWeight: 'bold', marginBottom: 10 }}>Biometric Authentication</Text>
            <Button title="Authenticate" onPress={handleBiometricAuth} />
        </View>
    );
};

export default BiometricAuth;
```

This code snippet demonstrates a simple component for biometric authentication using the Expo Local Authentication library.

Providing seamless wallet integration is another important UX consideration. Players need to be able to easily connect their wallets to the game, view their assets, and manage transactions. Supporting popular wallets, such as MetaMask, Trust Wallet, and Coinbase Wallet, ensures that players have multiple options. Additionally, simplifying the wallet connection process and providing clear instructions can enhance the overall experience.

Here's an example of integrating MetaMask with a React Native app:

```
import React from 'react';
import { View, Text, Button, Alert } from 'react-native';
import Web3 from 'web3';

const MetaMaskIntegration = ({ onConnected }) => {
    const handleConnectWallet = async () => {
        if (window.ethereum) {
            const web3 = new Web3(window.ethereum);
            try {
                await window.ethereum.enable();
                const accounts = await web3.eth.getAccounts();
                onConnected(accounts[0]);
```

```
            } catch (error) {
                Alert.alert('Connection failed', 'Please try again.');
            }
        } else {
            Alert.alert('MetaMask not installed', 'Please install MetaMask an
d try again.');
        }
    };

    return (
        <View style={{ padding: 20 }}>
            <Text style={{ fontSize: 24, fontWeight: 'bold', marginBottom: 10
 }}>Connect MetaMask</Text>
            <Button title="Connect Wallet" onPress={handleConnectWallet} />
        </View>
    );
};

export default MetaMaskIntegration;
```

This code snippet demonstrates how to connect a MetaMask wallet to a React Native app.

User education and support are also critical for a positive UX. Many players may be unfamiliar with NFTs and blockchain technology, so providing clear and concise information about how NFTs work, their benefits, and how to use them within the game is important. This can be achieved through in-game tutorials, FAQs, and support channels.

In conclusion, ensuring a positive user experience in mobile games that integrate NFTs involves designing intuitive interfaces, optimizing performance, implementing secure authentication methods, providing seamless wallet integration, and offering user education and support. By focusing on these UX considerations, developers can create engaging and satisfying experiences for players, enhancing the adoption and success of NFTs in mobile gaming.

9.3. Integrating Wallets and NFTs in Mobile Games

Integrating wallets and NFTs into mobile games is crucial for enabling players to securely manage their digital assets. This section explores the best practices and technical considerations for integrating wallets and NFTs into mobile gaming environments.

The first step in integrating wallets is to select the right wallet providers. Popular wallet options include MetaMask, Trust Wallet, and Coinbase Wallet. These wallets support major blockchain networks and provide robust security features. Supporting multiple wallets ensures that players have flexibility and choice, enhancing their overall experience.

To integrate a wallet into a mobile game, developers need to use the wallet's SDK or API. For example, MetaMask provides an API that allows developers to interact with the wallet and perform actions such as connecting the wallet, retrieving the user's address, and signing transactions.

Here's an example of integrating MetaMask with a React Native app:

```
import React from 'react';
import { View, Text, Button, Alert } from 'react-native';
import Web3 from 'web3';

const MetaMaskIntegration = ({ onConnected }) => {
    const handleConnectWallet = async () => {
        if (window.ethereum) {
            const web3 = new Web3(window.ethereum);
            try {
                await window.ethereum.enable();
                const accounts = await web3.eth.getAccounts();
                onConnected(accounts[0]);
            } catch (error) {
                Alert.alert('Connection failed', 'Please try again.');
            }
        } else {
            Alert.alert('MetaMask not installed', 'Please install MetaMask and try again.');
        }
    };

    return (
        <View style={{ padding: 20 }}>
            <Text style={{ fontSize: 24, fontWeight: 'bold', marginBottom: 10 }}>Connect MetaMask</Text>
            <Button title="Connect Wallet" onPress={handleConnectWallet} />
        </View>
    );
};

export default MetaMaskIntegration;
```

This code snippet demonstrates how to connect a MetaMask wallet to a React Native app, allowing users to interact with the blockchain directly from their mobile devices.

Once the wallet is connected, players should be able to view their NFTs and other digital assets. This requires retrieving and displaying the assets stored in the player's wallet. Using the Web3.js library, developers can interact with the Ethereum blockchain and retrieve the NFTs owned by the player's address.

Here's an example of fetching and displaying NFTs in a React Native app:

```
import React, { useEffect, useState } from 'react';
import { View, Text, FlatList, Image, ActivityIndicator } from 'react-native';
import Web3 from 'web3';
import { abi as erc721Abi } from './ERC721ABI.json';
```

```jsx
const NFTDisplay = ({ walletAddress }) => {
    const [nfts, setNfts] = useState([]);
    const [loading, setLoading] = useState(true);

    useEffect(() => {
        const fetchNFTs = async () => {
            const web3 = new Web3('https://mainnet.infura.io/v3/YOUR_INFURA_PROJECT_ID');
            const contract = new web3.eth.Contract(erc721Abi, '0xYourNFTContractAddress');

            const balance = await contract.methods.balanceOf(walletAddress).call();
            const nftPromises = [];

            for (let i = 0; i < balance; i++) {
                const tokenId = await contract.methods.tokenOfOwnerByIndex(walletAddress, i).call();
                const tokenURI = await contract.methods.tokenURI(tokenId).call();
                nftPromises.push(fetch(tokenURI).then((response) => response.json()));
            }

            const nftData = await Promise.all(nftPromises);
            setNfts(nftData);
            setLoading(false);
        };

        fetchNFTs();
    }, [walletAddress]);

    if (loading) {
        return <ActivityIndicator size="large" color="#0000ff" />;
    }

    return (
        <View style={{ padding: 20 }}>
            <Text style={{ fontSize: 24, fontWeight: 'bold', marginBottom: 10 }}>My NFTs</Text>
            <FlatList
                data={nfts}
                keyExtractor={(item, index) => index.toString()}
                renderItem={({ item }) => (
                    <View style={{ marginBottom: 10 }}>
                        <Image source={{ uri: item.image }} style={{ width: 100, height: 100 }} />
                        <Text>{item.name}</Text>
                        <Text>{item.description}</Text>
```

```
                    </View>
                )}
            />
        </View>
    );
};

export default NFTDisplay;
```

This code snippet demonstrates how to fetch and display NFTs owned by the player's wallet address.

Security is a critical aspect of wallet integration. Developers must ensure that sensitive data, such as private keys and transaction details, are handled securely. Using secure storage solutions and encryption can protect users' data. Additionally, implementing secure authentication methods, such as biometric authentication, can enhance security and user convenience.

Here's an example of implementing secure storage using the SecureStore module in React Native:

```
import React from 'react';
import { View, Text, Button, Alert } from 'react-native';
import * as SecureStore from 'expo-secure-store';

const SecureWallet = ({ onStored, onRetrieved }) => {
    const handleStoreData = async () => {
        try {
            await SecureStore.setItemAsync('walletAddress', '0xYourWalletAddress');
            onStored();
        } catch (error) {
            Alert.alert('Storage failed', 'Please try again.');
        }
    };

    const handleRetrieveData = async () => {
        try {
            const walletAddress = await SecureStore.getItemAsync('walletAddress');
            if (walletAddress) {
                onRetrieved(walletAddress);
            } else {
                Alert.alert('No data found', 'Please store your wallet address first.');
            }
        } catch (error) {
            Alert.alert('Retrieval failed', 'Please try again.');
        }
    };
```

```
    return (
        <View style={{ padding: 20 }}>
            <Text style={{ fontSize: 24, fontWeight: 'bold', marginBottom: 10
}}>Secure Wallet Storage</Text>
            <Button title="Store Wallet Address" onPress={handleStoreData} />
            <Button title="Retrieve Wallet Address" onPress={handleRetrieveDa
ta} />
        </View>
    );
};

export default SecureWallet;
```

This code snippet demonstrates how to securely store and retrieve wallet addresses using SecureStore in React Native.

User education is also important for a positive wallet integration experience. Many players may be unfamiliar with how to set up and use wallets. Providing clear instructions and guides within the game can help players navigate the process. This can include tutorials, FAQs, and support channels.

In conclusion, integrating wallets and NFTs into mobile games involves selecting the right wallet providers, implementing secure and user-friendly wallet connections, retrieving and displaying NFTs, ensuring security, and providing user education. By following these best practices, developers can create a seamless and engaging experience for players, enhancing the adoption and success of NFTs in mobile gaming.

9.4. Mobile Gaming NFT Marketplaces

Mobile gaming NFT marketplaces are essential for facilitating the buying, selling, and trading of NFTs within the mobile gaming ecosystem. These marketplaces provide a platform for players to interact with their digital assets, creating economic opportunities and enhancing player engagement. This section explores the key features, best practices, and technical considerations for developing mobile gaming NFT marketplaces.

One of the key features of an NFT marketplace is the ability to list NFTs for sale. Players should be able to easily list their NFTs with detailed descriptions, images, and pricing information. The marketplace should provide an intuitive interface for listing assets, ensuring that players can complete the process quickly and efficiently.

Here's an example of a Solidity contract for listing NFTs in a marketplace:

```
pragma solidity ^0.8.0;

import "@openzeppelin/contracts/token/ERC721/IERC721.sol";
import "@openzeppelin/contracts/access/Ownable.sol";

contract MobileNFTMarketplace is Ownable {
```

```solidity
    struct Listing {
        address seller;
        uint256 price;
    }

    mapping(uint256 => Listing) public listings;
    IERC721 public nftContract;

    constructor(address _nftContract) {
        nftContract = IERC721(_nftContract);
    }

    function listNFT(uint256 tokenId, uint256 price) public {
        require(nftContract.ownerOf(tokenId) == msg.sender, "Only the owner can list the NFT");
        listings[tokenId] = Listing({seller: msg.sender, price: price});
    }

    function buyNFT(uint256 tokenId) public payable {
        Listing memory listing = listings[tokenId];
        require(msg.value == listing.price, "Incorrect price");
        require(listing.seller != address(0), "NFT not listed");

        nftContract.safeTransferFrom(listing.seller, msg.sender, tokenId);
        payable(listing.seller).transfer(msg.value);
        delete listings[tokenId];
    }
}
```

This contract allows players to list and buy NFTs, creating a basic marketplace for mobile gaming.

A robust search and filtering system is crucial for a positive user experience. Players should be able to easily find specific NFTs based on various criteria such as rarity, price, and category. Implementing advanced search and filtering options enhances the usability of the marketplace and helps players discover the assets they are interested in.

Here's an example of implementing a search and filtering system in a React Native app:

```javascript
import React, { useState } from 'react';
import { View, Text, TextInput, FlatList, Button } from 'react-native';

const NFTMarketplace = ({ nfts, onBuy }) => {
    const [searchQuery, setSearchQuery] = useState('');
    const [filteredNfts, setFilteredNfts] = useState(nfts);

    const handleSearch = () => {
        const results = nfts.filter((nft) => nft.name.toLowerCase().includes(searchQuery.toLowerCase()));
        setFilteredNfts(results);
```

```
    };

    return (
        <View style={{ padding: 20 }}>
            <Text style={{ fontSize: 24, fontWeight: 'bold', marginBottom: 10 
}}>NFT Marketplace</Text>
            <TextInput
                placeholder="Search NFTs"
                value={searchQuery}
                onChangeText={setSearchQuery}
                style={{ borderWidth: 1, padding: 10, marginBottom: 10 }}
            />
            <Button title="Search" onPress={handleSearch} />
            <FlatList
                data={filteredNfts}
                keyExtractor={(item) => item.id.toString()}
                renderItem={({ item }) => (
                    <View style={{ marginBottom: 10 }}>
                        <Text>{item.name}</Text>
                        <Text>{item.price} ETH</Text>
                        <Button title="Buy" onPress={() => onBuy(item.id)} />
                    </View>
                )}
            />
        </View>
    );
};

export default NFTMarketplace;
```

This code snippet demonstrates a simple search and filtering system for an NFT marketplace.

Security is a critical aspect of any NFT marketplace. Developers must implement robust security measures to protect users' assets and transactions. This includes secure authentication methods, encryption, and regular security audits. Additionally, integrating secure payment gateways ensures that transactions are safe and reliable.

Another important feature is transaction transparency. Providing detailed transaction histories and receipts helps build trust with users. Players should be able to view their past transactions, including purchase details, prices, and timestamps. This transparency enhances the overall credibility of the marketplace.

Here's an example of implementing a transaction history feature in a React Native app:

```
import React, { useState, useEffect } from 'react';
import { View, Text, FlatList } from 'react-native';
import { ethers } from 'ethers';

const TransactionHistory = ({ walletAddress }) => {
```

```
    const [transactions, setTransactions] = useState([]);

    useEffect(() => {
        const fetchTransactions = async () => {
            const provider = new ethers.providers.JsonRpcProvider('https://mainnet.infura.io/v3/YOUR_INFURA_PROJECT_ID');
            const history = await provider.getHistory(walletAddress);
            setTransactions(history);
        };

        fetchTransactions();
    }, [walletAddress]);

    return (
        <View style={{ padding: 20 }}>
            <Text style={{ fontSize: 24, fontWeight: 'bold', marginBottom: 10 }}>Transaction History</Text>
            <FlatList
                data={transactions}
                keyExtractor={(item) => item.hash}
                renderItem={({ item }) => (
                    <View style={{ marginBottom: 10 }}>
                        <Text>Hash: {item.hash}</Text>
                        <Text>From: {item.from}</Text>
                        <Text>To: {item.to}</Text>
                        <Text>Value: {ethers.utils.formatEther(item.value)} ETH</Text>
                        <Text>Date: {new Date(item.timestamp * 1000).toLocaleDateString()}</Text>
                    </View>
                )}
            />
        </View>
    );
};

export default TransactionHistory;
```

This code snippet demonstrates how to fetch and display the transaction history of a wallet address.

User education and support are also important for a successful NFT marketplace. Providing clear instructions, FAQs, and customer support helps users understand how to use the marketplace and resolve any issues. This enhances the user experience and builds trust with the platform.

In conclusion, developing mobile gaming NFT marketplaces involves implementing features for listing and buying NFTs, robust search and filtering systems, security measures, transaction transparency, and user education. By following these best practices, developers can create a secure and engaging marketplace that enhances player interaction and economic opportunities within mobile games.

9.5. Future Prospects of NFTs in Mobile Gaming

The future prospects of NFTs in mobile gaming are promising, with potential for significant innovation and growth. As blockchain technology continues to evolve, NFTs are likely to become a more integral part of the mobile gaming landscape. This section explores the potential future developments and trends in NFTs for mobile gaming.

One of the most exciting prospects is the increasing interoperability of NFTs across different games and platforms. As more developers adopt standardized NFT protocols, players will be able to use their NFTs in multiple games, creating a seamless and interconnected gaming ecosystem. This interoperability enhances the value and utility of NFTs, as players can carry their assets and achievements across various gaming experiences.

The rise of decentralized finance (DeFi) applications integrated with NFTs will also play a significant role in the future of mobile gaming. Players will be able to leverage their in-game assets for financial activities such as staking, lending, and earning interest. This integration will create new economic opportunities and further incentivize player engagement.

Here's an example of a Solidity contract for staking NFTs in a DeFi application:

```solidity
pragma solidity ^0.8.0;

import "@openzeppelin/contracts/token/ERC721/IERC721.sol";
import "@openzeppelin/contracts/access/Ownable.sol";

contract NFTStaking is Ownable {
    struct Stake {
        address owner;
        uint256 startTime;
    }

    mapping(uint256 => Stake) public stakes;
    IERC721 public nftContract;

    constructor(address _nftContract) {
        nftContract = IERC721(_nftContract);
    }

    function stakeNFT(uint256 tokenId) public {
        require(nftContract.ownerOf(tokenId) == msg.sender, "Only the owner can stake the NFT");
        nftContract.transferFrom(msg.sender, address(this), tokenId);
        stakes[tokenId] = Stake({owner: msg.sender, startTime: block.timestamp});
```

```
    }

    function unstakeNFT(uint256 tokenId) public {
        Stake memory stakeInfo = stakes[tokenId];
        require(stakeInfo.owner == msg.sender, "Only the owner can unstake the NFT");

        nftContract.transferFrom(address(this), msg.sender, tokenId);
        delete stakes[tokenId];
    }

    function calculateRewards(uint256 tokenId) public view returns (uint256) {
        Stake memory stakeInfo = stakes[tokenId];
        uint256 stakingDuration = block.timestamp - stakeInfo.startTime;
        return stakingDuration * 1e18; // Example reward calculation
    }
}
```

This contract allows players to stake their NFTs and earn rewards based on the staking duration.

Augmented reality (AR) and virtual reality (VR) technologies are likely to further enhance the integration of NFTs in mobile gaming. AR and VR can create immersive gaming experiences where NFTs represent virtual items, environments, and characters. These technologies will enable players to interact with their NFTs in more engaging and realistic ways, blurring the lines between the virtual and physical worlds.

The development of more sophisticated AI-driven content generation will also impact NFTs in mobile gaming. AI can be used to create unique and dynamic NFTs, such as procedurally generated items, characters, and worlds. This will provide players with a continuous stream of fresh and personalized content, enhancing the replayability and longevity of games.

Social features and community-driven content will continue to grow in importance. Mobile games that integrate NFTs will increasingly focus on building strong player communities where users can create, share, and trade their own content. This collaborative environment will foster creativity and strengthen the social aspects of gaming.

Regulatory advancements and clearer legal frameworks will shape the future of NFTs in mobile gaming. As governments and regulatory bodies develop policies for digital assets and blockchain technology, developers will need to stay informed and compliant. This will provide greater security and legitimacy for NFTs, encouraging wider adoption and investment.

Scalability solutions, such as layer 2 protocols and sidechains, will address the current limitations of blockchain networks. These solutions will enable faster and more cost-effective transactions, making NFT interactions smoother and more accessible for mobile gamers. Improved scalability will support the growth of large-scale NFT ecosystems within mobile games.

Collaborations between game developers, blockchain companies, and other industries will drive innovation and create new use cases for NFTs. For example, partnerships with entertainment franchises, fashion brands, and sports organizations can bring exclusive and branded NFTs to mobile games, attracting a broader audience.

Environmental sustainability will also be a focus for the future of NFTs in mobile gaming. As concerns about the environmental impact of blockchain technology grow, developers will seek eco-friendly solutions. This includes adopting energy-efficient consensus mechanisms and supporting carbon offset initiatives to minimize the environmental footprint of NFTs.

In conclusion, the future prospects of NFTs in mobile gaming are bright, with opportunities for interoperability, DeFi integration, AR/VR enhancement, AI-driven content, social features, regulatory advancements, scalability solutions, industry collaborations, and environmental sustainability. As these trends and technologies continue to evolve, NFTs will become an increasingly important and innovative component of the mobile gaming industry.

Chapter 10: NFT Artwork and Digital Assets

10.1. The Art of Creating NFTs for Games

Creating NFTs for games involves a combination of artistic creativity, technical expertise, and an understanding of the gaming ecosystem. NFT artwork for games must not only be visually appealing but also integrate seamlessly into the game's environment and mechanics. This section explores the key considerations and best practices for creating compelling NFT artwork for games.

One of the first steps in creating NFT artwork for games is to develop a clear artistic vision. This involves defining the style, theme, and aesthetic of the NFTs to ensure consistency with the game's overall design. Artists should work closely with game designers and developers to ensure that the artwork aligns with the game's narrative and gameplay elements.

The use of high-quality, detailed artwork is essential for creating valuable and desirable NFTs. This includes paying attention to aspects such as color schemes, textures, and lighting to create visually stunning pieces. Artists should leverage advanced tools and software to produce high-resolution and intricate designs.

Here's an example of how to structure an NFT metadata file that includes artwork details:

```json
{
  "name": "Legendary Sword",
  "description": "A powerful sword forged in the fires of a volcanic mountain.",
  "image": "ipfs://QmExampleImageHash",
  "attributes": [
    {
      "trait_type": "Rarity",
      "value": "Legendary"
    },
    {
      "trait_type": "Damage",
      "value": 100
    },
    {
      "trait_type": "Element",
      "value": "Fire"
    }
  ]
}
```

This JSON file includes the name, description, image link, and attributes of an NFT sword, providing essential information for both players and marketplaces.

Animation and interactivity can significantly enhance the appeal of NFT artwork. Animated NFTs, such as characters or items with moving parts, add a dynamic element that static images lack. Interactive NFTs, where players can modify certain aspects or see changes based on in-game events, provide a deeper level of engagement.

Artists should also consider the rarity and uniqueness of their NFTs. Limited edition and one-of-a-kind pieces are more valuable and sought after by players and collectors. Creating a series of NFTs with varying levels of rarity can incentivize players to collect and trade, adding an economic layer to the game.

Collaborations with well-known artists or brands can further increase the value and desirability of NFT artwork. These collaborations bring in additional creativity and recognition, attracting a broader audience. For example, a popular artist could design a limited edition set of NFTs for a game, driving both art and game enthusiasts to participate.

Ensuring that the artwork integrates seamlessly with the game's mechanics is crucial. This includes considering how the NFTs will be used in the game, such as weapons, characters, or collectibles. The artwork should enhance the gameplay experience and provide tangible benefits to players, making the NFTs not just visually appealing but also functional.

Here's an example of a Solidity contract for minting an NFT with game-related attributes:

```solidity
pragma solidity ^0.8.0;

import "@openzeppelin/contracts/token/ERC721/ERC721.sol";
import "@openzeppelin/contracts/access/Ownable.sol";

contract GameNFT is ERC721, Ownable {
    struct NFTAttributes {
        uint256 damage;
        string element;
    }

    mapping(uint256 => NFTAttributes) public nftAttributes;

    uint256 public tokenCounter;

    constructor() ERC721("GameNFT", "GNFT") {
        tokenCounter = 0;
    }

    function mintNFT(address to, uint256 damage, string memory element) public onlyOwner returns (uint256) {
        uint256 newItemId = tokenCounter;
        _mint(to, newItemId);
        nftAttributes[newItemId] = NFTAttributes(damage, element);
        tokenCounter++;
        return newItemId;
```

```
    }
}
```

This contract allows the creation of NFTs with specific game-related attributes, such as damage and element type.

Another important aspect is the use of metadata to provide additional information about the NFTs. Metadata can include details such as the creator's name, creation date, and specific attributes related to the game's mechanics. This information enhances the value and transparency of the NFTs.

Here's an example of how to fetch and display NFT metadata in a web application:

```
import React, { useState, useEffect } from 'react';
import axios from 'axios';

const NFTDetails = ({ tokenId }) => {
    const [metadata, setMetadata] = useState(null);

    useEffect(() => {
        const fetchMetadata = async () => {
            const response = await axios.get(`https://ipfs.io/ipfs/QmExampleMetadataHash/${tokenId}`);
            setMetadata(response.data);
        };

        fetchMetadata();
    }, [tokenId]);

    if (!metadata) {
        return <div>Loading...</div>;
    }

    return (
        <div>
            <h1>{metadata.name}</h1>
            <p>{metadata.description}</p>
            <img src={metadata.image} alt={metadata.name} />
            <ul>
                {metadata.attributes.map((attr, index) => (
                    <li key={index}>{attr.trait_type}: {attr.value}</li>
                ))}
            </ul>
        </div>
    );
};

export default NFTDetails;
```

This code snippet fetches and displays NFT metadata, including the image, description, and attributes.

Finally, considering the long-term sustainability and relevance of the artwork is important. This includes thinking about how the NFTs will evolve with the game and ensuring that they remain valuable and engaging over time. Regular updates and new releases can keep the player base interested and invested in the game's NFT ecosystem.

In conclusion, creating NFTs for games involves a blend of artistic vision, technical skill, and an understanding of game mechanics. By focusing on high-quality artwork, rarity, interactivity, seamless integration, collaborations, detailed metadata, and long-term sustainability, artists and developers can create compelling NFTs that enhance the gaming experience and provide value to players.

10.2. Collaborating with Digital Artists

Collaborating with digital artists to create NFTs for games can bring a wealth of creativity and innovation to the project. Digital artists can provide unique visual styles and expertise that enhance the game's aesthetic appeal and attract a broader audience. This section explores the best practices and strategies for successful collaborations with digital artists.

One of the first steps in collaborating with digital artists is to clearly define the project's vision and goals. This includes outlining the game's theme, style, and the specific role that NFTs will play. Providing artists with a comprehensive brief helps ensure that their work aligns with the overall project objectives and artistic direction.

Finding the right digital artists for the collaboration is crucial. This involves researching and identifying artists whose style and portfolio match the game's aesthetic. Platforms such as ArtStation, Behance, and DeviantArt are excellent resources for discovering talented digital artists. Additionally, networking within the gaming and digital art communities can lead to valuable connections.

Once suitable artists are identified, reaching out with a well-crafted proposal is important. This proposal should include an overview of the project, the expected deliverables, timelines, and compensation details. Being transparent and professional in the initial communication sets a positive tone for the collaboration.

Here's an example of a proposal email to a digital artist:

```
Subject: Collaboration Opportunity for [Game Name]

Hi [Artist's Name],

I hope this message finds you well. My name is [Your Name], and I am the [You
r Position] at [Your Company]. We are currently working on an exciting new ga
me called [Game Name], and we are interested in collaborating with you to cre
ate unique NFT artwork for our game.

We have been impressed by your work, particularly your [mention specific artw
```

orks or style], and we believe your artistic vision would be a great fit for our project. The collaboration would involve creating [number and type of art works, e.g., character designs, items, environments] that align with our game's theme and aesthetic.

Here are some details about the project:
- Project Overview: [Brief description of the game and its theme]
- Deliverables: [List of expected deliverables]
- Timeline: [Estimated timeline for the project]
- Compensation: [Details about payment, royalties, or other forms of compensation]

We would love to discuss this opportunity with you in more detail and explore how we can work together to create something truly special. Please let us know if you are interested, and we can schedule a call at your convenience.

Thank you for considering this collaboration. We look forward to hearing from you soon.

Best regards,
[Your Name]
[Your Position]
[Your Contact Information]

This email provides a clear and professional proposal to the artist, outlining the project's details and expectations.

Establishing a collaborative workflow is essential for a smooth and productive partnership. This includes setting up regular communication channels, such as email, chat, or video calls, to discuss progress, provide feedback, and address any issues. Using project management tools like Trello, Asana, or Slack can help keep the collaboration organized and on track.

Providing constructive feedback is crucial for guiding the artistic process while respecting the artist's creative freedom. Feedback should be specific, actionable, and focused on how the artwork aligns with the project's goals. Encouraging an open dialogue where the artist feels comfortable sharing their ideas and suggestions can lead to innovative and high-quality results.

Here's an example of providing constructive feedback on an artwork draft:

Hi [Artist's Name],

Thank you for sharing the latest draft of the character design. The details and color palette look fantastic! I have a few suggestions to ensure it aligns with our game's theme:

1. Could we add more texture to the character's armor to give it a more rugged and worn look? This will emphasize their experience as a seasoned warrior.
2. The background elements are great, but could we make the colors slightly more muted to keep the focus on the character?

3. The facial expression is quite fierce, which I love. Maybe we can enhance the eyes to make them look even more intense and focused.

Overall, it's coming along beautifully, and I appreciate your hard work. Looking forward to seeing the next iteration!

Best,
[Your Name]

This feedback is specific, positive, and provides clear directions for the next steps.

Legal considerations are also important when collaborating with digital artists. This includes establishing clear contracts that outline the terms of the collaboration, ownership of the artwork, usage rights, and compensation. Ensuring that both parties understand and agree to these terms can prevent misunderstandings and disputes.

Here's an example of key points to include in a collaboration contract:

- **Scope of Work:** Detailed description of the artworks to be created and any specific requirements.
- **Timeline:** Deadlines for drafts, revisions, and final deliverables.
- **Compensation:** Payment terms, including rates, payment schedule, and any royalties or bonuses.
- **Ownership and Usage Rights:** Clarification of who owns the artwork and how it can be used by both parties.
- **Revisions:** Number of allowed revisions and the process for requesting changes.
- **Confidentiality:** Agreement to keep project details confidential until official release.

In conclusion, collaborating with digital artists to create NFTs for games involves clear communication, finding the right artists, providing constructive feedback, using project management tools, and ensuring legal clarity. By following these best practices, developers can harness the creativity and expertise of digital artists to enhance their games with unique and compelling NFT artwork.

10.3. Licensing and Copyrights in NFT Art

Licensing and copyrights are critical aspects to consider when creating and using NFT art in games. Properly managing these legal aspects ensures that artists and developers retain control over their work, avoid legal disputes, and establish clear usage rights for buyers. This section explores the key considerations and best practices for handling licensing and copyrights in NFT art.

The first step in managing licensing and copyrights is understanding the basic concepts. Copyright law protects original works of authorship, including visual art, from unauthorized use. This means that the creator of the artwork holds exclusive rights to reproduce, distribute, and display the work. Licensing, on the other hand, involves granting specific permissions to others to use the copyrighted work under defined conditions.

When creating NFT art for games, it's essential to establish clear ownership and usage rights from the outset. This involves creating a contract or agreement between the artist and the developer that outlines the terms of use, ownership, and any licensing arrangements. This contract should specify whether the artwork is being sold outright, licensed for use, or if the artist retains certain rights.

Here's an example of key points to include in a licensing agreement for NFT art:

- **Parties Involved:** Names and contact information of the artist and the developer.
- **Description of Artwork:** Detailed description of the artwork being licensed.
- **Grant of Rights:** Specific permissions granted to the developer, such as reproduction, distribution, and display rights.
- **Term and Territory:** Duration of the license and the geographical areas where the artwork can be used.
- **Compensation:** Payment terms, including any upfront fees, royalties, or profit-sharing arrangements.
- **Attribution:** Requirements for crediting the artist in the game or related materials.
- **Modification Rights:** Whether the developer can modify the artwork and under what conditions.
- **Termination:** Conditions under which the agreement can be terminated by either party.
- **Dispute Resolution:** Methods for resolving any disputes that may arise.

Here's an example clause for a licensing agreement:

```
Grant of Rights:
The Artist hereby grants to the Developer a non-exclusive, worldwide license to reproduce, distribute, and display the Artwork in connection with the game [Game Name]. This license includes the right to use the Artwork in promotional materials, advertisements, and merchandise related to the game. The Developer may not modify the Artwork without the Artist's prior written consent.
```

This clause specifies the rights granted to the developer and any restrictions on modifying the artwork.

When selling NFTs, it's important to include clear terms of sale that outline what rights are transferred to the buyer. Generally, purchasing an NFT provides ownership of the digital token, but not necessarily the underlying intellectual property (IP) rights to the artwork. Buyers should understand the scope of their rights, such as whether they can display the artwork, use it commercially, or create derivative works.

Here's an example of a terms of sale clause for an NFT:

```
Terms of Sale:
By purchasing this NFT, the Buyer obtains ownership of the digital token associated with the Artwork. This ownership does not transfer any intellectual property rights to the Artwork. The Buyer is granted a limited, non-exclusive license to display the Artwork for personal, non-commercial use. Any commercia
```

l use or modification of the Artwork requires the Artist's prior written consent.

This clause clarifies the buyer's rights and any restrictions on the use of the artwork.

Enforcing copyrights and licenses is another important aspect. This involves monitoring the use of the artwork and taking action against unauthorized use or infringement. Artists and developers can use blockchain technology to track the ownership and provenance of NFTs, making it easier to identify and address any violations.

Here's an example of how to monitor NFT usage using blockchain technology:

```
import Web3 from 'web3';

const web3 = new Web3('https://mainnet.infura.io/v3/YOUR_INFURA_PROJECT_ID');

const nftContractAddress = '0xYourNFTContractAddress';
const nftContractABI = [...]; // Replace with your contract ABI

const nftContract = new web3.eth.Contract(nftContractABI, nftContractAddress);

const checkOwnership = async (tokenId) => {
    const owner = await nftContract.methods.ownerOf(tokenId).call();
    console.log(`Owner of token ID ${tokenId}: ${owner}`);
};

// Example usage
checkOwnership(1);
```

This code snippet demonstrates how to check the ownership of an NFT using Web3.js, helping to monitor and enforce ownership rights.

In addition to enforcing rights, artists and developers should consider registering their copyrights with the appropriate authorities. Copyright registration provides legal benefits, such as the ability to sue for statutory damages and attorney's fees in case of infringement. It also serves as public notice of ownership, strengthening the creator's legal position.

In conclusion, managing licensing and copyrights in NFT art involves understanding the legal concepts, establishing clear agreements, defining terms of sale, enforcing rights, and considering copyright registration. By following these best practices, artists and developers can protect their work, avoid legal disputes, and ensure that all parties understand their rights and obligations.

10.4. 3D Models and Virtual Assets as NFTs

3D models and virtual assets play a significant role in the gaming industry, and their representation as NFTs can enhance player engagement, ownership, and economic activity. This section explores the process of creating, integrating, and managing 3D models and virtual assets as NFTs in games.

Creating 3D models for NFTs involves several steps, including concept design, modeling, texturing, rigging, and animation. Artists use specialized software such as Blender, Maya, or 3ds Max to create high-quality 3D assets that can be used in games. These models must be optimized for performance to ensure smooth integration and gameplay.

Here's an example workflow for creating a 3D model as an NFT:

1. **Concept Design:** Sketching the initial design and defining the visual style.
2. **Modeling:** Creating the 3D structure using modeling software.
3. **Texturing:** Applying textures to add details and realism to the model.
4. **Rigging:** Setting up a skeleton for the model to enable movement and animation.
5. **Animation:** Creating animations for the model, such as walking, running, or interacting with objects.
6. **Optimization:** Reducing the model's polygon count and optimizing textures for better performance.

Once the 3D model is created, it can be tokenized as an NFT. This involves minting the model on a blockchain platform, such as Ethereum, using a smart contract. The NFT metadata should include details about the model, such as its name, description, creator, and any special attributes or functionalities.

Here's an example of a Solidity contract for minting a 3D model NFT:

```solidity
pragma solidity ^0.8.0;

import "@openzeppelin/contracts/token/ERC721/ERC721.sol";
import "@openzeppelin/contracts/access/Ownable.sol";

contract VirtualAssetNFT is ERC721, Ownable {
    struct AssetAttributes {
        string modelURI;
        string textureURI;
        string animationURI;
    }

    mapping(uint256 => AssetAttributes) public assetAttributes;

    uint256 public tokenCounter;

    constructor() ERC721("VirtualAssetNFT", "VANFT") {
        tokenCounter = 0;
    }

    function mintAsset(address to, string memory modelURI, string memory textureURI, string memory animationURI) public onlyOwner returns (uint256) {
        uint256 newItemId = tokenCounter;
        _mint(to, newItemId);
        assetAttributes[newItemId] = AssetAttributes(modelURI, textureURI, an
```

```
imationURI);
        tokenCounter++;
        return newItemId;
    }
}
```

This contract allows the creation of NFTs with 3D model attributes, including model, texture, and animation URIs.

Integrating 3D model NFTs into a game involves ensuring that the game engine can read and display the models correctly. Popular game engines like Unity and Unreal Engine support the integration of blockchain-based assets through plugins and SDKs. Developers can use these tools to import the 3D models, apply the textures and animations, and make the assets interactive within the game environment.

Here's an example of integrating a 3D model NFT in Unity:

```
using UnityEngine;
using System.Collections;

public class NFTLoader : MonoBehaviour {
    public string modelURL = "https://ipfs.io/ipfs/QmExampleModelHash";
    public string textureURL = "https://ipfs.io/ipfs/QmExampleTextureHash";
    public string animationURL = "https://ipfs.io/ipfs/QmExampleAnimationHash";

    IEnumerator Start() {
        // Load model
        WWW modelWWW = new WWW(modelURL);
        yield return modelWWW;
        GameObject model = new GameObject("NFTModel");
        model.AddComponent<MeshFilter>().mesh = modelWWW.assetBundle.LoadAsset<Mesh>("ModelName");

        // Load texture
        WWW textureWWW = new WWW(textureURL);
        yield return textureWWW;
        model.GetComponent<MeshRenderer>().material.mainTexture = textureWWW.texture;

        // Load animation
        WWW animationWWW = new WWW(animationURL);
        yield return animationWWW;
        model.AddComponent<Animation>().clip = animationWWW.assetBundle.LoadAsset<AnimationClip>("AnimationName");

        // Add model to the scene
        model.transform.position = Vector3.zero;
    }
}
```

This script demonstrates how to load and display a 3D model NFT in Unity, including the model, texture, and animation.

Security and ownership are critical aspects of managing 3D model NFTs. Blockchain technology ensures that ownership of the NFTs is transparent and verifiable. However, developers must also implement security measures to protect the assets from unauthorized access and duplication. This includes using secure storage solutions for the model files and implementing robust authentication mechanisms.

Here's an example of secure storage using IPFS and encryption:

```javascript
const IPFS = require('ipfs-http-client');
const CryptoJS = require('crypto-js');

const ipfs = IPFS.create({ host: 'ipfs.infura.io', port: 5001, protocol: 'https' });

async function uploadEncryptedModel(fileBuffer, password) {
    const encryptedModel = CryptoJS.AES.encrypt(fileBuffer.toString('base64'), password).toString();
    const result = await ipfs.add(Buffer.from(encryptedModel));
    return result.path;
}

async function downloadEncryptedModel(hash, password) {
    const encryptedModel = await ipfs.cat(hash);
    const decryptedModel = CryptoJS.AES.decrypt(encryptedModel.toString(), password).toString(CryptoJS.enc.Utf8);
    return Buffer.from(decryptedModel, 'base64');
}

// Example usage
const modelBuffer = fs.readFileSync('path/to/model.fbx');
const password = 'securepassword';
uploadEncryptedModel(modelBuffer, password).then(hash => {
    console.log('Model uploaded to IPFS:', hash);
});
```

This code demonstrates how to upload and download encrypted 3D models using IPFS and AES encryption, ensuring secure storage of the assets.

In conclusion, creating, integrating, and managing 3D models and virtual assets as NFTs involves a multi-step process, including artistic creation, tokenization, game integration, and security measures. By following these best practices, developers can enhance their games with unique and valuable digital assets, providing players with a richer and more engaging experience.

10.5. Ensuring Authenticity and Rarity in NFT Art

Ensuring authenticity and rarity in NFT art is crucial for maintaining the value and trustworthiness of digital assets. Authenticity guarantees that the artwork is original and created by the stated artist, while rarity adds to the uniqueness and desirability of the NFT. This section explores strategies and best practices for ensuring the authenticity and rarity of NFT art.

One of the primary methods to ensure authenticity is through artist verification. Platforms that support NFT creation and trading should implement robust verification processes to confirm the identity of artists. This can include verifying social media accounts, conducting background checks, and requiring identity documentation. Verified artists can then be given a special badge or status that signifies their authenticity.

Blockchain technology itself provides a transparent and immutable record of ownership and provenance. By recording the creation, sale, and transfer of NFTs on the blockchain, it is possible to trace the entire history of the asset. This helps prevent fraud and ensures that buyers can verify the authenticity of their purchases.

Here's an example of how to check the provenance of an NFT using a smart contract:

```solidity
pragma solidity ^0.8.0;

contract Provenance {
    struct Ownership {
        address owner;
        uint256 timestamp;
    }

    mapping(uint256 => Ownership[]) public ownershipHistory;

    function recordOwnership(uint256 tokenId, address owner) public {
        ownershipHistory[tokenId].push(Ownership(owner, block.timestamp));
    }

    function getOwnershipHistory(uint256 tokenId) public view returns (Owners
hip[] memory) {
        return ownershipHistory[tokenId];
    }
}
```

This contract allows the recording and retrieval of ownership history for NFTs, providing a transparent provenance record.

Rarity can be ensured by limiting the number of editions or copies of an NFT. Artists and developers can create a fixed supply of an asset, making it scarce and more valuable. For example, a limited edition NFT might have only 10 copies, each with a unique identifier. This scarcity creates a sense of exclusivity and increases demand.

Here's an example of a Solidity contract for creating limited edition NFTs:

```solidity
pragma solidity ^0.8.0;

import "@openzeppelin/contracts/token/ERC721/ERC721.sol";
import "@openzeppelin/contracts/access/Ownable.sol";

contract LimitedEditionNFT is ERC721, Ownable {
    uint256 public maxSupply;
    uint256 public totalSupply;

    constructor(uint256 _maxSupply) ERC721("LimitedEditionNFT", "LENFT") {
        maxSupply = _maxSupply;
        totalSupply = 0;
    }

    function mintNFT(address to) public onlyOwner {
        require(totalSupply < maxSupply, "Max supply reached");
        _mint(to, totalSupply);
        totalSupply++;
    }
}
```

This contract ensures that only a limited number of NFTs can be minted, preserving their rarity.

Certifying the authenticity of NFT art can also involve integrating digital signatures. Artists can sign their digital artwork using cryptographic techniques, providing a verifiable proof of authenticity. This digital signature can be included in the NFT metadata, allowing buyers to confirm that the artwork was indeed created by the stated artist.

Here's an example of how to sign and verify a digital signature using JavaScript:

```javascript
const crypto = require('crypto');

function signData(data, privateKey) {
    const sign = crypto.createSign('SHA256');
    sign.update(data);
    sign.end();
    const signature = sign.sign(privateKey, 'hex');
    return signature;
}

function verifySignature(data, signature, publicKey) {
    const verify = crypto.createVerify('SHA256');
    verify.update(data);
    verify.end();
    return verify.verify(publicKey, signature, 'hex');
}
```

```
// Example usage
const data = 'This is my digital artwork';
const privateKey = 'your-private-key';
const publicKey = 'your-public-key';

const signature = signData(data, privateKey);
const isValid = verifySignature(data, signature, publicKey);

console.log('Signature:', signature);
console.log('Is valid:', isValid);
```

This code demonstrates how to sign and verify digital data, ensuring the authenticity of NFT art.

To further enhance authenticity, platforms can use watermarking techniques. Digital watermarks can be embedded into the artwork, visible or invisible, to indicate authenticity. These watermarks can be difficult to remove without damaging the artwork, providing an additional layer of protection against forgery.

Additionally, using smart contracts to enforce rarity and authenticity rules can help maintain trust in the NFT ecosystem. Smart contracts can automate the process of verifying artist identities, limiting supply, and recording provenance, reducing the risk of human error or manipulation.

In conclusion, ensuring authenticity and rarity in NFT art involves artist verification, transparent provenance records, limited editions, digital signatures, watermarking, and smart contracts. By implementing these strategies, artists and developers can protect the value of their NFTs, build trust with buyers, and create a sustainable and vibrant digital art ecosystem.

Chapter 11: Smart Contract Development for Gaming NFTs

11.1. Advanced Smart Contract Coding Techniques

Smart contract development for gaming NFTs involves using advanced coding techniques to ensure functionality, security, and efficiency. This section explores various advanced techniques and best practices to enhance smart contract development for gaming NFTs.

One advanced technique is the use of modular smart contract architecture. Modular contracts break down complex functionalities into smaller, reusable components. This approach makes the code more manageable, easier to understand, and facilitates code reuse across different projects.

For example, you can separate the core NFT logic from additional features like marketplace integration or staking mechanisms:

```solidity
// Core NFT Contract
pragma solidity ^0.8.0;

import "@openzeppelin/contracts/token/ERC721/ERC721.sol";
import "@openzeppelin/contracts/access/Ownable.sol";

contract CoreNFT is ERC721, Ownable {
    uint256 public tokenCounter;

    constructor() ERC721("CoreNFT", "CNFT") {
        tokenCounter = 0;
    }

    function mintNFT(address to) public onlyOwner returns (uint256) {
        uint256 newItemId = tokenCounter;
        _mint(to, newItemId);
        tokenCounter++;
        return newItemId;
    }
}

// Staking Contract
pragma solidity ^0.8.0;

import "./CoreNFT.sol";

contract NFTStaking {
    CoreNFT public nftContract;

    constructor(address nftAddress) {
        nftContract = CoreNFT(nftAddress);
    }
```

        // Staking logic here
}

This modularity allows developers to maintain and update each contract independently, enhancing flexibility and security.

Another advanced technique is the use of oracles to fetch off-chain data. Oracles provide smart contracts with external data, enabling more complex and dynamic functionalities. For example, in a game, an oracle can fetch real-time data for in-game events or rewards:

```solidity
pragma solidity ^0.8.0;

interface IOracle {
    function getGameEventData() external view returns (uint256);
}

contract GameEvent {
    IOracle public oracle;

    constructor(address oracleAddress) {
        oracle = IOracle(oracleAddress);
    }

    function fetchEventData() public view returns (uint256) {
        return oracle.getGameEventData();
    }
}
```

Using oracles, game developers can create more interactive and responsive gaming experiences by integrating real-world data.

Optimizing gas usage is another crucial aspect of advanced smart contract development. Efficient gas usage reduces transaction costs and improves the performance of the contract. Techniques such as minimizing storage operations, using packed variables, and optimizing loops can significantly reduce gas consumption:

```solidity
pragma solidity ^0.8.0;

contract GasOptimized {
    uint256[] public data;

    function addData(uint256 _data) public {
        data.push(_data);
    }

    function calculateSum() public view returns (uint256 sum) {
        uint256 length = data.length;
        for (uint256 i = 0; i < length; i++) {
            sum += data[i];
```

```
        }
    }
}
```

By storing the array length in a local variable (length), the loop reduces the number of storage reads, saving gas.

Security is paramount in smart contract development. Implementing advanced security measures such as reentrancy guards, proper access controls, and thorough testing can prevent vulnerabilities. For instance, using OpenZeppelin's ReentrancyGuard can protect against reentrancy attacks:

```
pragma solidity ^0.8.0;

import "@openzeppelin/contracts/security/ReentrancyGuard.sol";

contract SecureContract is ReentrancyGuard {
    mapping(address => uint256) public balances;

    function withdraw(uint256 amount) public nonReentrant {
        require(balances[msg.sender] >= amount, "Insufficient balance");
        balances[msg.sender] -= amount;
        payable(msg.sender).transfer(amount);
    }
}
```

In this example, the nonReentrant modifier prevents reentrancy attacks by ensuring that no reentrant calls to the withdraw function can occur.

Implementing upgradeable contracts is another advanced technique that allows for future modifications and improvements without disrupting the current contract state. The Proxy pattern is commonly used for this purpose, where a proxy contract delegates calls to an implementation contract:

```
// Proxy Contract
pragma solidity ^0.8.0;

contract Proxy {
    address public implementation;

    function setImplementation(address newImplementation) public {
        implementation = newImplementation;
    }

    fallback() external {
        address impl = implementation;
        require(impl != address(0), "Implementation not set");
        assembly {
            let ptr := mload(0x40)
            calldatacopy(ptr, 0, calldatasize())
```

```
            let result := delegatecall(gas(), impl, ptr, calldatasize(), 0, 0
)
            returndatacopy(ptr, 0, returndatasize())
            switch result
            case 0 { revert(ptr, returndatasize()) }
            default { return(ptr, returndatasize()) }
        }
    }
}
```

By separating the proxy and implementation contracts, developers can upgrade the implementation without changing the proxy address, maintaining the contract's state and user balances.

Finally, integrating automated testing and continuous integration (CI) pipelines is essential for maintaining high-quality smart contracts. Tools like Truffle, Hardhat, and Remix IDE provide robust testing frameworks, while CI tools like GitHub Actions and Travis CI automate testing and deployment processes:

```
const { expect } = require("chai");

describe("CoreNFT", function () {
    it("Should mint and return correct token count", async function () {
        const CoreNFT = await ethers.getContractFactory("CoreNFT");
        const coreNFT = await CoreNFT.deploy();
        await coreNFT.deployed();

        await coreNFT.mintNFT(owner.address);
        expect(await coreNFT.tokenCounter()).to.equal(1);
    });
});
```

In conclusion, advanced smart contract coding techniques for gaming NFTs involve modular architecture, oracles, gas optimization, security measures, upgradeable contracts, and automated testing. By leveraging these techniques, developers can create robust, efficient, and secure smart contracts for gaming applications.

11.2. Testing and Deploying Smart Contracts

Testing and deploying smart contracts are crucial steps in the development lifecycle to ensure they function correctly, securely, and efficiently. This section explores best practices and methodologies for testing and deploying smart contracts, with a focus on gaming NFTs.

Thorough testing is essential to identify and fix bugs, security vulnerabilities, and performance issues. Unit testing, integration testing, and end-to-end testing are the primary types of tests that should be conducted.

Unit testing focuses on individual functions and components of the smart contract. Tools like Truffle, Hardhat, and Remix IDE provide testing frameworks for writing and executing unit tests. Here's an example of a unit test for a minting function using Hardhat and Mocha:

```javascript
const { expect } = require("chai");

describe("CoreNFT", function () {
    let CoreNFT, coreNFT, owner, addr1;

    beforeEach(async function () {
        CoreNFT = await ethers.getContractFactory("CoreNFT");
        [owner, addr1] = await ethers.getSigners();
        coreNFT = await CoreNFT.deploy();
        await coreNFT.deployed();
    });

    it("Should mint a new NFT", async function () {
        await coreNFT.mintNFT(addr1.address);
        expect(await coreNFT.balanceOf(addr1.address)).to.equal(1);
    });

    it("Should increment tokenCounter", async function () {
        await coreNFT.mintNFT(addr1.address);
        expect(await coreNFT.tokenCounter()).to.equal(1);
    });
});
```

This unit test checks if the `mintNFT` function correctly mints a new NFT and increments the token counter.

Integration testing ensures that different parts of the smart contract work together as expected. This type of testing involves deploying the contract to a local or test network and interacting with it through various functions. Here's an example of an integration test:

```javascript
describe("Integration Test", function () {
    let CoreNFT, coreNFT, Marketplace, marketplace, owner, addr1;

    beforeEach(async function () {
        CoreNFT = await ethers.getContractFactory("CoreNFT");
        Marketplace = await ethers.getContractFactory("Marketplace");
        [owner, addr1] = await ethers.getSigners();
        coreNFT = await CoreNFT.deploy();
        await coreNFT.deployed();
        marketplace = await Marketplace.deploy(coreNFT.address);
        await marketplace.deployed();
    });

    it("Should list and buy an NFT", async function () {
        await coreNFT.mintNFT(owner.address);
        await coreNFT.approve(marketplace.address, 0);
        await marketplace.listNFT(0, ethers.utils.parseUnits("1", "ether"));

        await marketplace.connect(addr1).buyNFT(0, { value: ethers.utils.parseUnits("1", "ether") });
```

```
        expect(await coreNFT.ownerOf(0)).to.equal(addr1.address);
    });
});
```

This integration test verifies that an NFT can be listed and bought on the marketplace, ensuring the interaction between the NFT contract and the marketplace contract works correctly.

End-to-end testing involves testing the entire workflow, from deploying the contract to performing all the possible interactions users might execute. These tests simulate real-world usage and help identify any issues that might occur in a live environment.

Deploying smart contracts involves several steps, including preparing the deployment scripts, configuring the deployment environment, and executing the deployment. Hardhat and Truffle are popular tools for managing the deployment process.

Here's an example of a Hardhat deployment script:

```
async function main() {
    const [deployer] = await ethers.getSigners();

    console.log("Deploying contracts with the account:", deployer.address);

    const CoreNFT = await ethers.getContractFactory("CoreNFT");
    const coreNFT = await CoreNFT.deploy();
    await coreNFT.deployed();

    console.log("CoreNFT deployed to:", coreNFT.address);
}

main()
    .then(() => process.exit(0))
    .catch((error) => {
        console.error(error);
        process.exit(1);
    });
```

This script deploys the `CoreNFT` contract using the Hardhat runtime environment.

It's essential to deploy smart contracts to a test network (e.g., Ropsten, Rinkeby) before deploying them to the mainnet. This allows developers to conduct thorough testing in an environment that mimics the mainnet but without the associated costs and risks.

Security audits are a critical part of the deployment process. Before deploying to the mainnet, contracts should be audited by security experts to identify and fix any vulnerabilities. Audits can involve both automated tools and manual review by experienced auditors.

After deploying the contract, it's important to verify the contract on the blockchain explorer (e.g., Etherscan). Contract verification involves publishing the source code and metadata so that users can inspect the contract and verify its authenticity.

Here's an example of verifying a contract using Hardhat:

```
npx hardhat verify --network mainnet DEPLOYED_CONTRACT_ADDRESS "Constructor argument 1" "Constructor argument 2"
```

This command verifies the deployed contract on the specified network, making the source code and metadata publicly accessible.

In conclusion, testing and deploying smart contracts for gaming NFTs involves unit testing, integration testing, end-to-end testing, preparing deployment scripts, configuring the deployment environment, conducting security audits, and verifying the contract on blockchain explorers. By following these best practices, developers can ensure that their smart contracts are robust, secure, and ready for production use.

11.3. Smart Contract Optimization for Efficiency

Optimizing smart contracts for efficiency is crucial to minimize gas costs and improve performance. This section explores various optimization techniques and best practices to enhance the efficiency of smart contracts, particularly for gaming NFTs.

One of the primary optimization techniques is to minimize storage operations. Storage operations are the most expensive operations in terms of gas. Reducing the number of storage writes and reads can significantly lower gas costs. For example, instead of storing multiple variables separately, you can pack them into a single storage slot:

```
pragma solidity ^0.8.0;

contract StorageOptimization {
    struct PackedData {
        uint128 data1;
        uint128 data2;
    }

    PackedData public packedData;

    function setPackedData(uint128 _data1, uint128 _data2) public {
        packedData = PackedData(_data1, _data2);
    }
}
```

In this example, `data1` and `data2` are packed into a single storage slot, reducing the gas cost associated with storage operations.

Another optimization technique is to use events for logging data instead of storing it on-chain. Events are cheaper than storage and can be used to log important information that does not need to be stored persistently:

```solidity
pragma solidity ^0.8.0;

contract EventLogging {
    event DataLogged(address indexed user, uint256 data);

    function logData(uint256 data) public {
        emit DataLogged(msg.sender, data);
    }
}
```

In this example, the `logData` function logs data using an event, avoiding the higher gas cost of storing the data on-chain.

Using `memory` and `calldata` instead of `storage` for temporary variables and function parameters can also reduce gas costs. `Memory` and `calldata` are cheaper than `storage` because they do not persist after the function execution:

```solidity
pragma solidity ^0.8.0;

contract MemoryUsage {
    function processArray(uint256[] calldata data) public pure returns (uint256) {
        uint256 sum = 0;
        for (uint256 i = 0; i < data.length; i++) {
            sum += data[i];
        }
        return sum;
    }
}
```

In this example, the `data` array is passed as `calldata`, and the loop processes it in `memory`, reducing gas costs compared to using `storage`.

Optimizing loops is another important aspect of smart contract efficiency. Avoiding loops that run on `storage` variables and using fixed-size arrays or mappings where possible can save gas. Additionally, unrolling loops when the number of iterations is known in advance can improve performance:

```solidity
pragma solidity ^0.8.0;

contract LoopOptimization {
    uint256[5] public data;

    function unrolledLoop() public {
        data[0] = 1;
        data[1] = 2;
        data[2] = 3;
        data[3] = 4;
        data[4] = 5;
```

        }
}

In this example, the loop is unrolled, which can be more gas-efficient when the number of iterations is known.

Using libraries and inline assembly for critical sections of the code can also enhance efficiency. Libraries allow code reuse without duplicating it in every contract, and inline assembly provides more control over low-level operations:

```solidity
pragma solidity ^0.8.0;

library MathLib {
    function add(uint256 a, uint256 b) internal pure returns (uint256) {
        return a + b;
    }
}

contract LibraryUsage {
    using MathLib for uint256;

    function sum(uint256 a, uint256 b) public pure returns (uint256) {
        return a.add(b);
    }
}
```

In this example, `MathLib` is a library that provides a reusable `add` function, reducing code duplication and potentially saving gas.

Here's an example of using inline assembly for efficient calculations:

```solidity
pragma solidity ^0.8.0;

contract AssemblyOptimization {
    function multiply(uint256 a, uint256 b) public pure returns (uint256 result) {
        assembly {
            result := mul(a, b)
        }
    }
}
```

In this example, the `multiply` function uses inline assembly to perform the multiplication, which can be more gas-efficient.

Avoiding redundant computations and leveraging the `constant` and `immutable` keywords for state variables that do not change can also improve efficiency. These keywords ensure that the variables are stored in the contract's bytecode, reducing gas costs:

```solidity
pragma solidity ^0.8.0;
```

```
contract ConstantUsage {
    uint256 public constant FIXED_VALUE = 100;
    uint256 public immutable immutableValue;

    constructor(uint256 _value) {
        immutableValue = _value;
    }
}
```

In this example, `FIXED_VALUE` and `immutableValue` are optimized for gas efficiency.

Finally, it's essential to conduct thorough gas analysis and benchmarking using tools like `eth-gas-reporter` and Hardhat's built-in gas reporter. These tools provide insights into the gas costs of different functions and help identify areas for optimization:

```
npx hardhat test --network localhost
```

Running tests with gas reporting enabled helps developers understand the gas consumption of their contracts and optimize accordingly.

In conclusion, optimizing smart contracts for efficiency involves minimizing storage operations, using events for logging, leveraging `memory` and `calldata`, optimizing loops, using libraries and inline assembly, avoiding redundant computations, and conducting thorough gas analysis. By implementing these techniques, developers can create more efficient and cost-effective smart contracts for gaming NFTs.

11.4. Security Best Practices in Smart Contract Development

Security is a paramount concern in smart contract development, particularly for gaming NFTs, where significant value and user trust are at stake. This section explores various security best practices to protect smart contracts from vulnerabilities and ensure their integrity.

One of the foundational security practices is to use well-established libraries and frameworks. Libraries like OpenZeppelin provide audited and tested implementations of common smart contract components, reducing the risk of introducing vulnerabilities:

```
pragma solidity ^0.8.0;

import "@openzeppelin/contracts/token/ERC721/ERC721.sol";
import "@openzeppelin/contracts/access/Ownable.sol";

contract SecureNFT is ERC721, Ownable {
    uint256 public tokenCounter;

    constructor() ERC721("SecureNFT", "SNFT") {
        tokenCounter = 0;
    }

    function mintNFT(address to) public onlyOwner returns (uint256) {
```

```solidity
        uint256 newItemId = tokenCounter;
        _mint(to, newItemId);
        tokenCounter++;
        return newItemId;
    }
}
```

Using OpenZeppelin's ERC721 implementation ensures that the core NFT functionality is secure and compliant with industry standards.

Implementing proper access control is critical to prevent unauthorized access and modifications. The `Ownable` contract from OpenZeppelin provides a simple way to restrict access to certain functions:

```solidity
pragma solidity ^0.8.0;

import "@openzeppelin/contracts/access/Ownable.sol";

contract AccessControlled is Ownable {
    function restrictedFunction() public onlyOwner {
        // Restricted logic
    }
}
```

In this example, the `restrictedFunction` can only be called by the contract owner, ensuring that sensitive operations are protected.

Reentrancy attacks are a common vulnerability in smart contracts. Using the ReentrancyGuard contract from OpenZeppelin can prevent these attacks by ensuring that a function cannot be re-entered while it is still executing:

```solidity
pragma solidity ^0.8.0;

import "@openzeppelin/contracts/security/ReentrancyGuard.sol";

contract SecureWithdraw is ReentrancyGuard {
    mapping(address => uint256) public balances;

    function withdraw(uint256 amount) public nonReentrant {
        require(balances[msg.sender] >= amount, "Insufficient balance");
        balances[msg.sender] -= amount;
        payable(msg.sender).transfer(amount);
    }
}
```

The `nonReentrant` modifier ensures that the `withdraw` function cannot be called again before the first call completes.

Avoiding arithmetic overflows and underflows is another critical security measure. Using the `SafeMath` library from OpenZeppelin ensures that arithmetic operations are safe:

```solidity
pragma solidity ^0.8.0;

import "@openzeppelin/contracts/utils/math/SafeMath.sol";

contract SafeArithmetic {
    using SafeMath for uint256;

    function safeAdd(uint256 a, uint256 b) public pure returns (uint256) {
        return a.add(b);
    }
}
```

The `SafeMath` library provides safe versions of arithmetic operations that revert on overflow and underflow, preventing potential vulnerabilities.

Validating user inputs is essential to prevent invalid or malicious data from affecting the contract's logic. Input validation checks should be implemented to ensure that all inputs meet the expected criteria:

```solidity
pragma solidity ^0.8.0;

contract InputValidation {
    function validateInput(uint256 value) public pure {
        require(value > 0 && value < 100, "Invalid input");
        // Further logic
    }
}
```

In this example, the `validateInput` function ensures that the input value is within a valid range.

Ensuring that the contract's logic is clear and predictable is important for security. Avoid using complex and opaque constructs that can obscure the contract's behavior. Keeping the code simple and well-documented helps in identifying and preventing potential vulnerabilities.

Conducting thorough testing and auditing is crucial to identify and fix security issues. Automated testing tools like MythX, Slither, and Echidna can help detect common vulnerabilities and logical errors:

```
myth analyze contracts/SecureNFT.sol
```

Running security analysis tools on the contract code helps identify potential issues before deployment.

Engaging with professional security auditors for manual review is also highly recommended. Auditors with expertise in smart contract security can provide valuable insights and identify issues that automated tools might miss.

Implementing a bug bounty program can incentivize external security researchers to identify and report vulnerabilities. Platforms like HackerOne and Gitcoin offer frameworks for setting up and managing bug bounty programs.

In conclusion, security best practices in smart contract development include using established libraries, implementing proper access control, preventing reentrancy attacks, avoiding arithmetic overflows and underflows, validating user inputs, keeping the code simple and clear, conducting thorough testing and auditing, and engaging professional auditors and bug bounty programs. By following these practices, developers can enhance the security and integrity of their smart contracts for gaming NFTs.

11.5. Auditing and Quality Assurance of Game Smart Contracts

Auditing and quality assurance (QA) are critical steps in the development of game smart contracts to ensure they are secure, reliable, and function as intended. This section explores the methodologies, tools, and best practices for auditing and QA of game smart contracts.

The first step in auditing is to conduct a comprehensive code review. This involves examining the smart contract code line-by-line to identify potential vulnerabilities, logical errors, and inefficiencies. Key aspects to review include access controls, arithmetic operations, input validations, and the use of external calls.

Automated auditing tools can assist in identifying common vulnerabilities. Tools like MythX, Slither, and Echidna provide static analysis, symbolic execution, and fuzz testing to detect issues such as reentrancy, integer overflows, and unhandled exceptions:

```
# Using MythX for static analysis
myth analyze contracts/GameContract.sol
```

These tools generate detailed reports highlighting potential security issues and recommendations for remediation.

Manual auditing by experienced security professionals is crucial to identify complex vulnerabilities that automated tools might miss. Auditors should have expertise in smart contract security and be familiar with common attack vectors. They should also understand the specific requirements and constraints of the gaming context.

Here's a checklist for manual auditing of game smart contracts:

1. **Access Control:** Ensure that only authorized entities can perform sensitive operations.
2. **Reentrancy:** Check for reentrancy vulnerabilities, especially in functions involving external calls.
3. **Arithmetic Safety:** Verify the use of safe arithmetic operations to prevent overflows and underflows.
4. **Input Validation:** Ensure that all inputs are validated to meet expected criteria.

5. **State Consistency:** Verify that the contract's state transitions are consistent and predictable.
6. **Event Emissions:** Check that important state changes are accompanied by event emissions for transparency.
7. **Gas Optimization:** Identify and optimize any gas-intensive operations to reduce costs.
8. **External Calls:** Review the use of external calls to prevent attacks such as reentrancy and dependency on unreliable or malicious contracts.

Quality assurance involves rigorous testing to ensure the smart contract functions correctly under various scenarios. Unit testing, integration testing, and end-to-end testing are essential components of the QA process.

Unit testing focuses on individual functions to verify their correctness. Using testing frameworks like Hardhat and Truffle, developers can write and execute unit tests:

```
const { expect } = require("chai");

describe("GameContract", function () {
    let GameContract, gameContract, owner, player;

    beforeEach(async function () {
        GameContract = await ethers.getContractFactory("GameContract");
        [owner, player] = await ethers.getSigners();
        gameContract = await GameContract.deploy();
        await gameContract.deployed();
    });

    it("Should allow a player to join the game", async function () {
        await gameContract.joinGame(player.address);
        expect(await gameContract.isPlayer(player.address)).to.equal(true);
    });
});
```

This unit test checks if a player can successfully join the game.

Integration testing ensures that different components of the smart contract work together as expected. These tests typically involve deploying the contract to a local or test network and interacting with it through various functions:

```
describe("Integration Test", function () {
    let GameContract, gameContract, Marketplace, marketplace, owner, player;

    beforeEach(async function () {
        GameContract = await ethers.getContractFactory("GameContract");
        Marketplace = await ethers.getContractFactory("Marketplace");
        [owner, player] = await ethers.getSigners();
        gameContract = await GameContract.deploy();
        await gameContract.deployed();
```

```
        marketplace = await Marketplace.deploy(gameContract.address);
        await marketplace.deployed();
    });

    it("Should allow a player to buy an in-game item", async function () {
        await gameContract.joinGame(player.address);
        await gameContract.mintItem(owner.address, 1, "Sword");
        await gameContract.approve(marketplace.address, 1);
        await marketplace.connect(player).buyItem(1, { value: ethers.utils.pa
rseUnits("1", "ether") });
        expect(await gameContract.ownerOf(1)).to.equal(player.address);
    });
});
```

This integration test verifies that a player can buy an in-game item, ensuring the interaction between the game contract and the marketplace works correctly.

End-to-end testing involves testing the entire workflow from deployment to final user interactions. These tests simulate real-world usage and help identify any issues that might occur in a live environment.

In addition to testing and auditing, it's important to implement continuous integration (CI) and continuous deployment (CD) pipelines. CI/CD pipelines automate the testing, auditing, and deployment processes, ensuring that any changes to the codebase are thoroughly vetted before going live:

```
# Example GitHub Actions workflow for CI/CD
name: CI/CD

on: [push, pull_request]

jobs:
  build:
    runs-on: ubuntu-latest
    steps:
      - name: Checkout code
        uses: actions/checkout@v2

      - name: Setup Node.js
        uses: actions/setup-node@v2
        with:
          node-version: '14'

      - name: Install dependencies
        run: npm install

      - name: Run tests
        run: npx hardhat test
```

```yaml
      - name: Run linting
        run: npx hardhat lint

      - name: Deploy to testnet
        if: github.ref == 'refs/heads/main'
        run: npx hardhat run scripts/deploy.js --network ropsten
        env:
          INFURA_API_KEY: ${{ secrets.INFURA_API_KEY }}
          PRIVATE_KEY: ${{ secrets.PRIVATE_KEY }}
```

This GitHub Actions workflow automates the process of running tests, linting the code, and deploying the contract to a testnet.

Finally, engaging with the community through public bug bounties and audits can help identify and fix vulnerabilities. Platforms like Gitcoin and HackerOne provide frameworks for setting up and managing bug bounty programs, incentivizing external security researchers to report vulnerabilities.

In conclusion, auditing and quality assurance of game smart contracts involve comprehensive code reviews, automated and manual auditing, rigorous testing, CI/CD pipelines, and community engagement through bug bounties. By following these best practices, developers can ensure that their smart contracts are secure, reliable, and ready for deployment in the gaming environment.

Chapter 12: The Future of Gaming NFTs

12.1. Emerging Trends in NFT and Game Technology

The intersection of NFTs and gaming technology is constantly evolving, bringing forward new trends that shape the future of the industry. This section explores the most significant emerging trends in NFT and game technology, highlighting their potential impact and implications.

One of the most prominent trends is the rise of play-to-earn (P2E) gaming models. P2E games reward players with cryptocurrency or NFTs for their in-game activities, creating new economic opportunities for gamers. This model not only enhances player engagement but also offers a way for players to monetize their time and effort spent in the game. Successful examples like Axie Infinity and Splinterlands have demonstrated the viability of this approach.

Interoperability is another key trend, where NFTs can be used across multiple games and platforms. This allows players to take their assets from one game and use them in another, creating a more cohesive and interconnected gaming ecosystem. Standards like ERC-721 and ERC-1155 facilitate this interoperability, enabling developers to create NFTs that are compatible with various games and platforms.

The integration of DeFi (Decentralized Finance) elements into gaming is also gaining traction. DeFi enables financial activities like lending, borrowing, and staking within games. For instance, players can stake their NFTs to earn rewards or use them as collateral for loans. This fusion of gaming and finance creates new possibilities for player engagement and economic interaction.

Augmented Reality (AR) and Virtual Reality (VR) are set to revolutionize the way NFTs are experienced in games. AR and VR provide immersive environments where players can interact with their NFTs in real-time. Imagine walking through a virtual gallery of your NFT collectibles or using VR to explore a fantasy world where each item is a unique NFT. These technologies enhance the user experience and bring a new level of immersion to gaming.

Artificial Intelligence (AI) is another transformative technology in the NFT gaming space. AI can be used to create dynamic, personalized gaming experiences by generating unique in-game assets or tailoring game content to individual player preferences. AI-driven NFTs, which evolve based on player interactions, are also becoming a reality, adding depth and uniqueness to digital assets.

The concept of virtual land ownership is gaining popularity, with games like Decentraland and The Sandbox allowing players to buy, develop, and monetize virtual real estate. These virtual lands are represented as NFTs, giving players true ownership and the ability to trade or lease their properties. This trend is opening up new avenues for creativity and economic activity in the digital realm.

Blockchain scalability solutions, such as layer 2 protocols and sidechains, are addressing the scalability issues of traditional blockchains. These solutions enable faster and cheaper transactions, making it more feasible to use NFTs in high-volume gaming environments. Projects like Polygon and Immutable X are leading the way in providing scalable infrastructure for blockchain games.

Environmental sustainability is becoming an important consideration in the NFT and gaming industry. The high energy consumption of blockchain networks has raised concerns, leading to the adoption of more eco-friendly consensus mechanisms like Proof of Stake (PoS) and Proof of Authority (PoA). These methods significantly reduce the carbon footprint of blockchain operations, making NFT gaming more sustainable.

Here's an example of an eco-friendly smart contract using a PoS-based blockchain:

```solidity
pragma solidity ^0.8.0;

contract EcoFriendlyNFT {
    uint256 public tokenCounter;
    mapping(uint256 => address) public owners;

    constructor() {
        tokenCounter = 0;
    }

    function mint(address to) public returns (uint256) {
        tokenCounter++;
        owners[tokenCounter] = to;
        return tokenCounter;
    }
}
```

This simple contract mints NFTs on a PoS-based blockchain, reducing the environmental impact compared to traditional Proof of Work (PoW) systems.

The evolution of NFT marketplaces is another significant trend. Marketplaces are becoming more user-friendly and integrated with various payment solutions, including fiat currency and multiple cryptocurrencies. This accessibility encourages broader participation from both gamers and collectors, driving the growth of the NFT market.

Community-driven development is gaining momentum, with decentralized autonomous organizations (DAOs) playing a pivotal role. DAOs allow players and developers to collectively make decisions about game development, governance, and economics. This democratic approach fosters a strong sense of community and ownership among players.

In conclusion, the future of gaming NFTs is being shaped by trends like play-to-earn models, interoperability, DeFi integration, AR and VR experiences, AI-driven assets, virtual land ownership, blockchain scalability, environmental sustainability, evolving marketplaces, and community-driven development. These trends are driving innovation and creating new opportunities in the gaming industry.

12.2. NFTs in Augmented and Virtual Reality Games

The integration of NFTs in augmented reality (AR) and virtual reality (VR) games is a significant trend that promises to revolutionize the gaming experience. AR and VR technologies provide immersive environments where players can interact with NFTs in ways that were previously unimaginable. This section explores the potential of NFTs in AR and VR games, highlighting their benefits, challenges, and future prospects.

One of the primary benefits of integrating NFTs in AR and VR games is the enhanced user experience. In VR games, players can explore fully immersive 3D environments where NFTs serve as unique in-game assets, such as characters, items, or virtual real estate. For example, players can own and decorate virtual homes with NFT art or furniture, creating personalized spaces that reflect their identity and achievements.

In AR games, NFTs can be overlaid onto the real world, allowing players to interact with digital assets in their physical environment. This creates a seamless blend of the virtual and real worlds, enhancing the interactivity and engagement of the game. For instance, players can hunt for hidden NFTs in their neighborhood or display their NFT collections in augmented reality galleries.

The use of NFTs in AR and VR games also offers new economic opportunities for players. NFTs can be bought, sold, and traded on various marketplaces, allowing players to monetize their in-game assets. This adds a layer of financial value to the gaming experience, as players can earn real income through their virtual activities.

Here's an example of a basic VR game contract that integrates NFTs:

```solidity
pragma solidity ^0.8.0;

import "@openzeppelin/contracts/token/ERC721/ERC721.sol";
import "@openzeppelin/contracts/access/Ownable.sol";

contract VRGameNFT is ERC721, Ownable {
    uint256 public tokenCounter;

    constructor() ERC721("VRGameNFT", "VRNFT") {
        tokenCounter = 0;
    }

    function mintNFT(address to) public onlyOwner returns (uint256) {
        uint256 newItemId = tokenCounter;
        _mint(to, newItemId);
        tokenCounter++;
        return newItemId;
    }
}
```

This contract allows the minting of NFTs that can be used as unique assets in a VR game.

Despite the numerous benefits, there are also challenges associated with integrating NFTs in AR and VR games. One of the main challenges is the high cost and complexity of developing AR and VR experiences. These technologies require specialized hardware and software, which can be expensive and technically demanding to implement.

Interoperability is another challenge, as ensuring that NFTs can be used across different AR and VR platforms requires standardized protocols and collaboration among developers. Without interoperability, the utility of NFTs may be limited to specific games or platforms, reducing their overall value.

Security is a critical concern, as the integration of NFTs in AR and VR games introduces new vulnerabilities. Protecting user data, ensuring the authenticity of NFTs, and preventing fraud are essential to maintaining trust in the gaming ecosystem. Developers must implement robust security measures to safeguard against potential threats.

User adoption is also a challenge, as AR and VR technologies are still in the early stages of mainstream acceptance. Educating players about the benefits and usage of NFTs in these environments is crucial to driving adoption and engagement.

Despite these challenges, the future prospects of NFTs in AR and VR games are promising. As AR and VR technologies continue to advance, the integration of NFTs is likely to become more seamless and widespread. Innovations in hardware, such as more affordable and accessible VR headsets, will further drive the adoption of these immersive experiences.

Collaborations between game developers, blockchain platforms, and technology companies will play a pivotal role in advancing the integration of NFTs in AR and VR games. By working together, these stakeholders can develop standardized protocols, enhance interoperability, and create more engaging and secure gaming experiences.

In conclusion, the integration of NFTs in AR and VR games offers numerous benefits, including enhanced user experiences, new economic opportunities, and the potential for innovative gameplay. While challenges such as development costs, interoperability, security, and user adoption exist, the future prospects are bright. As technology continues to evolve, NFTs are set to play a significant role in shaping the future of AR and VR gaming.

12.3. The Impact of AI on NFT-Based Games

Artificial Intelligence (AI) is transforming various industries, and its impact on NFT-based games is profound. AI technologies can enhance the gaming experience, create dynamic and personalized content, and introduce new forms of interaction and engagement. This section explores the role of AI in NFT-based games, highlighting its potential benefits, applications, and challenges.

One of the primary benefits of AI in NFT-based games is the ability to create dynamic and adaptive gameplay. AI algorithms can analyze player behavior and preferences to tailor the gaming experience to individual players. This personalization can involve adjusting the difficulty level, generating customized quests, or offering tailored rewards. By providing a more engaging and immersive experience, AI can significantly enhance player retention and satisfaction.

AI can also be used to generate unique and evolving NFTs. Instead of static assets, AI-driven NFTs can change and grow based on player interactions and game events. For example, an AI-powered pet NFT could learn and adapt to a player's actions, developing new skills and behaviors over time. This dynamic nature adds a layer of depth and uniqueness to NFTs, making them more valuable and interesting to players.

Here's an example of an AI-driven NFT contract:

```solidity
pragma solidity ^0.8.0;

import "@openzeppelin/contracts/token/ERC721/ERC721.sol";
import "@openzeppelin/contracts/access/Ownable.sol";

contract AIDrivenNFT is ERC721, Ownable {
    struct Attributes {
        uint256 level;
        uint256 experience;
    }

    mapping(uint256 => Attributes) public nftAttributes;

    constructor() ERC721("AIDrivenNFT", "AINFT") {}

    function mintNFT(address to) public onlyOwner returns (uint256) {
        uint256 newItemId = totalSupply();
        _mint(to, newItemId);
        nftAttributes[newItemId] = Attributes(1, 0);
        return newItemId;
    }

    function updateAttributes(uint256 tokenId, uint256 experience) public onlyOwner {
        Attributes storage attrs = nftAttributes[tokenId];
        attrs.experience += experience;
        if (attrs.experience >= 100) {
            attrs.level++;
            attrs.experience = 0;
        }
    }
}
```

This contract allows the minting of NFTs with attributes that can be updated based on player interactions.

AI can enhance NPC (Non-Player Character) behavior and interactions in NFT-based games. Intelligent NPCs can provide more realistic and engaging interactions, creating a richer and more immersive game world. AI-powered NPCs can respond to player actions in more nuanced ways, offer complex dialogues, and adapt their behavior based on the game context.

Predictive analytics is another application of AI in NFT-based games. By analyzing player data, AI can predict player behavior and preferences, allowing developers to optimize game design and marketing strategies. For example, AI can identify patterns in player spending, helping developers to create targeted in-game offers and promotions.

AI can also play a role in enhancing the security of NFT-based games. Machine learning algorithms can detect unusual patterns and behaviors that may indicate fraudulent activities or security breaches. By continuously monitoring the game environment, AI can help prevent cheating, hacking, and other malicious activities, ensuring a fair and secure gaming experience.

Despite the numerous benefits, integrating AI into NFT-based games presents several challenges. One of the main challenges is the complexity and cost of developing AI algorithms. AI development requires specialized expertise and significant computational resources, which can be a barrier for smaller game developers.

Ensuring the transparency and explainability of AI algorithms is another challenge. Players need to understand how AI decisions are made, especially when it comes to generating rewards or determining game outcomes. Transparent and explainable AI fosters trust and ensures that players feel confident in the fairness of the game.

Data privacy is a critical concern when using AI in games. AI algorithms often rely on large amounts of player data to function effectively. Developers must implement robust data protection measures to ensure that player data is collected, stored, and used responsibly. Compliance with data privacy regulations, such as GDPR, is essential to maintain player trust and avoid legal issues.

In conclusion, AI has the potential to significantly enhance NFT-based games by creating dynamic gameplay, generating unique NFTs, improving NPC interactions, enabling predictive analytics, and enhancing security. While challenges such as development complexity, transparency, and data privacy exist, the benefits of AI integration are substantial. As AI technology continues to advance, its impact on NFT-based games will likely grow, offering new possibilities for innovation and engagement.

12.4. Predictions: The Next Decade of Gaming NFTs

The next decade of gaming NFTs is poised to bring significant advancements and transformations to the gaming industry. As technology continues to evolve, NFTs will play an increasingly central role in shaping the future of gaming. This section explores predictions for the next ten years, highlighting key trends, innovations, and potential developments in the world of gaming NFTs.

One of the most anticipated trends is the mainstream adoption of gaming NFTs. As blockchain technology becomes more accessible and user-friendly, a larger number of game developers and players will embrace NFTs. This widespread adoption will lead to a more integrated and cohesive gaming ecosystem, where NFTs are a standard component of most games.

Interoperability will be a major focus, with NFTs being used seamlessly across different games and platforms. Players will be able to carry their NFTs from one game to another, creating a unified gaming experience. This interoperability will be facilitated by standardized protocols and collaboration among developers, blockchain platforms, and industry stakeholders.

The evolution of play-to-earn (P2E) models will continue to gain momentum. More games will adopt P2E mechanisms, offering players various ways to earn real income through in-game activities. This shift will transform gaming from a purely recreational activity to a viable source of income for many players. The rise of decentralized finance (DeFi) elements within games will further enhance these economic opportunities.

Virtual reality (VR) and augmented reality (AR) will become more prevalent in gaming, with NFTs playing a crucial role in these immersive experiences. Players will interact with NFTs in fully immersive VR environments or see them overlaid in their physical surroundings through AR. These technologies will create new dimensions of interactivity and engagement, making the gaming experience more immersive and realistic.

AI-driven NFTs will become more sophisticated, offering unique and evolving digital assets that adapt based on player interactions. These dynamic NFTs will provide deeper and more personalized gaming experiences, with AI algorithms generating content tailored to individual player preferences. This will add a new layer of depth and uniqueness to digital assets, increasing their value and appeal.

Environmental sustainability will be a key consideration, with the gaming industry adopting more eco-friendly blockchain technologies. Proof of Stake (PoS) and other energy-efficient consensus mechanisms will replace the energy-intensive Proof of Work (PoW) systems. This shift will reduce the carbon footprint of blockchain operations, making NFT gaming more sustainable and responsible.

Here's an example of an eco-friendly NFT contract using a PoS-based blockchain:

```solidity
pragma solidity ^0.8.0;

contract GreenNFT {
    uint256 public tokenCounter;
    mapping(uint256 => address) public owners;

    constructor() {
        tokenCounter = 0;
    }

    function mint(address to) public returns (uint256) {
        tokenCounter++;
        owners[tokenCounter] = to;
        return tokenCounter;
    }
}
```

This contract mints NFTs on a PoS-based blockchain, promoting environmental sustainability.

The rise of decentralized autonomous organizations (DAOs) will democratize game development and governance. Players and developers will collectively make decisions about game updates, governance, and economic policies. This community-driven approach will foster a strong sense of ownership and involvement, enhancing player engagement and loyalty.

NFT marketplaces will continue to evolve, becoming more user-friendly and integrated with various payment solutions. These marketplaces will offer seamless experiences for buying, selling, and trading NFTs, attracting a broader audience. Enhanced security measures and regulatory compliance will ensure the safety and legitimacy of transactions.

The gaming industry will see an increase in collaborations and partnerships across different sectors. Game developers will collaborate with artists, celebrities, and brands to create exclusive and branded NFTs. These collaborations will drive innovation and attract new audiences, further expanding the reach and appeal of gaming NFTs.

Education and awareness about NFTs and blockchain technology will grow, reducing barriers to entry for new players and developers. As more people understand the benefits and potential of NFTs, the adoption rate will increase, leading to a more vibrant and diverse gaming ecosystem.

In conclusion, the next decade of gaming NFTs will be marked by mainstream adoption, interoperability, the evolution of play-to-earn models, the rise of VR and AR, AI-driven NFTs, environmental sustainability, decentralized governance, evolving marketplaces, cross-sector collaborations, and increased education and awareness. These developments will drive innovation and transform the gaming industry, offering new opportunities and experiences for players and developers alike.

12.5. Ethical and Social Implications of Future NFT Gaming

The rapid growth and evolution of NFT gaming bring with them a range of ethical and social implications that must be carefully considered. As the industry continues to expand, addressing these issues is crucial to ensure that NFT gaming develops in a responsible and inclusive manner. This section explores the ethical and social implications of future NFT gaming, highlighting key concerns and potential solutions.

One of the primary ethical concerns is the environmental impact of blockchain technology. Traditional blockchain networks, particularly those using Proof of Work (PoW) consensus mechanisms, consume significant amounts of energy, contributing to carbon emissions and environmental degradation. To mitigate this impact, the industry is moving towards more energy-efficient consensus mechanisms like Proof of Stake (PoS). Developers and platforms must prioritize sustainability by adopting eco-friendly technologies and promoting responsible practices.

Another ethical issue is the potential for economic inequality. While play-to-earn (P2E) models offer new economic opportunities, they can also exacerbate existing inequalities.

Players from wealthier backgrounds may have more resources to invest in NFTs, gaining advantages over those with fewer resources. To address this, game developers should design balanced economic systems that offer fair opportunities for all players, regardless of their financial background.

The commercialization of gaming through NFTs raises concerns about the commodification of leisure. As gaming becomes more financially driven, the focus may shift from enjoyment and creativity to profit and competition. This shift can impact the intrinsic value of gaming as a form of entertainment and artistic expression. Developers should strive to maintain a balance between economic incentives and the core principles of gaming, ensuring that fun and creativity remain central to the experience.

Data privacy is a critical concern in NFT gaming. The integration of AI and blockchain technologies often involves the collection and analysis of large amounts of player data. Ensuring that this data is handled responsibly, with strict adherence to privacy regulations, is essential. Developers must implement robust data protection measures and be transparent about data collection practices, giving players control over their personal information.

The rise of decentralized autonomous organizations (DAOs) in gaming introduces new governance models that empower players. While this democratization is positive, it also raises questions about decision-making processes and accountability. Ensuring that DAOs operate transparently and inclusively, with mechanisms to prevent abuse and ensure fair representation, is crucial for their success.

Inclusivity and accessibility are important ethical considerations in NFT gaming. The industry must strive to create inclusive environments that welcome players from diverse backgrounds, including those with disabilities. This includes designing games that are accessible and providing tools and resources to support diverse player communities. By prioritizing inclusivity, developers can ensure that NFT gaming is enjoyed by a broad and diverse audience.

The speculative nature of NFTs raises concerns about financial risks for players. The volatility of NFT markets can lead to significant financial losses, particularly for those who invest without fully understanding the risks. Developers and platforms have a responsibility to educate players about the potential risks and provide clear information to help them make informed decisions. Implementing measures to protect players from excessive speculation and financial harm is also important.

The impact of NFT gaming on mental health is another area of concern. The pressures of earning and competition, combined with the addictive nature of gaming, can affect players' mental well-being. Developers should consider the potential mental health implications and design games that promote healthy gaming habits. Providing resources and support for players who may be struggling with addiction or mental health issues is essential.

The ethical use of AI in NFT gaming is also crucial. AI algorithms should be designed and implemented in ways that respect players' rights and avoid biases. Ensuring transparency and explainability in AI decision-making processes can help build trust and prevent potential abuses.

In conclusion, the ethical and social implications of future NFT gaming are multifaceted and complex. Addressing these concerns requires a collaborative effort from developers, platforms, and the broader gaming community. By prioritizing sustainability, fairness, inclusivity, data privacy, responsible governance, financial education, mental health, and ethical AI use, the industry can develop in a way that is both innovative and responsible.

Chapter 13: User Experience and Interface Design for NFT Games

13.1. Designing Intuitive NFT User Interfaces

Designing intuitive user interfaces (UIs) for NFT games is crucial for ensuring that players can easily interact with the game's features and enjoy a seamless experience. This section explores best practices and strategies for creating user-friendly UIs in NFT games.

A key aspect of intuitive UI design is simplicity. Keeping the interface clean and uncluttered helps players navigate the game without feeling overwhelmed. Use clear and concise labels, minimalistic icons, and ample whitespace to create a visually appealing and easy-to-understand layout. Group related elements together and prioritize the most important features to guide players' attention.

For example, in an NFT marketplace within a game, the main screen could feature categories like "New Listings," "Top Sellers," and "Your NFTs," with each section clearly separated and labeled. A search bar at the top allows players to quickly find specific items.

Navigation should be straightforward and consistent throughout the game. Use familiar UI patterns, such as tab bars, side menus, and breadcrumbs, to help players understand how to move between different sections. Ensure that navigation elements are always accessible and clearly indicate the current location within the game.

Here's an example of a simple navigation bar in HTML and CSS:

```
<nav>
    <ul>
        <li><a href="#home">Home</a></li>
        <li><a href="#marketplace">Marketplace</a></li>
        <li><a href="#inventory">Inventory</a></li>
        <li><a href="#profile">Profile</a></li>
    </ul>
</nav>

<style>
    nav ul {
        list-style-type: none;
        margin: 0;
        padding: 0;
        overflow: hidden;
        background-color: #333;
    }

    nav ul li {
        float: left;
    }

    nav ul li a {
```

```css
        display: block;
        color: white;
        text-align: center;
        padding: 14px 16px;
        text-decoration: none;
    }

    nav ul li a:hover {
        background-color: #111;
    }
</style>
```

This code creates a simple navigation bar with links to different sections of the game.

Feedback is essential for an intuitive UI. Provide immediate and clear feedback for player actions, such as clicking a button, making a purchase, or completing a quest. Use animations, sound effects, and visual cues to confirm actions and keep players informed about the status of their interactions.

For instance, when a player purchases an NFT, a confirmation dialog could appear, followed by a success message and a brief animation showing the NFT being added to their inventory.

Consistency in design elements, such as color schemes, typography, and iconography, helps create a cohesive and intuitive experience. Stick to a limited color palette and font family to maintain visual harmony. Use icons that are easily recognizable and convey their meaning effectively.

Here's an example of a consistent color scheme and typography setup in CSS:

```css
body {
    font-family: 'Arial, sans-serif';
    color: #333;
    background-color: #f9f9f9;
}

h1, h2, h3 {
    color: #2c3e50;
}

a {
    color: #2980b9;
}

button {
    background-color: #3498db;
    color: white;
    border: none;
    padding: 10px 20px;
    cursor: pointer;
```

```
}
button:hover {
    background-color: #2980b9;
}
```

This CSS defines a consistent color scheme and typography for the game's UI.

Accessibility is a crucial consideration in UI design. Ensure that the game is accessible to players with disabilities by following best practices for web accessibility, such as using semantic HTML, providing alternative text for images, and ensuring sufficient color contrast. Implement keyboard navigation and screen reader support to make the game usable for everyone.

Here's an example of an accessible button in HTML:

```
<button aria-label="Purchase NFT">Buy Now</button>
```

The `aria-label` attribute provides a descriptive label for screen readers, making the button accessible to visually impaired players.

Usability testing is an essential step in the UI design process. Conduct tests with real players to identify any usability issues and gather feedback on the interface. Use this feedback to refine and improve the UI, ensuring that it meets the needs and expectations of the players.

In conclusion, designing intuitive UIs for NFT games involves simplicity, straightforward navigation, clear feedback, consistency, accessibility, and usability testing. By following these best practices, developers can create user-friendly interfaces that enhance the overall gaming experience and ensure that players can easily interact with the game's features.

13.2. User Experience Principles in NFT Integration

Integrating NFTs into games requires careful consideration of user experience (UX) principles to ensure that the addition enhances rather than detracts from the overall gameplay. This section explores key UX principles that should guide the integration of NFTs into games, ensuring a seamless and enjoyable experience for players.

One of the fundamental principles of good UX is to prioritize the player's needs and goals. When integrating NFTs, it's important to ensure that they add meaningful value to the game. NFTs should enhance the gameplay experience by providing unique items, characters, or features that offer real benefits to players. Avoid making NFTs feel like unnecessary add-ons or purely financial instruments.

Transparency is crucial in NFT integration. Players should clearly understand what NFTs are, how they can be used, and what benefits they offer. Provide detailed information about each NFT, including its attributes, rarity, and potential uses within the game. Transparency builds trust and helps players make informed decisions about purchasing and using NFTs.

Here's an example of providing detailed NFT information in HTML:

```html
<div class="nft-details">
    <h2>Legendary Sword</h2>
    <p>Rarity: Legendary</p>
    <p>Damage: 100</p>
    <p>Special Ability: Fire Strike</p>
    <p>This legendary sword grants the wielder the ability to unleash a powerful fire strike, dealing massive damage to enemies.</p>
</div>
```

This HTML snippet provides clear and detailed information about an NFT item in the game.

Seamless integration is key to a positive UX. NFTs should be naturally incorporated into the game, without disrupting the flow of gameplay. Players should be able to acquire, use, and trade NFTs without having to leave the game environment or navigate complex processes. Use intuitive in-game interfaces and ensure that NFT transactions are straightforward and user-friendly.

Here's an example of a simple in-game interface for purchasing an NFT:

```html
<div class="nft-purchase">
    <h3>Buy Legendary Sword</h3>
    <button onclick="purchaseNFT()">Purchase for 0.5 ETH</button>
</div>

<script>
    function purchaseNFT() {
        // Logic to handle NFT purchase
        alert('NFT purchased successfully!');
    }
</script>
```

This interface allows players to purchase an NFT with a single click, providing a seamless experience.

Security and trust are paramount when integrating NFTs. Ensure that all transactions are secure and transparent, protecting players' assets and personal information. Implement robust security measures, such as encryption and two-factor authentication, to safeguard against fraud and hacking. Clearly communicate these measures to players to build confidence in the system.

Providing a balanced and fair game economy is essential. Avoid creating a pay-to-win environment where players who spend more money on NFTs have a significant advantage. Instead, design a balanced system where NFTs offer unique benefits but do not overshadow skill and strategy. This ensures that the game remains enjoyable and fair for all players, regardless of their spending.

Inclusivity is another important principle. Ensure that the integration of NFTs does not exclude or disadvantage certain groups of players. Consider offering a mix of free and purchasable NFTs, allowing players to earn NFTs through gameplay as well as through purchases. This approach ensures that all players can enjoy the benefits of NFTs, regardless of their financial situation.

Feedback and iteration are crucial components of good UX design. Gather feedback from players about their experiences with NFTs in the game. Use surveys, focus groups, and analytics to understand how players are interacting with NFTs and identify any pain points or areas for improvement. Continuously iterate on the design based on this feedback to enhance the overall experience.

Here's an example of a simple feedback form for gathering player input:

```html
<div class="feedback-form">
    <h3>Share Your Feedback</h3>
    <form>
        <label for="feedback">What do you think about the NFT integration?</label><br>
        <textarea id="feedback" name="feedback" rows="4" cols="50"></textarea><br>
        <button type="submit">Submit</button>
    </form>
</div>
```

This form allows players to provide feedback on their experiences with NFTs in the game.

In conclusion, integrating NFTs into games successfully requires a focus on player needs, transparency, seamless integration, security, balanced economy, inclusivity, and continuous feedback. By adhering to these UX principles, developers can ensure that NFTs enhance the gaming experience and provide real value to players.

13.3. Accessibility and Inclusivity in NFT Gaming

Ensuring accessibility and inclusivity in NFT gaming is essential for creating an inclusive environment where all players, regardless of their abilities or backgrounds, can participate and enjoy the game. This section explores strategies and best practices for making NFT games accessible and inclusive.

One of the fundamental principles of accessibility is to design games that can be played by individuals with various disabilities. This includes providing options for players with visual, auditory, motor, and cognitive impairments. Implementing features like adjustable text sizes, high-contrast color schemes, and screen reader compatibility can make the game accessible to players with visual impairments.

Here's an example of a high-contrast color scheme in CSS:

```css
body {
    background-color: #000;
    color: #FFF;
}

a {
```

```css
    color: #00F;
}

button {
    background-color: #FFF;
    color: #000;
    border: 2px solid #00F;
    padding: 10px 20px;
    cursor: pointer;
}

button:hover {
    background-color: #00F;
    color: #FFF;
}
```

This CSS code provides a high-contrast color scheme that improves readability for visually impaired players.

For players with auditory impairments, providing subtitles or text alternatives for in-game audio cues is crucial. Ensure that all important audio information is also conveyed visually. Additionally, allowing players to adjust or mute background music and sound effects can help accommodate different auditory needs.

Here's an example of providing subtitles for in-game dialogue:

```html
<div class="subtitles">
    <p>[Character]: Welcome to the game! Your adventure begins here.</p>
</div>
```

This HTML snippet displays subtitles for an in-game dialogue, ensuring that players with auditory impairments can follow along.

Motor impairments can affect a player's ability to interact with the game using standard input devices. Providing customizable control schemes, including options for alternative input devices such as gamepads or voice commands, can enhance accessibility. Additionally, ensuring that all game functions can be performed using keyboard shortcuts can make the game more accessible to players with limited mobility.

Here's an example of implementing keyboard shortcuts for game controls:

```html
<script>
    document.addEventListener('keydown', function(event) {
        switch(event.key) {
            case 'ArrowUp':
                // Move character up
                break;
            case 'ArrowDown':
                // Move character down
                break;
```

```
            case 'ArrowLeft':
                // Move character left
                break;
            case 'ArrowRight':
                // Move character right
                break;
            case 'Enter':
                // Select option
                break;
            default:
                break;
        }
    });
</script>
```

This script allows players to control the game using keyboard shortcuts.

Cognitive impairments can affect a player's ability to process complex information and instructions. Simplifying game mechanics, providing clear and concise instructions, and using intuitive design elements can help make the game more accessible. Avoiding excessive use of flashing lights and rapid movements can also reduce the risk of triggering seizures in players with photosensitive epilepsy.

Inclusivity goes beyond accessibility by ensuring that the game environment is welcoming and supportive for players from diverse backgrounds. This includes offering diverse character options, representing various ethnicities, genders, and cultures. Creating an inclusive community where all players feel valued and respected is essential for fostering a positive gaming experience.

Providing multiple language options is another important aspect of inclusivity. Localizing the game for different languages allows players from various regions to enjoy the game in their native language. This includes translating not only the game text but also subtitles, menus, and tutorials.

Here's an example of providing language options in a game:

```
<select id="language-select" onchange="changeLanguage()">
    <option value="en">English</option>
    <option value="es">Español</option>
    <option value="fr">Français</option>
    <option value="de">Deutsch</option>
</select>

<script>
    function changeLanguage() {
        var selectedLanguage = document.getElementById('language-select').value;
        // Logic to change the game language
    }
</script>
```

This interface allows players to select their preferred language, enhancing inclusivity.

Economic inclusivity is also important in NFT gaming. While NFTs often involve financial transactions, it's important to ensure that players who cannot afford to purchase NFTs can still enjoy the game. Offering a mix of free and purchasable NFTs, as well as opportunities to earn NFTs through gameplay, can make the game more inclusive for players from different economic backgrounds.

Community support and moderation are crucial for maintaining an inclusive gaming environment. Implementing robust community guidelines and moderation tools can help prevent harassment and discrimination. Providing players with tools to report inappropriate behavior and ensuring prompt action is taken to address issues can create a safer and more welcoming community.

In conclusion, ensuring accessibility and inclusivity in NFT gaming involves designing for various disabilities, offering diverse character options, localizing the game for different languages, providing economic inclusivity, and maintaining a supportive community. By following these best practices, developers can create an inclusive environment where all players can participate and enjoy the game.

13.4. Personalization and Customization with NFTs

Personalization and customization are key aspects of enhancing the player experience in NFT games. By leveraging NFTs, developers can offer unique and personalized content that caters to individual player preferences. This section explores strategies and best practices for incorporating personalization and customization features in NFT games.

One of the primary ways to offer personalization is through customizable avatars and characters. NFTs can represent unique character skins, outfits, accessories, and other cosmetic items that players can use to personalize their in-game appearance. Allowing players to mix and match different NFT items to create their own unique look enhances their connection to the game and promotes self-expression.

Here's an example of a customizable avatar interface in HTML:

```html
<div class="avatar-customization">
    <h3>Customize Your Avatar</h3>
    <div class="avatar-preview">
        <img id="avatar-image" src="default-avatar.png" alt="Avatar Preview">
    </div>
    <div class="customization-options">
        <label for="skin-select">Skin:</label>
        <select id="skin-select" onchange="updateAvatar()">
            <option value="default">Default</option>
            <option value="skin1">Skin 1</option>
            <option value="skin2">Skin 2</option>
        </select>
        <label for="outfit-select">Outfit:</label>
        <select id="outfit-select" onchange="updateAvatar()">
```

```html
            <option value="default">Default</option>
            <option value="outfit1">Outfit 1</option>
            <option value="outfit2">Outfit 2</option>
        </select>
        <label for="accessory-select">Accessory:</label>
        <select id="accessory-select" onchange="updateAvatar()">
            <option value="default">Default</option>
            <option value="accessory1">Accessory 1</option>
            <option value="accessory2">Accessory 2</option>
        </select>
    </div>
</div>

<script>
    function updateAvatar() {
        // Logic to update avatar preview based on selected options
    }
</script>
```

This interface allows players to customize their avatars by selecting different skins, outfits, and accessories.

Personalization can also extend to in-game items and equipment. NFTs can represent unique weapons, tools, vehicles, and other items that players can acquire and customize. Offering various options for modifying and upgrading these items, such as changing colors, adding enhancements, or attaching special effects, allows players to tailor their in-game assets to their preferences.

Creating personalized in-game environments is another effective way to enhance the player experience. Players can use NFTs to customize their virtual spaces, such as homes, gardens, or entire worlds. Providing a wide range of decorative items, furniture, and architectural elements as NFTs enables players to create unique and personalized environments that reflect their style and creativity.

Dynamic NFTs that evolve based on player interactions add an additional layer of personalization. These NFTs can change in appearance, attributes, or abilities as players progress through the game. For example, a pet NFT could grow and develop new skills based on how the player interacts with it. This dynamic nature makes NFTs more engaging and creates a deeper connection between players and their digital assets.

Here's an example of a Solidity contract for a dynamic NFT:

```solidity
pragma solidity ^0.8.0;

import "@openzeppelin/contracts/token/ERC721/ERC721.sol";
import "@openzeppelin/contracts/access/Ownable.sol";

contract DynamicNFT is ERC721, Ownable {
    struct Attributes {
        uint256 level;
```

```solidity
        uint256 experience;
    }

    mapping(uint256 => Attributes) public nftAttributes;

    constructor() ERC721("DynamicNFT", "DNFT") {}

    function mintNFT(address to) public onlyOwner returns (uint256) {
        uint256 newItemId = totalSupply();
        _mint(to, newItemId);
        nftAttributes[newItemId] = Attributes(1, 0);
        return newItemId;
    }

    function updateAttributes(uint256 tokenId, uint256 experience) public onlyOwner {
        Attributes storage attrs = nftAttributes[tokenId];
        attrs.experience += experience;
        if (attrs.experience >= 100) {
            attrs.level++;
            attrs.experience = 0;
        }
    }
}
```

This contract allows the minting of NFTs with attributes that can evolve based on player interactions.

Providing players with personalized rewards based on their achievements and activities is another effective strategy. Tailoring rewards to match player preferences and play styles enhances the sense of accomplishment and motivates continued engagement. For example, players who prefer combat might receive unique weapons, while those who enjoy exploration might receive special maps or travel gear.

Offering personalization options in the game's user interface can also enhance the player experience. Allowing players to customize the layout, color scheme, and other UI elements ensures that the game environment suits their preferences. This level of customization can make the game more comfortable and enjoyable for individual players.

Here's an example of a customizable UI in HTML and CSS:

```html
<div class="ui-customization">
    <h3>Customize Your UI</h3>
    <label for="theme-select">Theme:</label>
    <select id="theme-select" onchange="updateTheme()">
        <option value="light">Light</option>
        <option value="dark">Dark</option>
    </select>
</div>
```

```
<style>
    body.light-theme {
        background-color: #fff;
        color: #000;
    }

    body.dark-theme {
        background-color: #000;
        color: #fff;
    }
</style>

<script>
    function updateTheme() {
        var selectedTheme = document.getElementById('theme-select').value;
        document.body.className = selectedTheme + '-theme';
    }
</script>
```

This code allows players to switch between light and dark themes, customizing the game's appearance to their liking.

In conclusion, personalization and customization with NFTs involve offering customizable avatars, in-game items, environments, dynamic NFTs, personalized rewards, and customizable UIs. By providing these options, developers can enhance the player experience and create a more engaging and enjoyable game.

13.5. Feedback Loops and Player Engagement Strategies

Implementing effective feedback loops and engagement strategies is essential for maintaining player interest and fostering a vibrant gaming community. This section explores various methods for creating positive feedback loops and engaging players in NFT games.

A key component of effective feedback loops is providing timely and meaningful feedback for player actions. This includes visual, auditory, and textual cues that acknowledge achievements, rewards, and progress. Positive reinforcement encourages continued engagement and helps players understand the impact of their actions within the game.

Here's an example of providing visual feedback for completing a quest:

```
<div class="quest-completion">
    <h3>Quest Complete!</h3>
    <p>You have earned 100 XP and a Rare Sword.</p>
</div>

<style>
    .quest-completion {
        background-color: #4caf50;
        color: white;
```

```
        padding: 10px;
        border-radius: 5px;
        display: none;
    }
</style>

<script>
    function showQuestCompletion() {
        var completionMessage = document.querySelector('.quest-completion');
        completionMessage.style.display = 'block';
    }
</script>
```

This interface provides visual feedback for completing a quest, rewarding the player and encouraging further participation.

Engagement strategies should focus on creating a sense of progression and accomplishment. Implementing leveling systems, skill trees, and achievement badges gives players clear goals to strive for and a sense of growth as they progress through the game. Offering exclusive NFTs as rewards for reaching certain milestones can further incentivize player engagement.

Here's an example of an achievement system:

```
<div class="achievements">
    <h3>Achievements</h3>
    <ul>
        <li>First Kill: <span id="first-kill-status">Not Achieved</span></li>
        <li>Treasure Hunter: <span id="treasure-hunter-status">Not Achieved</span></li>
    </ul>
</div>

<script>
    function unlockAchievement(achievement) {
        document.getElementById(achievement + '-status').innerText = 'Achieved';
        // Additional logic to grant rewards
    }
</script>
```

This system tracks achievements and updates the status when specific goals are met, providing players with a sense of accomplishment.

Community engagement is crucial for creating a vibrant and active player base. Encouraging social interactions through guilds, chat systems, and multiplayer features fosters a sense of community and belonging. Organizing events, such as tournaments, competitions, and collaborative quests, provides opportunities for players to interact and work together towards common goals.

Here's an example of a simple chat system for in-game communication:

```html
<div class="chat">
    <h3>Game Chat</h3>
    <div id="chat-messages"></div>
    <input type="text" id="chat-input" placeholder="Type a message...">
    <button onclick="sendMessage()">Send</button>
</div>

<script>
    function sendMessage() {
        var input = document.getElementById('chat-input');
        var message = input.value;
        var chatMessages = document.getElementById('chat-messages');
        chatMessages.innerHTML += '<p>' + message + '</p>';
        input.value = '';
    }
</script>
```

This chat system allows players to communicate in real-time, enhancing social interactions within the game.

Regular updates and new content are essential for keeping the game fresh and exciting. Introducing new quests, items, characters, and features on a regular basis keeps players engaged and eager to explore new content. Announcing updates and involving the community in the development process through feedback and suggestions can further strengthen player engagement.

Personalizing the gaming experience based on player preferences and behaviors can enhance engagement. Implementing AI-driven recommendations for quests, items, and activities tailored to individual players can make the game more relevant and enjoyable. Tracking player behavior and using this data to provide personalized experiences can lead to higher retention and satisfaction.

Here's an example of recommending quests based on player preferences:

```html
<div class="recommended-quests">
    <h3>Recommended Quests</h3>
    <ul id="quest-list"></ul>
</div>

<script>
    var quests = [
        { name: 'Defeat the Dragon', type: 'combat' },
        { name: 'Find the Hidden Treasure', type: 'exploration' },
        { name: 'Craft a Magic Potion', type: 'crafting' }
    ];

    function recommendQuests(preferredType) {
        var questList = document.getElementById('quest-list');
```

```
        questList.innerHTML = '';
        quests.forEach(function (quest) {
            if (quest.type === preferredType) {
                questList.innerHTML += '<li>' + quest.name + '</li>';
            }
        });
    }

    // Example usage: recommend quests based on player's preferred type
    recommendQuests('combat');
</script>
```

This script recommends quests based on the player's preferred type, personalizing the gaming experience.

In conclusion, creating effective feedback loops and engagement strategies involves providing timely feedback, implementing progression systems, fostering community interactions, regularly updating content, and personalizing the gaming experience. By employing these strategies, developers can maintain player interest and create a dynamic and engaging NFT game environment.

Chapter 14: Marketing and Promoting NFT Games

14.1. Crafting a Unique Selling Proposition for NFT Games

Creating a unique selling proposition (USP) for an NFT game is essential for differentiating it in the competitive gaming market. A well-crafted USP highlights the game's distinctive features and benefits, attracting players and investors. This section explores strategies for developing a compelling USP for NFT games.

The first step in crafting a USP is to identify the core strengths and unique features of the game. These could include innovative gameplay mechanics, exclusive NFT assets, a vibrant community, or partnerships with well-known brands or artists. Highlighting these aspects helps to create a clear and attractive message for potential players.

For example, if the game offers a unique play-to-earn (P2E) model that allows players to earn real income, this should be prominently featured in the USP. Similarly, if the game has a rich narrative and immersive world-building, these elements should be emphasized to attract players who value story-driven experiences.

Here's an example of a USP for a fantasy NFT game:

```
"Embark on an epic adventure in a richly detailed fantasy world where your ac
tions shape the realm. Earn valuable NFTs and real-world rewards as you explo
re, battle, and build your legend. Join a thriving community of adventurers a
nd create your unique story in our immersive play-to-earn universe."
```

This USP highlights the game's immersive world, the ability to earn NFTs and rewards, and the community aspect, making it appealing to a broad audience.

Understanding the target audience is crucial for crafting an effective USP. Conduct market research to identify the demographics, preferences, and behaviors of potential players. Tailor the USP to address their specific needs and desires, ensuring that the message resonates with the intended audience.

For instance, if the target audience consists of casual gamers who enjoy social interactions, the USP should emphasize the game's social features, such as multiplayer modes, in-game chat, and community events. If the audience is more competitive, highlight the game's strategic elements and competitive gameplay.

Differentiation is key to a strong USP. Analyze competing NFT games to identify gaps and opportunities. Highlight what sets the game apart, whether it's unique NFT assets, superior graphics, innovative gameplay, or a robust play-to-earn system. Clearly articulating these differences helps to position the game as a standout choice in the market.

Here's an example of a differentiated USP for a sci-fi NFT game:

```
"Experience the future of gaming with our groundbreaking sci-fi NFT adventure
. Collect rare, high-fidelity NFT spacecraft and weapons, each with unique at
tributes. Engage in intense, skill-based battles in stunning environments, an
```

d earn crypto rewards in our dynamic play-to-earn ecosystem. Join a community of pioneers and redefine what's possible in the metaverse."

This USP emphasizes the game's unique assets, high-quality graphics, and competitive gameplay, setting it apart from other NFT games.

Communicating the value proposition clearly and concisely is essential. Use simple and compelling language to convey the benefits of the game. Avoid jargon and overly technical terms that might confuse potential players. The goal is to create an easily understandable and memorable message that captures the essence of the game.

Incorporating social proof into the USP can enhance credibility and appeal. Highlighting positive reviews, endorsements from influencers, or impressive player statistics can help build trust and attract new players. If the game has received awards or recognition, this should be prominently featured in the USP.

Here's an example of incorporating social proof into a USP:

"Join over 500,000 players in our award-winning NFT game, praised for its innovative gameplay and stunning visuals. Earn rave reviews and endorsements from top gaming influencers. Dive into a world where your skills and strategy earn you real-world rewards. Don't miss out on the game that's redefining the future of gaming."

This USP leverages social proof to build credibility and attract new players.

Consistency is crucial when communicating the USP across various marketing channels. Ensure that the core message is reflected in all promotional materials, including the website, social media, advertisements, and press releases. A consistent message reinforces the game's unique value proposition and helps build brand recognition.

Testing and refining the USP is an ongoing process. Gather feedback from players and analyze the effectiveness of marketing campaigns to identify what resonates most with the audience. Use this information to refine and enhance the USP, ensuring that it remains relevant and compelling.

In conclusion, crafting a unique selling proposition for NFT games involves identifying core strengths, understanding the target audience, differentiating from competitors, communicating value clearly, incorporating social proof, maintaining consistency, and continuously refining the message. By following these strategies, developers can create a compelling USP that attracts players and sets their game apart in the competitive NFT gaming market.

14.2. Digital Marketing Strategies for Blockchain Games

Effective digital marketing strategies are crucial for promoting blockchain games and attracting a broad audience. This section explores various digital marketing tactics and best practices for successfully promoting blockchain games.

One of the most effective digital marketing strategies is leveraging social media platforms. Platforms like Twitter, Discord, Instagram, and TikTok offer extensive reach and engagement opportunities. Creating engaging content, such as game teasers, behind-the-scenes videos, and player testimonials, can attract attention and build a following. Regularly posting updates and interacting with the community helps to maintain interest and engagement.

Here's an example of a social media post for a blockchain game:

"□ Get ready for an epic adventure in [Game Name]! □ Collect unique NFTs, earn rewards, and join a thriving community. Are you up for the challenge? □ #BlockchainGaming #NFTs #PlayToEarn"

This post uses emojis, hashtags, and a call-to-action to engage the audience and encourage them to learn more about the game.

Content marketing is another powerful strategy. Creating high-quality, informative content such as blog posts, articles, and videos can help educate potential players about the game and blockchain technology. Topics might include gameplay tips, NFT guides, developer interviews, and industry trends. Sharing this content on the game's website and social media channels can attract organic traffic and build authority.

Here's an example of a blog post introduction for a blockchain game:

"Welcome to the ultimate guide to [Game Name]! In this post, we'll explore everything you need to know about our innovative blockchain game, from collecting rare NFTs to mastering the play-to-earn mechanics. Whether you're a seasoned gamer or new to the world of blockchain, this guide has something for everyone. Let's dive in!"

This introduction sets the tone for an informative and engaging blog post that provides value to the reader.

Influencer marketing can significantly boost the visibility of a blockchain game. Collaborating with gaming influencers and content creators can help reach a wider audience and build credibility. Influencers can create gameplay videos, reviews, and live streams, showcasing the game's features and engaging their followers. Choose influencers whose audience aligns with the target demographic of the game for maximum impact.

Email marketing is a valuable tool for nurturing relationships with potential players. Building an email list through sign-ups on the game's website allows for direct communication with interested individuals. Regular newsletters can keep subscribers informed about game updates, upcoming events, and exclusive offers. Personalizing emails based on player behavior and preferences can enhance engagement.

Here's an example of an email marketing campaign:

Subject: "Exclusive Early Access to [Game Name] - Join the Adventure!"

"Hi [Player Name],

We're excited to offer you exclusive early access to [Game Name]! As a valued member of our community, you'll be among the first to experience our innovative blockchain game and collect unique NFTs. Don't miss out on this limited-time opportunity - click the link below to get started!

[Get Early Access]

See you in the game!

Best regards,
The [Game Name] Team"

This email creates a sense of exclusivity and urgency, encouraging recipients to take action.

Search engine optimization (SEO) is essential for improving the game's visibility on search engines. Conduct keyword research to identify terms and phrases that potential players are searching for. Optimize the game's website and content for these keywords to increase organic traffic. Additionally, creating high-quality backlinks from reputable websites can improve search engine rankings.

Paid advertising can also be effective in promoting blockchain games. Platforms like Google Ads, Facebook Ads, and Twitter Ads offer targeted advertising options to reach specific demographics. Creating compelling ad copy and visuals that highlight the game's unique features can attract clicks and conversions. Monitor and analyze ad performance to optimize campaigns for better results.

Here's an example of a Google Ad for a blockchain game:

Title: "Play [Game Name] - Earn NFTs and Rewards"
Description: "Join the adventure in [Game Name]! Collect unique NFTs, compete in challenges, and earn real-world rewards. Play now!"
URL: "[Game Website]"

This ad highlights the game's key features and includes a clear call-to-action.

Engaging with online communities and forums can help promote the game and build a loyal following. Platforms like Reddit, Bitcointalk, and gaming forums offer opportunities to share updates, answer questions, and participate in discussions. Being active in these communities helps to establish a presence and build relationships with potential players.

Participating in events and webinars can also enhance the game's visibility. Speaking at industry conferences, hosting live Q&A sessions, and participating in virtual expos can showcase the game to a broader audience. These events provide opportunities to network with industry professionals and attract media coverage.

Finally, offering incentives and rewards can encourage players to spread the word about the game. Referral programs, in-game rewards for sharing content, and exclusive bonuses for early adopters can motivate players to promote the game to their friends and followers.

In conclusion, effective digital marketing strategies for blockchain games include leveraging social media, content marketing, influencer marketing, email marketing, SEO, paid advertising, community engagement, events, and incentives. By implementing these tactics, developers can successfully promote their blockchain games and attract a broad and engaged player base.

14.3. Community Engagement and Loyalty Programs

Building and maintaining a strong community is crucial for the success of NFT games. Engaged communities not only enhance player experience but also drive growth and longevity for the game. This section explores strategies for effective community engagement and loyalty programs to foster a loyal player base.

One of the fundamental strategies for community engagement is creating multiple channels for communication and interaction. Platforms like Discord, Telegram, and dedicated forums provide spaces where players can discuss the game, share experiences, and connect with the development team. Active and responsive participation from developers in these channels builds trust and a sense of community.

Hosting regular events and activities is another effective way to engage the community. In-game events, tournaments, and challenges encourage participation and provide opportunities for players to showcase their skills and earn rewards. These events can be themed around holidays, game milestones, or community achievements, adding variety and excitement to the game.

Here's an example of an announcement for an in-game event:

```
"🎉 Join us for the [Game Name] Winter Festival! ❄️

From December 20th to January 3rd, participate in exclusive challenges, earn
limited-edition NFTs, and celebrate the season with your fellow adventurers.
Don't miss out on the fun and rewards!

#WinterFestival #NFTGaming #PlayToEarn"
```

This announcement creates excitement and encourages players to participate in the event.

Recognizing and rewarding community members for their contributions is essential for fostering loyalty. Highlighting player achievements, featuring community creations, and offering rewards for active participation can make players feel valued and appreciated. Implementing a system for recognizing top contributors, such as a "Player of the Month" or "Top Guild," can further incentivize engagement.

Loyalty programs can significantly enhance player retention and satisfaction. These programs reward players for their continued participation and support, offering exclusive benefits and rewards. Tiered loyalty programs, where players can unlock higher levels of rewards based on their activity, create a sense of progression and achievement.

Here's an example of a tiered loyalty program:

```
"Welcome to the [Game Name] Loyalty Program!

Level 1: Novice Adventurer
- Earn 10% bonus rewards on all in-game activities
- Access to exclusive weekly challenges

Level 2: Skilled Explorer
- Earn 20% bonus rewards on all in-game activities
- Access to monthly exclusive NFT drops
- Early access to new game content

Level 3: Master Legend
- Earn 30% bonus rewards on all in-game activities
- Access to bi-weekly exclusive NFT drops
- Personalized in-game title and badge
- VIP support and direct communication with the dev team"
```

This loyalty program offers increasing rewards and benefits, encouraging players to remain active and engaged.

Transparency and openness are crucial for building trust within the community. Regularly sharing updates about game development, upcoming features, and addressing player feedback demonstrates that the developers are committed to the community's interests. Hosting "Ask Me Anything" (AMA) sessions or developer diaries can provide insights into the development process and foster a closer connection with the players.

Encouraging user-generated content (UGC) can enhance community engagement and creativity. Players can create fan art, write stories, or develop mods that add to the game's universe. Recognizing and showcasing UGC on official channels can motivate players to contribute and feel more connected to the game.

Here's an example of a call for user-generated content:

```
"Calling all artists and creators! □

We want to see your amazing [Game Name] fan art, stories, and mods. Share you
r creations with us using #GameNameUGC for a chance to be featured on our off
icial channels and win exclusive rewards!

#FanArt #GamingCommunity #NFTGaming"
```

This call to action encourages players to share their creations and participate in the community.

Creating opportunities for collaborative decision-making can also enhance community engagement. Implementing voting systems or community councils where players can provide input on game updates, new features, and events gives players a sense of ownership and involvement. This collaborative approach can lead to better game design and increased player satisfaction.

Providing excellent customer support is vital for maintaining a positive community experience. Quick and helpful responses to player inquiries and issues demonstrate that the developers care about their players. Implementing a comprehensive support system with FAQs, guides, and dedicated support staff can enhance the overall player experience.

Finally, celebrating milestones and achievements with the community can strengthen the bond between players and developers. Acknowledging anniversaries, player milestones, and community accomplishments with special events, rewards, and public recognition fosters a sense of pride and loyalty.

In conclusion, effective community engagement and loyalty programs involve creating multiple communication channels, hosting regular events, recognizing contributions, implementing loyalty programs, maintaining transparency, encouraging user-generated content, enabling collaborative decision-making, providing excellent support, and celebrating milestones. By following these strategies, developers can build a strong and loyal community that supports and grows with the game.

14.4. Collaborations and Partnerships in the NFT Space

Collaborations and partnerships are powerful strategies for expanding the reach and impact of NFT games. By working with other companies, brands, and influencers, developers can leverage new opportunities and enhance the gaming experience. This section explores the benefits and strategies for successful collaborations and partnerships in the NFT space.

One of the primary benefits of collaborations is increased exposure. Partnering with well-known brands or influencers can introduce the game to new audiences and generate buzz. For example, collaborating with a popular gaming influencer to create exclusive in-game content or hosting a live stream event can attract their followers to the game.

Here's an example of an announcement for a collaboration with an influencer:

```
"We're thrilled to announce our collaboration with [Influencer Name]! 

Join us for an exclusive live stream event on [Date] where [Influencer Name] will explore [Game Name], complete challenges, and give away unique NFTs. Don't miss out on this exciting event! 

#GamingCollab #NFTGaming #LiveStream"
```

This announcement creates excitement and encourages the influencer's followers to participate.

Collaborations with other NFT projects can also enhance the game's value and appeal. For example, integrating NFTs from another successful project into the game can attract fans of that project and create unique cross-platform experiences. These collaborations can also involve joint events, where players can earn rewards and participate in activities that span both games.

Strategic partnerships with technology providers can improve the game's infrastructure and features. Collaborating with blockchain platforms, wallet providers, or payment processors can enhance the game's functionality and user experience. These partnerships can provide technical support, improve security, and offer new features such as seamless wallet integration or advanced NFT marketplaces.

Here's an example of a partnership announcement with a blockchain platform:

```
"We're excited to partner with [Blockchain Platform] to bring enhanced securi
ty and seamless transactions to [Game Name]. Our collaboration will provide p
layers with a smoother and more secure gaming experience, including easy wall
et integration and advanced NFT features. Stay tuned for more updates! 🔗

#BlockchainPartnership #NFTGaming #GameName"
```

This announcement highlights the benefits of the partnership and reassures players about the enhanced security and features.

Collaborating with artists and creators can add unique and valuable content to the game. Commissioning exclusive NFT artworks, skins, or items from renowned artists can attract art collectors and enhance the game's aesthetic appeal. These collaborations can also involve co-branded merchandise or limited-edition collectibles that appeal to both gaming and art communities.

Partnerships with non-gaming brands can create unique promotional opportunities and expand the game's reach beyond traditional gaming audiences. For example, collaborating with fashion brands, sports teams, or entertainment franchises can introduce the game to new markets and create co-branded experiences that attract diverse audiences.

Here's an example of a collaboration announcement with a fashion brand:

```
"Introducing the [Fashion Brand] x [Game Name] collaboration! 👗🎮

Discover exclusive in-game outfits and accessories designed by [Fashion Brand
], available for a limited time. Dress your avatar in style and stand out in
the world of [Game Name]. Don't miss out on this unique fashion and gaming ex
perience!

#FashionGaming #NFTCollab #GameName"
```

This announcement highlights the unique content created through the collaboration and appeals to both fashion and gaming enthusiasts.

Creating co-branded marketing campaigns can amplify the impact of collaborations and partnerships. Joint promotions, social media campaigns, and cross-platform events can generate buzz and attract attention from both partners' audiences. Coordinated marketing efforts ensure that the collaboration reaches a wider audience and creates a cohesive and compelling message.

Establishing clear goals and expectations is crucial for successful collaborations. Both parties should have a shared understanding of the objectives, target audience, and desired outcomes. Clearly defined roles, responsibilities, and timelines ensure that the collaboration runs smoothly and achieves its goals.

Here's an example of a collaboration agreement outline:

1. Objectives: Define the goals and desired outcomes of the collaboration.
2. Target Audience: Identify the primary audience for the collaboration.
3. Roles and Responsibilities: Outline each party's responsibilities and tasks.
4. Timeline: Establish key milestones and deadlines.
5. Promotion: Plan joint marketing efforts and promotional activities.
6. Evaluation: Define metrics for success and methods for evaluating the collaboration's impact.

This outline provides a framework for planning and executing a successful collaboration.

Maintaining open communication and flexibility throughout the collaboration is essential. Regular check-ins, progress updates, and feedback sessions ensure that both parties are aligned and can address any challenges promptly. Being open to adjustments and new ideas can also enhance the collaboration's effectiveness and impact.

In conclusion, collaborations and partnerships in the NFT space offer numerous benefits, including increased exposure, enhanced content, improved infrastructure, and expanded reach. By leveraging strategic partnerships with influencers, other NFT projects, technology providers, artists, and non-gaming brands, developers can create unique and valuable experiences for players. Successful collaborations require clear goals, open communication, and coordinated marketing efforts to maximize their impact.

14.5. Navigating Regulatory Compliance in Marketing

Navigating regulatory compliance in marketing is crucial for NFT games to ensure that promotional activities adhere to legal standards and protect both the developers and players. This section explores key considerations and best practices for maintaining regulatory compliance in marketing NFT games.

One of the primary regulatory concerns in marketing NFT games is adherence to advertising standards. Many jurisdictions have specific guidelines for advertising, including requirements for truthfulness, non-deception, and substantiation of claims. Developers must ensure that all marketing materials accurately represent the game and its features, avoiding any false or misleading statements.

Here's an example of a compliant marketing statement:

"Discover the innovative world of [Game Name], where you can collect unique NFTs, participate in engaging quests, and earn real rewards. Start your adventure today!"

This statement accurately describes the game without making exaggerated or false claims.

Transparency is essential in marketing, especially when promoting NFTs and play-to-earn (P2E) models. Clearly communicate the mechanics, risks, and potential rewards associated with NFTs and P2E elements. Providing detailed information about how players can earn, trade, and use NFTs within the game helps build trust and ensures compliance with regulatory requirements.

Disclosures are a critical aspect of regulatory compliance. When collaborating with influencers or running paid promotions, it's important to disclose any material connections. Influencers must clearly indicate when content is sponsored or if they have received compensation or free products for promoting the game. This transparency helps maintain credibility and trust with the audience.

Here's an example of a disclosure statement for influencer marketing:

"Join me as I explore [Game Name], an exciting new NFT game! This video is sponsored by [Game Name], and I received compensation to share my experience with you. Check out the game and start your adventure today! #Ad"

This disclosure clearly indicates the sponsorship and ensures compliance with advertising guidelines.

Data privacy is another crucial consideration. Collecting and using player data for marketing purposes must comply with data protection regulations, such as the General Data Protection Regulation (GDPR) in the European Union or the California Consumer Privacy Act (CCPA) in the United States. Obtain explicit consent from players before collecting their data and provide clear information about how their data will be used.

Here's an example of a data privacy consent statement:

"By signing up for our newsletter, you agree to receive updates and promotional emails from [Game Name]. We value your privacy and will never share your information with third parties. You can unsubscribe at any time. [Privacy Policy Link]"

This statement ensures that players are informed about data collection and their rights.

Compliance with anti-money laundering (AML) regulations is essential, especially in the context of NFT transactions. Implementing robust KYC (Know Your Customer) procedures and monitoring transactions for suspicious activity helps prevent money laundering and ensures regulatory compliance. Collaborating with reputable payment processors and blockchain platforms that adhere to AML regulations can further enhance compliance.

Here's an example of a KYC process for NFT transactions:

1. User Registration: Collect basic information, including name, email, and date of birth.
2. Identity Verification: Request government-issued ID and perform identity verification checks.
3. Address Verification: Collect and verify residential address using utility bills or bank statements.

4. **Transaction Monitoring**: Monitor transactions for unusual patterns or large sums and flag suspicious activity for review.

This process ensures that the game complies with AML regulations and protects against fraudulent activities.

Consumer protection laws also play a significant role in marketing compliance. Ensure that players have clear and accurate information about the terms and conditions of in-game purchases, refunds, and exchanges. Providing a comprehensive and easily accessible terms of service document helps protect both the developers and players.

Here's an example of a key point from a terms of service document:

"Purchases of in-game items, including NFTs, are final and non-refundable. By completing a purchase, you agree to the terms and conditions outlined in this document. For more information, please refer to our full Terms of Service [Link]."

This statement clearly communicates the non-refundable nature of purchases and directs players to the full terms of service.

Monitoring and staying updated on regulatory changes is essential for ongoing compliance. Regulations surrounding NFTs, blockchain technology, and digital marketing are continuously evolving. Regularly review and update marketing practices to ensure they align with the latest legal requirements. Consulting with legal experts who specialize in blockchain and gaming law can provide valuable guidance.

In conclusion, navigating regulatory compliance in marketing NFT games involves adhering to advertising standards, ensuring transparency, providing disclosures, protecting data privacy, complying with AML regulations, and safeguarding consumer rights. By following these best practices and staying informed about regulatory changes, developers can conduct marketing activities that are both effective and legally compliant.

Chapter 15: Legal Considerations in NFT Game Development

15.1. Intellectual Property Rights in NFTs

Intellectual property (IP) rights play a crucial role in NFT game development. Understanding and managing these rights is essential to ensure that all parties involved are protected and that the game operates within the bounds of the law. This section explores the key aspects of intellectual property rights in NFTs and how they apply to game development.

NFTs, or non-fungible tokens, represent ownership of unique digital assets on a blockchain. These assets can include artwork, in-game items, characters, and other digital content. When creating or selling NFTs, it's important to address the intellectual property rights associated with these assets.

Creators of digital assets used in NFTs retain their intellectual property rights unless explicitly transferred or licensed to another party. This means that the original artist or developer holds the copyright to their work, even if it is sold as an NFT. Buyers of NFTs typically purchase ownership of the token and a license to use the associated digital asset, but they do not automatically acquire the underlying IP rights.

Here's an example of a license agreement for an NFT:

```
By purchasing this NFT, you are granted a limited, non-exclusive license to u
se, display, and enjoy the associated digital asset for personal, non-commerc
ial purposes. The creator retains all intellectual property rights to the dig
ital asset, including the right to reproduce, distribute, and create derivati
ve works.
```

This agreement clarifies that the buyer does not receive full IP rights to the asset.

For game developers, it is important to ensure that they have the necessary rights to use and distribute any digital assets included in their NFTs. This may involve obtaining licenses from artists, musicians, and other content creators. Clear agreements should be in place to define the scope of these rights and any royalties or compensation that the creators will receive.

If a game includes user-generated content (UGC), developers need to establish terms that address the ownership and use of this content. Players who create UGC, such as custom characters or items, should understand how their creations can be used within the game and any associated IP rights. Developers might require users to grant a license to use their UGC within the game and for promotional purposes.

Here's an example of a UGC license agreement:

```
By submitting your content to [Game Name], you grant [Developer Name] a world
wide, royalty-free, sublicensable, and transferable license to use, reproduce
, distribute, prepare derivative works of, display, and perform the content i
```

n connection with the game and its promotion. You retain ownership of the underlying intellectual property rights to your content.

This agreement allows the developer to use player-created content while respecting the player's IP rights.

Enforcing IP rights in the context of NFTs can be challenging due to the decentralized nature of blockchain technology. However, developers can take steps to protect their rights by monitoring the market for unauthorized uses of their assets and pursuing legal action when necessary. This might include filing DMCA takedown requests or seeking legal remedies for infringement.

In addition to copyright, trademarks play a significant role in protecting brand identity. Game developers should register trademarks for their game titles, logos, and other distinctive elements to prevent unauthorized use by others. This helps maintain brand integrity and ensures that players can trust the authenticity of the game and its associated NFTs.

Patents may also be relevant in NFT game development, particularly for novel technological solutions or gameplay mechanics. Developers who create innovative features may consider patenting their inventions to protect their intellectual property and gain a competitive advantage.

In conclusion, intellectual property rights in NFTs encompass various aspects, including copyright, trademarks, and patents. Game developers must navigate these rights carefully, obtaining necessary licenses, establishing clear agreements with content creators, and taking steps to protect their own IP. By doing so, they can ensure that their NFT game operates legally and ethically while respecting the rights of all parties involved.

15.2. Legal Frameworks Governing Digital Assets

The legal frameworks governing digital assets, including NFTs, are evolving rapidly as governments and regulatory bodies strive to keep pace with technological advancements. Understanding these frameworks is crucial for NFT game developers to ensure compliance and avoid legal pitfalls. This section explores key legal considerations and regulations that impact the development and use of digital assets in games.

One of the primary legal challenges in the NFT space is the classification of digital assets. Different jurisdictions may classify NFTs differently, impacting how they are regulated. For example, some countries may consider NFTs as digital goods, while others might classify them as securities or financial instruments. Developers must stay informed about the legal definitions and classifications in their target markets to ensure compliance.

In the United States, the Securities and Exchange Commission (SEC) has provided guidance on the classification of digital assets. The Howey Test is commonly used to determine whether an asset qualifies as a security. Under this test, an asset is considered a security if it involves an investment of money in a common enterprise with an expectation of profits derived from the efforts of others. NFT game developers should evaluate their assets against this test to determine if they fall under securities regulation.

Here's an example of a disclaimer addressing potential classification as a security:

```
The NFTs offered in [Game Name] are intended to be used solely within the game environment for entertainment purposes. They do not represent an investment opportunity and should not be purchased with the expectation of financial return.
```

This disclaimer clarifies the intended use of the NFTs and addresses potential regulatory concerns.

Consumer protection laws also play a significant role in the regulation of digital assets. These laws aim to protect consumers from unfair practices and ensure transparency in transactions. Developers must provide clear and accurate information about their NFTs, including details about the asset, its functionality, and any associated risks. Additionally, refund policies and terms of service should be easily accessible and understandable.

Data privacy regulations, such as the General Data Protection Regulation (GDPR) in the European Union and the California Consumer Privacy Act (CCPA) in the United States, impose strict requirements on the collection, storage, and use of personal data. NFT game developers must implement robust data protection measures and obtain explicit consent from users before collecting their data. Compliance with these regulations is essential to avoid significant fines and reputational damage.

Anti-money laundering (AML) and know your customer (KYC) regulations are increasingly being applied to digital assets to prevent illegal activities such as money laundering and terrorist financing. Developers must implement procedures to verify the identity of their users and monitor transactions for suspicious activity. Partnering with compliant payment processors and blockchain platforms can help ensure adherence to these regulations.

Here's an example of a basic KYC process:

```
1. User Registration: Collect basic information, including name, email, and date of birth.
2. Identity Verification: Request government-issued ID and perform identity verification checks.
3. Address Verification: Collect and verify residential address using utility bills or bank statements.
4. Transaction Monitoring: Monitor transactions for unusual patterns or large sums and flag suspicious activity for review.
```

This process helps ensure compliance with AML and KYC regulations.

Intellectual property (IP) laws govern the creation, use, and distribution of digital assets. Developers must ensure they have the necessary rights to use any third-party content in their NFTs and establish clear agreements with content creators. Protecting their own IP through copyrights, trademarks, and patents is also crucial to prevent unauthorized use and maintain control over their assets.

Taxation is another important consideration in the regulation of digital assets. The tax treatment of NFTs can vary depending on the jurisdiction and the nature of the transactions. Developers and users may be subject to taxes on income, capital gains, or sales, depending on how the assets are used and traded. Consulting with tax professionals and staying informed about relevant tax laws can help ensure compliance.

Contract law is fundamental in the creation and transfer of NFTs. Smart contracts, which are self-executing contracts with the terms of the agreement directly written into code, play a key role in NFT transactions. Developers must ensure that smart contracts are legally enforceable and that they accurately reflect the terms of the agreement between parties.

Here's an example of a simple smart contract for an NFT sale:

```solidity
pragma solidity ^0.8.0;

contract NFTSale {
    address public seller;
    address public buyer;
    uint256 public price;
    uint256 public tokenId;

    constructor(address _seller, uint256 _price, uint256 _tokenId) {
        seller = _seller;
        price = _price;
        tokenId = _tokenId;
    }

    function purchase() public payable {
        require(msg.value == price, "Incorrect price");
        buyer = msg.sender;
        // Transfer NFT from seller to buyer
    }
}
```

This smart contract facilitates the sale of an NFT by transferring ownership upon receipt of the specified payment.

In conclusion, the legal frameworks governing digital assets encompass a wide range of considerations, including classification, consumer protection, data privacy, AML/KYC, intellectual property, taxation, and contract law. NFT game developers must navigate these regulations carefully to ensure compliance and protect their interests. Staying informed about legal developments and seeking professional advice can help developers operate within the law and build a successful and sustainable NFT game.

15.3. Privacy and Data Security in NFT Transactions

Privacy and data security are critical concerns in NFT transactions, as they involve sensitive personal information and valuable digital assets. Ensuring robust privacy and security measures is essential to protect users and maintain trust in the NFT ecosystem.

This section explores best practices and strategies for safeguarding privacy and data security in NFT transactions.

One of the primary steps in protecting privacy is minimizing the collection of personal data. Collect only the information necessary for the transaction and avoid gathering excessive or unrelated data. This principle of data minimization reduces the risk of data breaches and ensures compliance with data protection regulations such as GDPR and CCPA.

Implementing strong encryption protocols is crucial for securing data during transmission and storage. Use end-to-end encryption to protect data as it travels between users and the server, ensuring that unauthorized parties cannot intercept or access the information. Additionally, encrypt sensitive data stored on servers to prevent unauthorized access in the event of a data breach.

Here's an example of encrypting data in transit using HTTPS:

```html
<form action="https://example.com/submit" method="post">
    <input type="text" name="username" placeholder="Username">
    <input type="password" name="password" placeholder="Password">
    <button type="submit">Submit</button>
</form>
```

Using HTTPS ensures that the data submitted through the form is encrypted during transmission.

Access control measures are essential for protecting sensitive data and ensuring that only authorized personnel can access it. Implement role-based access controls (RBAC) to restrict access based on users' roles and responsibilities. Regularly review and update access permissions to reflect changes in roles or employment status.

Here's an example of a basic access control list (ACL) in a web application:

```json
{
    "admin": {
        "can_view": ["all"],
        "can_edit": ["all"],
        "can_delete": ["all"]
    },
    "user": {
        "can_view": ["own_profile", "own_transactions"],
        "can_edit": ["own_profile"],
        "can_delete": []
    }
}
```

This ACL defines different permissions for admin and user roles, restricting access based on the role.

Regularly updating and patching software is crucial to protect against known vulnerabilities. Ensure that all systems, applications, and dependencies are kept up-to-date with the latest security patches. Implementing automated patch management tools can help streamline this process and reduce the risk of unpatched vulnerabilities.

Conducting regular security audits and penetration testing helps identify and address potential weaknesses in the system. Security audits involve reviewing the system architecture, code, and configurations to ensure compliance with security best practices. Penetration testing simulates real-world attacks to evaluate the system's defenses and identify vulnerabilities.

Here's an example of using a security audit tool for a smart contract:

```
# Using MythX for smart contract security analysis
myth analyze contracts/MyNFT.sol
```

This command runs a security analysis on the specified smart contract to identify potential vulnerabilities.

Implementing multi-factor authentication (MFA) adds an additional layer of security for user accounts. MFA requires users to provide two or more forms of verification, such as a password and a one-time code sent to their mobile device. This reduces the risk of unauthorized access, even if a user's password is compromised.

Here's an example of enabling MFA for user login:

```
<form action="/login" method="post">
    <input type="text" name="username" placeholder="Username">
    <input type="password" name="password" placeholder="Password">
    <button type="submit">Login</button>
</form>
<form action="/verify-otp" method="post">
    <input type="text" name="otp" placeholder="One-Time Password">
    <button type="submit">Verify</button>
</form>
```

This example includes a second form for verifying a one-time password as part of the MFA process.

Implementing secure smart contract development practices is essential to protect NFT transactions. Use well-established libraries and frameworks, conduct thorough code reviews, and follow best practices for smart contract security. Tools like OpenZeppelin provide audited and secure implementations of common smart contract components.

Here's an example of a secure NFT contract using OpenZeppelin:

```
pragma solidity ^0.8.0;

import "@openzeppelin/contracts/token/ERC721/ERC721.sol";
import "@openzeppelin/contracts/access/Ownable.sol";

contract SecureNFT is ERC721, Ownable {
    uint256 public tokenCounter;
```

```
    constructor() ERC721("SecureNFT", "SNFT") {
        tokenCounter = 0;
    }

    function mintNFT(address to) public onlyOwner returns (uint256) {
        uint256 newItemId = tokenCounter;
        _mint(to, newItemId);
        tokenCounter++;
        return newItemId;
    }
}
```

This contract uses OpenZeppelin's ERC721 implementation, ensuring a secure and compliant NFT standard.

Ensuring compliance with data protection regulations is crucial for maintaining privacy and avoiding legal issues. Implement transparent data handling practices, obtain explicit consent from users, and provide clear information about how their data will be used. Regularly review and update privacy policies to reflect any changes in data handling practices.

Educating users about privacy and security best practices can help them protect their own data. Provide resources and guidance on topics such as creating strong passwords, recognizing phishing attempts, and safely managing their digital assets. Empowering users with knowledge enhances overall security.

In conclusion, ensuring privacy and data security in NFT transactions involves minimizing data collection, implementing strong encryption, access controls, regular updates, security audits, multi-factor authentication, secure smart contract development, compliance with regulations, and user education. By following these best practices, developers can protect sensitive information and maintain trust in the NFT ecosystem.

15.4. Consumer Protection Laws and NFTs

Consumer protection laws are designed to safeguard consumers' rights and ensure fair practices in the marketplace. These laws are increasingly relevant in the context of NFTs, as they govern transactions involving digital assets and protect consumers from fraud, misleading information, and unfair practices. This section explores key consumer protection considerations for NFT developers and how to ensure compliance.

One of the primary concerns under consumer protection laws is the transparency of information provided to consumers. Developers must ensure that all marketing materials, product descriptions, and terms of service are clear, accurate, and not misleading. This includes providing detailed information about the nature of the NFTs, their intended use, and any associated risks.

Here's an example of a clear and transparent NFT product description:

"This NFT represents ownership of a unique digital artwork created by [Artist Name]. The artwork is stored on the Ethereum blockchain and can be viewed and displayed on compatible platforms. By purchasing this NFT, you are granted a limited license to use and display the artwork for personal, non-commercial purposes. The artist retains all intellectual property rights."

This description provides clear information about the NFT, its use, and the retention of IP rights by the artist.

Refund policies and terms of service should be easily accessible and understandable to consumers. Clearly outline the conditions under which refunds are available, any applicable fees, and the process for requesting a refund. Terms of service should cover important aspects such as user rights, responsibilities, and dispute resolution mechanisms.

Here's an example of a straightforward refund policy:

"All sales of NFTs are final. Refunds are not available except in cases of technical issues that prevent the NFT from being delivered or used as described. If you experience a technical issue, please contact our support team within 14 days of purchase to request a refund. Our support team will review your request and, if eligible, process the refund within 7 business days."

This policy clearly states the conditions under which refunds are available and the process for requesting one.

Protecting consumers from fraud and ensuring the authenticity of NFTs is another critical aspect of consumer protection. Developers should implement measures to verify the identity of sellers, authenticate digital assets, and provide proof of ownership. Utilizing blockchain technology to create immutable records of ownership and transaction history helps ensure the authenticity and traceability of NFTs.

Here's an example of verifying NFT authenticity using a blockchain explorer:

"To verify the authenticity of your NFT, visit [Blockchain Explorer] and enter the contract address and token ID provided in your purchase confirmation. This will display the transaction history and confirm the ownership of your NFT on the blockchain."

This example guides consumers on how to verify the authenticity of their NFT using a blockchain explorer.

Ensuring fair pricing practices is important to protect consumers from exploitation. Developers should avoid artificially inflating prices or creating scarcity through deceptive practices. Transparent pricing mechanisms and the use of reputable marketplaces can help maintain fair pricing and protect consumers.

Implementing robust security measures to protect consumer data and digital assets is essential. Developers should ensure that their platforms are secure from cyber threats and that personal information is handled in accordance with data protection regulations. This includes using encryption, access controls, and regular security audits to safeguard sensitive information.

Dispute resolution mechanisms should be clearly defined and accessible to consumers. Provide a process for addressing complaints and resolving disputes, including contact information for customer support and details on how to escalate issues if necessary. Offering transparent and fair dispute resolution helps build trust and protect consumer rights.

Here's an example of a dispute resolution process:

"If you have a complaint or dispute regarding your NFT purchase, please contact our customer support team at [Support Email] within 30 days of the transaction. Our team will review your complaint and work with you to resolve the issue. If you are not satisfied with the resolution, you may escalate the dispute to [Dispute Resolution Service] for further review."

This process outlines the steps for resolving disputes and provides contact information for support.

Compliance with consumer protection laws also involves staying informed about legal developments and regulatory changes. As the legal landscape for digital assets and NFTs evolves, developers must adapt their practices to ensure ongoing compliance. Consulting with legal experts and participating in industry forums can provide valuable insights and guidance.

In conclusion, consumer protection laws play a crucial role in ensuring fair practices and safeguarding consumers' rights in the context of NFTs. Developers must focus on transparency, clear terms of service, fraud prevention, fair pricing, robust security measures, and accessible dispute resolution mechanisms to ensure compliance. By adhering to these principles, developers can build trust with consumers and create a secure and fair marketplace for NFTs.

15.5. Global Regulatory Landscape for NFT Gaming

The global regulatory landscape for NFT gaming is complex and constantly evolving. Different countries have varying approaches to regulating digital assets, including NFTs, which can impact how NFT games operate internationally. This section explores key regulatory considerations for NFT game developers and how to navigate the global regulatory environment.

In the United States, the regulation of digital assets, including NFTs, is primarily overseen by the Securities and Exchange Commission (SEC) and the Commodity Futures Trading Commission (CFTC). The SEC applies the Howey Test to determine whether a digital asset qualifies as a security. If an NFT is deemed a security, it must comply with securities regulations, including registration and disclosure requirements. Developers should carefully evaluate their NFTs against the Howey Test to determine their regulatory obligations.

In the European Union, the regulation of digital assets is governed by the European Securities and Markets Authority (ESMA) and the Markets in Crypto-Assets (MiCA) regulation. MiCA aims to provide a comprehensive regulatory framework for digital assets, including NFTs, to ensure consumer protection and market integrity. Developers operating in the EU must comply with MiCA requirements, including transparency, disclosure, and consumer protection measures.

In Asia, regulatory approaches to digital assets vary significantly between countries. For example, Japan has established a clear regulatory framework for digital assets under the Financial Services Agency (FSA), which requires registration and compliance with anti-money laundering (AML) and know your customer (KYC) regulations. In contrast, China has imposed strict restrictions on cryptocurrency activities, including the issuance and trading of digital assets.

Navigating the global regulatory landscape requires a thorough understanding of the specific regulations in each jurisdiction where the game operates. Developers should conduct comprehensive legal research and seek advice from legal experts to ensure compliance with local laws. This may involve obtaining licenses, registering with regulatory authorities, and implementing specific compliance measures.

Here's an example of a compliance statement for an NFT game operating in multiple jurisdictions:

```
"[Game Name] complies with all applicable regulations in the jurisdictions where it operates. Our NFTs are designed to meet the requirements of securities, consumer protection, and data privacy laws. We have implemented robust AML and KYC procedures to ensure the security and integrity of our platform. For more information about our compliance measures, please contact [Compliance Contact]."
```

This statement communicates the game's commitment to regulatory compliance and provides contact information for further inquiries.

Anti-money laundering (AML) and know your customer (KYC) regulations are critical considerations for NFT game developers. These regulations aim to prevent illegal activities such as money laundering and terrorist financing. Developers must implement procedures to verify the identity of users and monitor transactions for suspicious activity. Compliance with AML and KYC regulations is essential to maintain the integrity of the platform and avoid legal penalties.

Here's an example of an AML and KYC process for an NFT game:

```
1. User Registration: Collect basic information, including name, email, and date of birth.
2. Identity Verification: Request government-issued ID and perform identity verification checks.
3. Address Verification: Collect and verify residential address using utility bills or bank statements.
4. Transaction Monitoring: Monitor transactions for unusual patterns or large sums and flag suspicious activity for review.
```

This process helps ensure compliance with AML and KYC regulations.

Data privacy regulations, such as the General Data Protection Regulation (GDPR) in the European Union and the California Consumer Privacy Act (CCPA) in the United States, impose strict requirements on the collection, storage, and use of personal data. Developers must implement robust data protection measures and obtain explicit consent from users before collecting their data. Compliance with these regulations is essential to avoid significant fines and reputational damage.

Intellectual property (IP) laws are also a key consideration in the global regulatory landscape for NFT gaming. Developers must ensure that they have the necessary rights to use any third-party content in their NFTs and establish clear agreements with content creators. Protecting their own IP through copyrights, trademarks, and patents is also crucial to prevent unauthorized use and maintain control over their assets.

Taxation is another important regulatory consideration. The tax treatment of NFTs can vary depending on the jurisdiction and the nature of the transactions. Developers and users may be subject to taxes on income, capital gains, or sales, depending on how the assets are used and traded. Consulting with tax professionals and staying informed about relevant tax laws can help ensure compliance.

Here's an example of a tax compliance statement for an NFT game:

"All transactions involving NFTs in [Game Name] are subject to applicable tax regulations in the jurisdictions where the transactions occur. Users are responsible for reporting and paying any taxes due on their NFT transactions. For more information about tax compliance, please consult with a tax professional."

This statement clarifies the tax responsibilities of users and emphasizes the importance of compliance.

In conclusion, navigating the global regulatory landscape for NFT gaming involves understanding and complying with a wide range of regulations, including securities, consumer protection, AML/KYC, data privacy, intellectual property, and taxation. Developers must conduct thorough legal research, seek advice from legal experts, and implement robust compliance measures to operate successfully in multiple jurisdictions. By adhering to these regulatory requirements, developers can build a secure and trustworthy platform for NFT gaming.

Chapter 16: Economics and Financial Analysis of NFT Gaming

16.1. Economic Models in NFT Gaming

Economic models in NFT gaming are crucial for creating sustainable and engaging game ecosystems. These models determine how value is generated, distributed, and maintained within the game, impacting player engagement, developer revenue, and overall game success. This section explores various economic models used in NFT gaming and their implications.

One of the most prominent economic models in NFT gaming is the play-to-earn (P2E) model. In this model, players earn rewards in the form of cryptocurrency or NFTs by participating in the game. These rewards can be traded or sold on external marketplaces, providing players with real-world income opportunities. The P2E model incentivizes active participation and can significantly boost player retention and engagement.

For example, in Axie Infinity, players earn Smooth Love Potion (SLP) tokens by battling, breeding, and raising their Axies. These tokens can be sold on cryptocurrency exchanges, allowing players to earn income. This model has proven successful in attracting a large player base and generating substantial revenue.

Another economic model is the free-to-play (F2P) model with optional in-game purchases. In this model, the game is free to access, but players can purchase NFTs to enhance their gameplay experience. These purchases might include unique characters, skins, weapons, or other in-game items. The F2P model lowers the barrier to entry, attracting a broader audience while generating revenue through microtransactions.

Here's an example of a smart contract for an in-game NFT purchase:

```solidity
pragma solidity ^0.8.0;

import "@openzeppelin/contracts/token/ERC721/ERC721.sol";
import "@openzeppelin/contracts/access/Ownable.sol";

contract GameItem is ERC721, Ownable {
    uint256 public nextTokenId;
    uint256 public itemPrice;

    constructor(uint256 _itemPrice) ERC721("GameItem", "GMI") {
        nextTokenId = 1;
        itemPrice = _itemPrice;
    }

    function purchaseItem() public payable {
        require(msg.value == itemPrice, "Incorrect value sent");
        _mint(msg.sender, nextTokenId);
        nextTokenId++;
    }
```

```
    function withdrawFunds() public onlyOwner {
        payable(owner()).transfer(address(this).balance);
    }
}
```

This contract allows players to purchase in-game items by sending the specified item price in cryptocurrency.

Subscription-based models are also gaining traction in NFT gaming. In this model, players pay a recurring fee to access exclusive content, events, or features. This model provides a steady revenue stream for developers and can enhance player loyalty by offering ongoing value. Subscription models can be combined with other models, such as F2P or P2E, to create hybrid economic systems.

The virtual goods economy model focuses on the creation, distribution, and trading of virtual goods within the game. Players can buy, sell, and trade NFTs representing various in-game assets. This model leverages the scarcity and uniqueness of NFTs to create value. The marketplace dynamics, such as supply and demand, significantly influence the value of these virtual goods.

For example, Decentraland operates a virtual goods economy where players can buy, sell, and trade virtual real estate, clothing, and other items. The value of these goods is driven by their scarcity, utility, and player demand, creating a dynamic and engaging economic environment.

Tokenomics, or the economic principles governing the creation and distribution of tokens within the game, are fundamental to many NFT gaming models. Tokenomics involves designing token supply, distribution mechanisms, and utility within the game. Properly designed tokenomics can incentivize desirable behaviors, such as active participation, long-term engagement, and community building.

Here's an example of a basic tokenomics model for an in-game currency:

```
pragma solidity ^0.8.0;

import "@openzeppelin/contracts/token/ERC20/ERC20.sol";

contract GameToken is ERC20 {
    uint256 public initialSupply = 1000000 * (10 ** 18);

    constructor() ERC20("GameToken", "GTK") {
        _mint(msg.sender, initialSupply);
    }

    function distributeTokens(address recipient, uint256 amount) public onlyOwner {
        _transfer(msg.sender, recipient, amount);
```

```
        }
}
```

This contract defines an in-game currency with an initial supply, allowing the owner to distribute tokens to players.

Decentralized finance (DeFi) elements are increasingly being integrated into NFT games. DeFi features, such as staking, lending, and yield farming, can provide additional income opportunities for players and enhance the game's economic ecosystem. For example, players might stake their NFTs to earn rewards or use them as collateral for loans.

In conclusion, economic models in NFT gaming, including play-to-earn, free-to-play, subscription-based, virtual goods economy, and tokenomics, are essential for creating sustainable and engaging game ecosystems. By carefully designing and implementing these models, developers can attract and retain players, generate revenue, and ensure the long-term success of their games.

16.2. Financial Planning and Budgeting for NFT Projects

Financial planning and budgeting are critical components of developing and launching successful NFT projects. Proper financial management ensures that resources are allocated effectively, potential risks are mitigated, and the project remains financially viable. This section explores key aspects of financial planning and budgeting for NFT projects.

The first step in financial planning is creating a comprehensive budget that outlines all projected expenses and revenues. This budget should cover various stages of the project, including development, marketing, operations, and maintenance. Detailed budgeting helps identify funding needs and ensures that the project remains on track financially.

For example, a budget for an NFT game might include the following categories:

- Development costs: Salaries for developers, designers, and other team members; software and tools; testing and quality assurance.
- Marketing expenses: Advertising campaigns, influencer partnerships, social media management, and promotional events.
- Operational costs: Server hosting, blockchain transaction fees, customer support, and administrative expenses.
- Legal and regulatory costs: Legal consultations, compliance with regulations, and intellectual property protection.
- Contingency funds: Reserves for unexpected expenses or delays.

Creating a detailed budget spreadsheet can help track and manage these expenses. Here's an example of a simple budget template:

```
| Category        | Estimated Cost | Actual Cost | Variance |
|-----------------|----------------|-------------|----------|
| Development     | $200,000       | $           | $        |
| Marketing       | $100,000       | $           | $        |
| Operations      | $50,000        | $           | $        |
```

```
| Legal & Regulatory  | $20,000         | $            | $         |
| Contingency         | $30,000         | $            | $         |
|---------------------|-----------------|--------------|-----------|
| Total               | $400,000        | $            | $         |
```

This template helps track estimated and actual costs, highlighting variances that need attention.

Revenue projections are another essential aspect of financial planning. Estimating potential revenue streams from NFT sales, in-game transactions, subscriptions, and other sources helps assess the project's financial viability. These projections should be based on market research, competitor analysis, and historical data from similar projects.

For instance, revenue projections for an NFT game might include:

- Initial NFT sales: Revenue from the sale of limited-edition NFTs or pre-sale events.
- In-game transactions: Revenue from players purchasing in-game items, skins, or other assets.
- Subscription fees: Recurring revenue from players subscribing to premium content or services.
- Secondary market sales: Royalties from the resale of NFTs on secondary marketplaces.

Cash flow management is critical to ensure that the project has sufficient liquidity to cover expenses as they arise. Monitoring cash flow helps identify potential shortfalls and allows for timely adjustments. Maintaining a cash reserve or securing additional funding can provide a buffer against unexpected expenses.

Risk management is an integral part of financial planning. Identifying potential risks, such as regulatory changes, market volatility, or technical challenges, helps develop mitigation strategies. Diversifying revenue streams, obtaining insurance, and maintaining a contingency fund are effective risk management practices.

Securing funding is often necessary to cover the initial costs of developing an NFT project. This funding can come from various sources, including personal savings, investments, grants, or crowdfunding. Developing a compelling pitch deck and business plan can help attract investors and secure funding.

Here's an example of key components for an NFT project pitch deck:

1. Project Overview: A brief introduction to the project, its goals, and its unique value proposition.
2. Market Analysis: An overview of the target market, trends, and potential opportunities.
3. Business Model: A detailed explanation of the revenue streams and economic model.
4. Development Plan: A timeline and roadmap for the project's development stages.
5. Team: Information about the project's team members and their relevant experience.
6. Financial Projections: Revenue projections, budget, and funding requirements.

7. Risk Management: Identification of potential risks and mitigation strategies.

Effective cost management involves regularly reviewing and adjusting the budget to reflect actual expenditures and changing circumstances. Monitoring financial performance against the budget helps identify areas where costs can be reduced or reallocated. Utilizing financial management software can streamline this process and provide real-time insights.

In conclusion, financial planning and budgeting are essential for the successful development and launch of NFT projects. By creating a comprehensive budget, projecting revenue, managing cash flow, identifying risks, securing funding, and effectively managing costs, developers can ensure their projects remain financially viable and achieve their goals.

16.3. Analyzing Market Trends and Player Spending Habits

Understanding market trends and player spending habits is crucial for the success of NFT games. Analyzing these factors helps developers make informed decisions about game design, marketing strategies, and economic models. This section explores key methods and insights for analyzing market trends and player spending habits in NFT gaming.

One of the primary methods for analyzing market trends is conducting market research. This involves collecting data on the current state of the NFT gaming market, including popular games, emerging trends, and player demographics. Market research can be conducted through surveys, focus groups, industry reports, and competitor analysis.

For example, a market research report might reveal that collectible card games are gaining popularity in the NFT space. This insight could influence a developer to incorporate collectible elements into their game to attract a broader audience.

Tracking sales data and transaction volumes on NFT marketplaces provides valuable insights into player spending habits. Analyzing which types of NFTs are most popular, their average selling prices, and the frequency of transactions can help developers understand what players value and are willing to spend money on.

Here's an example of analyzing sales data:

NFT Type	Average Price	Total Sales	Transaction Volume
Character Skins	0.5 ETH	1,000	500 ETH
In-Game Weapons	1.0 ETH	500	500 ETH
Virtual Land	2.5 ETH	200	500 ETH
Collectible Cards	0.3 ETH	1,500	450 ETH

This table provides an overview of sales data for different types of NFTs, helping identify the most lucrative categories.

Social media analysis is another effective method for understanding market trends and player preferences. Monitoring discussions on platforms like Twitter, Discord, and Reddit can provide real-time insights into player sentiment, popular topics, and emerging trends.

Social media analysis tools can help track mentions, hashtags, and engagement metrics related to the game.

Here's an example of tracking social media mentions:

Platform	Mentions	Positive Sentiment	Negative Sentiment
Twitter	5,000	70%	30%
Discord	2,000	80%	20%
Reddit	1,500	65%	35%

This data helps developers understand how their game is perceived on different social media platforms.

Player behavior analytics involve collecting and analyzing data on how players interact with the game. This includes metrics such as playtime, in-game purchases, progression, and engagement levels. Understanding player behavior helps identify patterns and preferences, enabling developers to tailor the game experience to meet player needs.

Here's an example of player behavior metrics:

Metric	Value
Average Playtime	2 hours/day
In-Game Purchase Rate	20%
Level Completion Rate	75%
Daily Active Users	10,000

These metrics provide insights into player engagement and spending habits.

Surveys and feedback from players are valuable sources of information for understanding player preferences and spending habits. Conducting regular surveys and encouraging feedback helps gather qualitative data on player motivations, satisfaction levels, and desired features. This feedback can guide game design and feature development.

Here's an example of a player survey question:

"Which in-game items do you find most valuable? (Select all that apply)
- Character Skins
- Weapons
- Virtual Land
- Collectible Cards"

The responses to this question help identify the most valued in-game items.

Analyzing secondary market activity provides insights into the value and demand for NFTs beyond the initial sale. Tracking the resale prices, trading volumes, and frequency of transactions on secondary marketplaces helps understand the long-term value of NFTs and player interest in trading.

Here's an example of secondary market data:

```
| NFT Type            | Average Resale Price | Total Resale Volume |
|---------------------|----------------------|---------------------|
| Character Skins     | 0.8 ETH              | 400 ETH             |
| In-Game Weapons     | 1.2 ETH              | 600 ETH             |
| Virtual Land        | 3.0 ETH              | 600 ETH             |
| Collectible Cards   | 0.5 ETH              | 750 ETH             |
```

This data provides insights into the demand and value of NFTs on the secondary market.

In conclusion, analyzing market trends and player spending habits involves conducting market research, tracking sales data, monitoring social media, analyzing player behavior, collecting feedback, and examining secondary market activity. By leveraging these methods, developers can make informed decisions that enhance the game's appeal, optimize revenue, and ensure long-term success.

16.4. Risk Management in NFT Investments

Risk management is a critical aspect of NFT investments, as the market is characterized by volatility, regulatory uncertainty, and technological risks. Effective risk management strategies help mitigate potential losses and ensure the sustainability of investments. This section explores key risk management practices for NFT investments.

One of the primary risks in NFT investments is market volatility. NFT prices can fluctuate significantly due to changes in demand, market sentiment, and external factors such as regulatory announcements. To manage this risk, investors should diversify their portfolio by investing in a variety of NFT categories and projects. Diversification helps spread risk and reduces the impact of price volatility on the overall portfolio.

Conducting thorough due diligence is essential before investing in NFTs. This involves researching the project's team, technology, market potential, and community engagement. Evaluating the project's roadmap, partnerships, and previous achievements provides insights into its credibility and long-term viability. Due diligence helps identify potential red flags and make informed investment decisions.

Here's an example of a due diligence checklist:

1. Team: Research the background and experience of the project team.
2. Technology: Evaluate the underlying technology and its scalability.
3. Market Potential: Assess the market demand and competition.
4. Roadmap: Review the project's roadmap and milestones.
5. Partnerships: Identify strategic partnerships and collaborations.
6. Community: Analyze community engagement and support.

This checklist helps investors conduct comprehensive due diligence on NFT projects.

Understanding the regulatory environment is crucial for managing legal and compliance risks. NFT regulations vary across jurisdictions and can impact the legality and tax treatment of investments. Staying informed about regulatory developments and seeking legal advice ensures compliance and helps avoid potential legal issues.

Implementing security measures is vital to protect NFT investments from cyber threats. Using secure wallets, enabling two-factor authentication, and keeping private keys safe are essential practices. Additionally, investors should be cautious of phishing attacks and scams, verifying the authenticity of NFT marketplaces and transactions.

Here's an example of securing an NFT wallet:

```
1. Choose a reputable wallet provider with strong security features.
2. Enable two-factor authentication for added security.
3. Store private keys in a secure, offline location.
4. Regularly update software to protect against vulnerabilities.
```

These steps help secure NFT wallets and protect investments.

Monitoring market trends and staying informed about industry developments is important for managing market risks. Regularly reviewing market data, news, and analyst reports helps investors anticipate potential market movements and adjust their strategies accordingly. Participating in industry forums and following influential voices in the NFT space provides valuable insights.

Implementing a risk management framework involves setting clear investment goals, risk tolerance, and exit strategies. Defining these parameters helps investors make disciplined decisions and avoid emotional reactions to market fluctuations. A well-defined risk management framework provides a structured approach to managing investments.

Here's an example of a risk management framework:

```
1. Investment Goals: Define short-term and long-term investment objectives.
2. Risk Tolerance: Assess the level of risk you are willing to accept.
3. Diversification: Allocate investments across different NFT categories.
4. Exit Strategies: Establish criteria for selling or holding investments.
5. Monitoring: Regularly review and adjust the investment portfolio.
```

This framework guides investors in managing their NFT investments effectively.

Insurance products are emerging as a way to mitigate certain risks in the NFT space. Some platforms offer insurance coverage for digital assets, protecting against loss, theft, or damage. Evaluating the availability and terms of insurance products can provide an additional layer of security for NFT investments.

In conclusion, risk management in NFT investments involves diversifying the portfolio, conducting due diligence, understanding regulatory requirements, implementing security measures, monitoring market trends, and establishing a risk management framework. By following these practices, investors can mitigate potential risks and enhance the sustainability of their NFT investments.

16.5. Valuation of NFTs in the Gaming Context

Valuing NFTs in the gaming context is a complex process influenced by various factors such as rarity, utility, demand, and market trends. Accurate valuation is essential for making informed investment decisions, pricing in-game items, and ensuring a fair and sustainable game economy. This section explores key factors and methods for valuing NFTs in gaming.

Rarity is one of the primary factors affecting the value of NFTs. Rare items are generally more valuable due to their limited supply. The scarcity of an NFT can be determined by its total supply, the distribution frequency, and the conditions under which it can be obtained. For example, a limited-edition character skin released during a special event will likely have a higher value due to its exclusivity.

Utility refers to the practical use and benefits an NFT provides within the game. NFTs with significant in-game advantages, such as powerful weapons, rare abilities, or access to exclusive areas, tend to have higher value. The more impactful the utility, the more players are willing to pay for the NFT.

For example, in a role-playing game (RPG), a legendary sword that grants a significant boost in combat performance will be highly valued by players seeking to enhance their gameplay experience.

Market demand is another critical factor in NFT valuation. The value of an NFT is influenced by the number of players interested in acquiring it. High demand can drive up prices, especially for rare and valuable items. Analyzing market trends, player preferences, and transaction volumes helps gauge the demand for specific NFTs.

Here's an example of tracking market demand for an NFT:

```
| NFT Type          | Average Price | Total Sales | Transaction Volume |
|-------------------|---------------|-------------|--------------------|
| Character Skins   | 0.5 ETH       | 1,000       | 500 ETH            |
| In-Game Weapons   | 1.0 ETH       | 500         | 500 ETH            |
| Virtual Land      | 2.5 ETH       | 200         | 500 ETH            |
| Collectible Cards | 0.3 ETH       | 1,500       | 450 ETH            |
```

This table provides insights into the demand and value of different types of NFTs.

Historical sales data is a valuable resource for determining the value of NFTs. Analyzing past transactions, including initial sale prices and resale values, provides a benchmark for future valuations. Historical data helps identify trends and patterns, enabling more accurate pricing and valuation.

Community sentiment and player engagement also play a role in NFT valuation. Positive sentiment and active engagement within the game's community can enhance the perceived value of NFTs. Developers can foster a positive community by maintaining transparent communication, regularly updating the game, and organizing events that promote player interaction.

Secondary market activity provides additional insights into NFT valuation. Monitoring the resale prices and trading volumes on secondary marketplaces helps understand the long-term value and liquidity of NFTs. High resale prices and active trading indicate strong demand and potential appreciation in value.

Here's an example of secondary market data:

NFT Type	Average Resale Price	Total Resale Volume
Character Skins	0.8 ETH	400 ETH
In-Game Weapons	1.2 ETH	600 ETH
Virtual Land	3.0 ETH	600 ETH
Collectible Cards	0.5 ETH	750 ETH

This data helps assess the demand and value of NFTs on the secondary market.

Partnerships and collaborations can enhance the value of NFTs by associating them with reputable brands or influencers. Exclusive NFTs created in collaboration with well-known artists, celebrities, or brands can attract higher prices due to their added prestige and desirability.

Future potential and speculative value also influence NFT valuation. Players may be willing to pay a premium for NFTs they believe will appreciate in value or provide future benefits. Developers can enhance this potential by outlining clear roadmaps, introducing new features, and continuously improving the game.

Economic models within the game, such as play-to-earn (P2E) mechanics, can impact NFT value. NFTs that generate ongoing income or rewards, such as virtual land that earns rental income or characters that participate in profitable activities, can have higher value due to their revenue-generating potential.

External factors, such as overall market conditions and trends in the broader NFT and cryptocurrency markets, can also affect NFT valuation. Bullish market conditions and positive sentiment towards NFTs and blockchain technology can drive up prices, while bearish conditions may lead to lower valuations.

In conclusion, valuing NFTs in the gaming context involves considering factors such as rarity, utility, market demand, historical sales data, community sentiment, secondary market activity, partnerships, future potential, and economic models. By analyzing these factors, developers and investors can make informed decisions about pricing and valuing NFTs, ensuring a fair and sustainable game economy.

Chapter 17: Community and Social Impact of Gaming NFTs

17.1. Building Inclusive Gaming Communities with NFTs

Building inclusive gaming communities is essential for fostering a positive and engaging environment for all players. NFTs can play a significant role in promoting inclusivity by providing unique opportunities for customization, representation, and engagement. This section explores strategies for leveraging NFTs to build inclusive gaming communities.

One of the primary ways to promote inclusivity through NFTs is by offering a diverse range of customizable avatars and characters. Players should be able to create avatars that reflect their identities, including different genders, ethnicities, body types, and abilities. This representation ensures that all players feel seen and valued within the game.

For example, a game could offer NFTs representing a wide range of character traits and accessories, allowing players to mix and match features to create unique avatars. This customization enhances player engagement and fosters a sense of belonging.

Inclusivity can also be promoted by creating accessible gameplay features. Games should be designed to accommodate players with various disabilities, providing options such as customizable controls, subtitles, and visual aids. NFTs can be used to unlock these accessibility features, ensuring that all players can enjoy the game.

Here's an example of an accessibility feature unlocked through an NFT:

```html
<div class="accessibility-options">
    <h3>Accessibility Options</h3>
    <label for="subtitles">Enable Subtitles</label>
    <input type="checkbox" id="subtitles">
    <label for="high-contrast">High Contrast Mode</label>
    <input type="checkbox" id="high-contrast">
</div>

<script>
    function unlockAccessibilityFeatures(nftOwned) {
        if (nftOwned) {
            document.getElementById('accessibility-options').style.display = 'block';
        }
    }
    unlockAccessibilityFeatures(true); // Example: NFT is owned
</script>
```

This script enables accessibility options if the player owns the relevant NFT.

Community events and activities can also enhance inclusivity. Hosting events that celebrate different cultures, holidays, and traditions can bring players together and promote understanding and appreciation of diversity. NFTs can be used as rewards or participation tokens in these events, adding an element of excitement and engagement.

Creating safe and welcoming online spaces is crucial for fostering inclusivity. Implementing robust moderation tools and community guidelines helps prevent harassment and discrimination. Players should feel safe expressing themselves and participating in community discussions. NFTs can be used to reward positive behavior and community contributions.

Here's an example of a community guideline enforcement system:

```
<div class="community-guidelines">
    <h3>Community Guidelines</h3>
    <p>Respect all players. No harassment, discrimination, or hate speech.</p>
    <p>Follow the rules. Keep discussions on topic and constructive.</p>
</div>

<script>
    function enforceGuidelines(userBehavior) {
        if (userBehavior.violatesGuidelines) {
            // Take action (e.g., mute, ban)
            console.log('Action taken: User muted');
        } else {
            // Reward positive behavior
            console.log('Reward given: Positive behavior NFT');
        }
    }
    enforceGuidelines({violatesGuidelines: false}); // Example: Positive behavior
</script>
```

This script enforces community guidelines and rewards positive behavior.

Collaborations with diverse creators and influencers can also promote inclusivity. Partnering with artists, writers, and influencers from various backgrounds ensures that different perspectives are represented in the game. These collaborations can lead to the creation of exclusive NFTs that reflect the diversity and richness of different cultures.

Supporting player-driven content creation can further enhance inclusivity. Allowing players to create and share their own NFTs, such as custom skins, items, and stories, encourages creativity and self-expression. Player-generated content can reflect a wide range of experiences and identities, enriching the game environment.

In conclusion, building inclusive gaming communities with NFTs involves offering diverse customization options, creating accessible gameplay features, hosting inclusive events, ensuring safe online spaces, collaborating with diverse creators, and supporting player-driven content. By leveraging NFTs in these ways, developers can foster a positive and engaging environment for all players.

17.2. Social Dynamics and Player Interaction in NFT Games

Social dynamics and player interaction are fundamental aspects of NFT games, shaping the overall gaming experience and community culture. Understanding these dynamics is crucial for creating engaging and inclusive games that foster positive interactions among players. This section explores key elements of social dynamics and player interaction in NFT games.

One of the primary ways NFT games facilitate social interaction is through multiplayer gameplay. Cooperative and competitive modes encourage players to collaborate or compete with one another, fostering a sense of community and camaraderie. NFTs can be used as rewards for team achievements or as items to be traded among players, enhancing social bonds.

For example, in a multiplayer battle game, players might earn unique NFTs as rewards for team victories. These NFTs could represent special weapons, armor, or other in-game assets that players can trade or use to enhance their gameplay.

Social hubs and virtual spaces are essential for player interaction. These areas allow players to gather, chat, trade NFTs, and participate in community events. Creating immersive and interactive social spaces encourages players to spend time socializing and building relationships within the game.

Here's an example of a virtual social hub in HTML:

```html
<div class="social-hub">
    <h3>Welcome to the Social Hub</h3>
    <div id="chat-box">
        <!-- Chat messages will appear here -->
    </div>
    <input type="text" id="chat-input" placeholder="Type a message...">
    <button onclick="sendMessage()">Send</button>
</div>

<script>
    function sendMessage() {
        var message = document.getElementById('chat-input').value;
        var chatBox = document.getElementById('chat-box');
        chatBox.innerHTML += '<p>' + message + '</p>';
        document.getElementById('chat-input').value = '';
    }
</script>
```

This script creates a simple chat interface for players to communicate in the social hub.

Player-driven economies are another key aspect of social dynamics in NFT games. Allowing players to create, buy, sell, and trade NFTs within the game fosters a vibrant and interactive economy. Players can set up virtual shops, participate in auctions, and negotiate trades, creating dynamic social interactions.

In-game events and activities can enhance social dynamics by bringing players together for shared experiences. These events might include tournaments, treasure hunts, and seasonal celebrations. Offering exclusive NFTs as rewards for participation encourages players to engage in these events and interact with their peers.

Here's an example of an in-game event announcement:

```
<div class="event-announcement">
    <h3>Join the Great Treasure Hunt!</h3>
    <p>Embark on an epic quest to find hidden treasures across the game world. Collect exclusive NFTs and earn rewards along the way. The event starts on [Date] - don't miss out!</p>
</div>
```

This announcement creates excitement and encourages players to participate in the event.

Guilds and player groups are important for fostering a sense of belonging and community. Allowing players to form or join guilds creates opportunities for collaboration, mentorship, and social interaction. Guilds can have their own exclusive NFTs, events, and challenges, enhancing the group experience.

Player feedback and involvement in game development can also strengthen social dynamics. Encouraging players to provide feedback, suggest features, and participate in beta testing fosters a sense of ownership and engagement. Developers can reward active participants with exclusive NFTs or recognition within the game.

Here's an example of a feedback submission form:

```
<div class="feedback-form">
    <h3>We Value Your Feedback</h3>
    <form>
        <label for="feedback">Share your thoughts:</label><br>
        <textarea id="feedback" rows="4" cols="50"></textarea><br>
        <button type="submit">Submit</button>
    </form>
</div>
```

This form allows players to submit feedback and suggestions.

Positive reinforcement and recognition are crucial for promoting healthy social interactions. Rewarding players for positive behavior, such as helping others, creating content, or contributing to the community, encourages a supportive and inclusive environment. NFTs can be used as rewards for these positive actions, providing tangible recognition.

In conclusion, social dynamics and player interaction in NFT games involve multiplayer gameplay, social hubs, player-driven economies, in-game events, guilds, player feedback, and positive reinforcement. By incorporating these elements, developers can create engaging and inclusive games that foster positive social interactions and build strong communities.

17.3. NFTs and Their Role in Digital Identity

NFTs play a significant role in shaping digital identity, providing unique opportunities for self-expression, ownership, and personalization in virtual environments. This section explores how NFTs contribute to digital identity and the implications for players and developers.

One of the primary ways NFTs influence digital identity is through customizable avatars and characters. Players can use NFTs to create and personalize their in-game personas, reflecting their individuality and preferences. These avatars can include unique traits, outfits, accessories, and other visual elements, allowing players to express their identities in the virtual world.

For example, a player might own an NFT representing a rare outfit or accessory that they can equip on their avatar. This customization enhances the player's connection to their digital persona and allows for unique self-expression.

Ownership of digital assets is a key aspect of digital identity. NFTs provide verifiable proof of ownership for virtual items, art, and other digital content. This ownership is recorded on the blockchain, ensuring authenticity and immutability. Players can showcase their NFTs as part of their digital identity, displaying their collections, achievements, and personal tastes.

Here's an example of displaying owned NFTs on a player profile:

```html
<div class="profile">
    <h3>Player Profile</h3>
    <div class="nft-collection">
        <h4>My NFT Collection</h4>
        <img src="nft1.png" alt="NFT 1">
        <img src="nft2.png" alt="NFT 2">
        <img src="nft3.png" alt="NFT 3">
    </div>
</div>
```

This profile section showcases the player's NFT collection, enhancing their digital identity.

NFTs also enable players to participate in and contribute to virtual economies. By creating, buying, and selling NFTs, players can build reputations as collectors, traders, or creators within the game community. These economic activities become part of their digital identity, reflecting their skills, expertise, and interests.

Digital achievements and milestones can be represented by NFTs, serving as badges or trophies that players can display. These NFTs recognize accomplishments such as completing challenging quests, participating in events, or reaching high ranks. Displaying these achievement NFTs on profiles or social media platforms reinforces the player's digital identity and status.

Here's an example of an achievement NFT displayed on a profile:

```html
<div class="achievements">
    <h4>Achievements</h4>
    <img src="achievement-nft.png" alt="Achievement Badge">
    <p>Completed the Great Treasure Hunt - [Date]</p>
</div>
```

This example highlights an achievement NFT earned by the player.

Interoperability between different games and platforms enhances the role of NFTs in digital identity. Players can use their NFTs across multiple virtual environments, maintaining consistent digital identities. This interoperability allows for seamless transitions between games and platforms, enriching the overall player experience.

For instance, a rare avatar skin owned as an NFT might be usable in multiple games, allowing the player to maintain their unique appearance across different virtual worlds.

NFTs also enable players to participate in decentralized governance and decision-making processes. Ownership of specific NFTs can grant voting rights or influence over game development and community decisions. This participation becomes part of the player's digital identity, reflecting their involvement and contributions to the game's ecosystem.

Here's an example of NFT-based voting:

```html
<div class="voting">
    <h4>Community Vote</h4>
    <p>Select the next in-game event:</p>
    <button>Option 1: Treasure Hunt</button>
    <button>Option 2: Battle Tournament</button>
</div>

<script>
    function castVote(option) {
        console.log('Vote cast for: ' + option);
    }
</script>
```

This interface allows players to vote on game events, with their votes tied to NFT ownership.

In conclusion, NFTs play a vital role in digital identity by enabling customization, ownership, economic participation, achievement recognition, interoperability, and decentralized governance. These elements contribute to a richer and more personalized digital experience, allowing players to express their individuality and engage meaningfully with virtual environments.

17.4. Ethical Gaming Practices and Player Welfare

Ethical gaming practices and player welfare are paramount in the development and management of NFT games. Ensuring a fair, safe, and supportive environment for players promotes long-term engagement and a positive community culture. This section explores key ethical considerations and strategies for safeguarding player welfare in NFT games.

One of the primary ethical concerns in NFT gaming is ensuring fair gameplay. Developers must implement mechanisms to prevent cheating, exploitation, and unfair advantages. This includes detecting and mitigating bots, hacks, and other forms of cheating. Fair gameplay ensures that all players have an equal opportunity to succeed based on their skills and efforts.

Transparency is crucial for maintaining player trust. Developers should provide clear and accurate information about game mechanics, NFT functionalities, and transaction processes. Transparent communication helps players make informed decisions and understand the potential risks and rewards associated with their actions.

Here's an example of a transparency statement for an NFT game:

"We are committed to transparency and fairness in [Game Name]. Our game mechanics, NFT functionalities, and transaction processes are clearly outlined in our documentation. We encourage players to review this information and reach out with any questions or concerns."

This statement emphasizes the commitment to transparency and encourages player engagement.

Protecting player data and privacy is essential for ethical gaming practices. Developers must implement robust data protection measures to safeguard personal information and ensure compliance with data privacy regulations. This includes using encryption, secure storage, and obtaining explicit consent for data collection and usage.

Supporting player well-being involves creating a balanced and healthy gaming environment. Developers should encourage responsible gaming practices, such as setting playtime limits, providing breaks, and promoting a healthy balance between gaming and other activities. Implementing features that remind players to take breaks and monitor their gaming habits can help prevent addiction and burnout.

Here's an example of a reminder feature to promote responsible gaming:

```
<div class="reminder">
    <p>You've been playing for 2 hours. It's time to take a break and stretch!</p>
    <button>Continue Playing</button>
    <button>Take a Break</button>
</div>
```

This reminder encourages players to take breaks and promotes healthy gaming habits.

Fostering a positive and inclusive community is crucial for player welfare. Developers should establish clear community guidelines and enforce them consistently to prevent harassment, discrimination, and toxic behavior. Providing tools for players to report misconduct and ensuring swift and fair action against violators helps maintain a safe and welcoming environment.

Here's an example of community guidelines enforcement:

```html
<div class="community-guidelines">
    <h3>Community Guidelines</h3>
    <p>Respect all players. No harassment, discrimination, or hate speech.</p>
    <p>Follow the rules. Keep discussions on topic and constructive.</p>
</div>

<script>
    function enforceGuidelines(userBehavior) {
        if (userBehavior.violatesGuidelines) {
            // Take action (e.g., mute, ban)
            console.log('Action taken: User muted');
        } else {
            // Reward positive behavior
            console.log('Reward given: Positive behavior NFT');
        }
    }
    enforceGuidelines({violatesGuidelines: false}); // Example: Positive behavior
</script>
```

This script enforces community guidelines and rewards positive behavior.

Ethical monetization practices are essential to ensure that in-game purchases and NFT transactions are fair and transparent. Developers should avoid exploitative pricing models, such as pay-to-win mechanics, that create imbalances and frustrate players. Providing value through meaningful content and fair pricing fosters trust and satisfaction.

Ensuring accessibility is another important aspect of ethical gaming. Games should be designed to accommodate players with various disabilities, providing options such as customizable controls, subtitles, and visual aids. Accessible design ensures that all players can enjoy the game and participate fully.

Supporting mental health and providing resources for players in need is crucial for player welfare. Developers can offer information about mental health resources, support hotlines, and online counseling services. Creating partnerships with mental health organizations can provide additional support for players experiencing difficulties.

Here's an example of providing mental health resources:

```html
<div class="mental-health-resources">
    <h3>Mental Health Resources</h3>
    <p>If you need support, please reach out to these resources:</p>
    <ul>
        <li><a href="https://www.mentalhealth.org">Mental Health Foundation</
```

```
a></li>
        <li><a href="https://www.supporthotline.org">Support Hotline</a></li>
        <li><a href="https://www.onlinecounseling.org">Online Counseling Serv
ices</a></li>
    </ul>
</div>
```

This section provides links to mental health resources for players in need.

In conclusion, ethical gaming practices and player welfare in NFT games involve ensuring fair gameplay, transparency, data protection, responsible gaming, positive community culture, ethical monetization, accessibility, and mental health support. By prioritizing these considerations, developers can create a safe, fair, and supportive environment that promotes player well-being and long-term engagement.

17.5. The Role of NFTs in Charitable Initiatives and Social Causes

NFTs have significant potential to support charitable initiatives and social causes, providing new ways to raise funds, increase awareness, and engage communities. This section explores how NFTs can be leveraged for philanthropy and social impact, highlighting key strategies and examples.

One of the primary ways NFTs can support charitable initiatives is through fundraising. Organizations can create and sell NFTs, with proceeds going directly to their causes. These NFTs can be unique artworks, collectibles, or virtual experiences that appeal to donors and supporters. The transparency of blockchain technology ensures that funds are tracked and used for their intended purposes.

For example, a charity might collaborate with a well-known artist to create exclusive NFT art pieces. These pieces can be auctioned, with all proceeds supporting the charity's mission. The uniqueness and exclusivity of the NFTs can attract higher bids, increasing the funds raised.

Here's an example of a charity NFT auction announcement:

```
<div class="auction-announcement">
    <h3>Support Our Cause: Charity NFT Auction</h3>
    <p>Bid on exclusive NFT artworks created by renowned artist [Artist Name]
. All proceeds will support [Charity Name] and our mission to [Charity Missio
n].</p>
    <button>View Auction</button>
</div>
```

This announcement promotes the charity auction and encourages participation.

NFTs can also be used to create awareness and engage communities around social causes. Organizations can mint NFTs that symbolize their causes, such as environmental conservation, social justice, or health initiatives. Supporters can purchase or earn these NFTs to show their commitment and spread awareness through their digital networks.

For instance, an environmental organization might create NFTs representing endangered species. By collecting these NFTs, supporters contribute to conservation efforts and raise awareness about the importance of protecting wildlife.

Tokenizing impact is another innovative approach, where NFTs represent real-world actions or contributions. For example, an NFT could represent a tree planted, a meal provided, or a donation made. These impact tokens can be collected, traded, or used to unlock additional content, creating a gamified approach to philanthropy.

Here's an example of a tokenized impact NFT:

```
<div class="impact-nft">
    <h3>Plant a Tree NFT</h3>
    <p>Each NFT represents a tree planted in [Location]. Collect this NFT to contribute to reforestation efforts and track the impact of your contribution.</p>
    <button>Get NFT</button>
</div>
```

This NFT represents a tree planted, encouraging contributions to reforestation.

Collaborations with influencers and celebrities can amplify the reach and impact of NFT-based charitable initiatives. High-profile individuals can create or endorse NFTs, attracting their followers and increasing awareness and funds for the cause. These collaborations can generate significant media attention and engage a broader audience.

Creating virtual events and experiences using NFTs can also support social causes. Organizations can host virtual concerts, art exhibitions, or conferences, where attendees purchase NFTs as tickets or souvenirs. These events can raise funds and provide unique experiences that engage supporters and promote the cause.

Here's an example of a virtual event announcement:

```
<div class="event-announcement">
    <h3>Virtual Charity Concert</h3>
    <p>Join us for a live virtual concert featuring [Artist Name]. Purchase an NFT ticket to attend and support [Charity Name]. All proceeds will benefit our mission to [Charity Mission].</p>
    <button>Get Ticket</button>
</div>
```

This announcement promotes a virtual charity concert and encourages NFT ticket purchases.

Transparency and accountability are crucial for NFT-based charitable initiatives. Organizations must ensure that the funds raised through NFTs are used responsibly and transparently. Providing regular updates and reports on the impact of the donations helps build trust and encourages continued support.

Here's an example of an impact report update:

```html
<div class="impact-report">
    <h3>Impact Report: NFT Fundraiser</h3>
    <p>Thanks to your support, we have raised [Amount] through our NFT fundraiser. These funds have been used to [Describe Impact].</p>
    <button>Read Full Report</button>
</div>
```

This report provides an update on the impact of the NFT fundraiser.

In conclusion, NFTs play a valuable role in charitable initiatives and social causes by enabling fundraising, creating awareness, engaging communities, and providing transparency. By leveraging NFTs, organizations can innovate their philanthropic efforts, reach new supporters, and make a meaningful impact on the world.

Chapter 18: Technical Challenges and Solutions in NFT Gaming

18.1. Scalability Issues in Blockchain Games

Scalability is a significant challenge in blockchain-based games, especially those utilizing NFTs. As the number of transactions increases, the blockchain can become congested, leading to slower transaction times and higher fees. This section explores the scalability issues in blockchain games and potential solutions to address these challenges.

One of the primary scalability issues in blockchain games is the limited throughput of most blockchain networks. For example, Ethereum, one of the most popular blockchains for NFTs, can process around 15 transactions per second (TPS). In contrast, traditional gaming platforms can handle thousands of transactions per second. This limitation can result in delays and increased costs during peak usage times.

To address these issues, developers can consider using layer 2 scaling solutions. Layer 2 solutions, such as sidechains and state channels, operate on top of the main blockchain, allowing for faster and cheaper transactions. These solutions can significantly increase the throughput while reducing the load on the main chain.

For example, a game could implement a sidechain to handle in-game transactions. Players could transfer their assets to the sidechain, where transactions are processed more quickly and at lower costs. Periodically, the sidechain's state is synchronized with the main chain, ensuring security and transparency.

Here's an example of integrating a sidechain with a blockchain game:

```solidity
// Mainnet contract
pragma solidity ^0.8.0;

contract MainnetBridge {
    address public sidechainContract;

    function setSidechainContract(address _sidechainContract) public {
        sidechainContract = _sidechainContract;
    }

    function depositToSidechain(uint256 amount) public {
        // Transfer tokens to the sidechain
    }

    function syncFromSidechain(uint256 amount) public {
        // Sync state from the sidechain
    }
}
```

This contract sets up a bridge between the mainnet and the sidechain for asset transfers and state synchronization.

Another solution is sharding, which involves dividing the blockchain into smaller, more manageable pieces called shards. Each shard processes a portion of the transactions, allowing the network to handle more transactions in parallel. Sharding can significantly improve scalability, but it also introduces complexity in maintaining consistency across shards.

Optimizing smart contracts for efficiency can also help alleviate scalability issues. Writing efficient code, minimizing gas usage, and avoiding unnecessary computations can reduce the load on the blockchain. Developers should regularly audit and optimize their smart contracts to ensure they are as efficient as possible.

For example, consider a simple NFT minting function:

```solidity
pragma solidity ^0.8.0;

contract SimpleNFT {
    uint256 public tokenCounter;
    mapping(uint256 => address) public tokenOwners;

    function mint() public {
        tokenCounter++;
        tokenOwners[tokenCounter] = msg.sender;
    }
}
```

Optimizing this function to batch minting multiple NFTs can reduce transaction costs and improve efficiency.

```solidity
function batchMint(uint256 numberOfTokens) public {
    for (uint256 i = 0; i < numberOfTokens; i++) {
        tokenCounter++;
        tokenOwners[tokenCounter] = msg.sender;
    }
}
```

This optimized function mints multiple NFTs in a single transaction, reducing the overall gas cost.

Using alternative blockchains designed for higher scalability, such as Solana or Binance Smart Chain, can also be a solution. These blockchains offer higher throughput and lower transaction fees, making them suitable for high-transaction-volume applications like blockchain games.

Finally, implementing off-chain solutions for non-critical operations can reduce the load on the blockchain. For example, game logic that does not require the security of the blockchain can be processed off-chain, with only critical transactions recorded on the blockchain. This hybrid approach can balance the benefits of blockchain technology with the need for scalability.

In conclusion, addressing scalability issues in blockchain games involves leveraging layer 2 solutions, sharding, optimizing smart contracts, using scalable blockchains, and implementing off-chain solutions. By adopting these strategies, developers can create more scalable and efficient blockchain games that can handle higher transaction volumes and provide a better user experience.

18.2. Interoperability Challenges with NFTs

Interoperability is a crucial aspect of the NFT ecosystem, enabling assets to be used across different platforms and applications. However, achieving seamless interoperability poses several technical challenges. This section explores these challenges and potential solutions to enhance NFT interoperability.

One of the primary challenges of NFT interoperability is the varying standards across different blockchains. While Ethereum's ERC-721 and ERC-1155 standards are widely adopted, other blockchains have their own standards, such as Binance Smart Chain's BEP-721 and BEP-1155. These differing standards can create compatibility issues, making it difficult to transfer NFTs between blockchains.

To address this challenge, developers can use cross-chain bridges. Cross-chain bridges facilitate the transfer of assets between different blockchains by locking the original asset on the source chain and minting a corresponding asset on the destination chain. This approach allows NFTs to move across chains while maintaining their unique properties.

Here's an example of a basic cross-chain bridge concept:

```solidity
// Ethereum contract
pragma solidity ^0.8.0;

contract EthereumBridge {
    address public bscBridge;

    function setBSCBridge(address _bscBridge) public {
        bscBridge = _bscBridge;
    }

    function lockNFT(uint256 tokenId) public {
        // Logic to lock the NFT on Ethereum
    }

    function mintNFTOnBSC(uint256 tokenId, address owner) public {
        require(msg.sender == bscBridge, "Only BSC bridge can call this");
        // Logic to mint corresponding NFT on BSC
    }
}
```

This contract outlines the concept of locking an NFT on Ethereum and minting a corresponding NFT on Binance Smart Chain.

Another challenge is the lack of standardized metadata across platforms. NFTs often contain metadata that describes their properties, such as images, attributes, and provenance. However, different platforms may use varying metadata structures, making it difficult to interpret and display the information consistently.

Developing common metadata standards can help address this issue. The InterPlanetary File System (IPFS) is a decentralized storage solution commonly used for storing NFT metadata. By adopting standardized metadata formats and storing them on IPFS, developers can ensure consistent interpretation across different platforms.

Here's an example of a standardized metadata format stored on IPFS:

```
{
    "name": "Rare Sword",
    "description": "A rare and powerful sword.",
    "image": "ipfs://QmExampleHash",
    "attributes": [
        {
            "trait_type": "Power",
            "value": 100
        },
        {
            "trait_type": "Durability",
            "value": 80
        }
    ]
}
```

This JSON format provides a consistent structure for NFT metadata, facilitating interoperability.

Smart contract compatibility is another hurdle. Different blockchains use different virtual machines and smart contract languages, which can create compatibility issues. For example, Ethereum uses the Ethereum Virtual Machine (EVM) and Solidity, while Solana uses the Solana Runtime and Rust. This diversity complicates the deployment of interoperable smart contracts.

To overcome this, developers can use interoperability frameworks like Polkadot or Cosmos. These frameworks enable communication and asset transfers between different blockchains by providing a common infrastructure. Polkadot's parachains and Cosmos's zones allow developers to build specialized blockchains that can interoperate with others within the network.

Creating cross-platform wallets and interfaces is also essential for interoperability. Users should be able to manage their NFTs across different blockchains using a single wallet or interface. Wallets like MetaMask and Trust Wallet are expanding their support to multiple blockchains, enabling users to interact with various NFT ecosystems seamlessly.

Lastly, fostering collaboration between blockchain communities can drive interoperability. Open standards, shared protocols, and collaborative projects can help create a more cohesive and interoperable NFT ecosystem. Initiatives like the Ethereum Improvement Proposals (EIPs) and cross-chain working groups can facilitate this collaboration.

In conclusion, addressing interoperability challenges with NFTs involves using cross-chain bridges, developing common metadata standards, leveraging interoperability frameworks, creating cross-platform wallets, and fostering collaboration. By implementing these solutions, developers can enhance the interoperability of NFTs, enabling seamless use across different platforms and applications.

18.3. Overcoming Latency and Performance Hurdles

Latency and performance issues can significantly impact the user experience in NFT games, especially those with real-time interactions. Overcoming these hurdles is crucial for creating responsive and engaging games. This section explores strategies to address latency and performance challenges in NFT gaming.

One of the primary causes of latency in blockchain-based games is the time required to confirm transactions on the blockchain. Public blockchains, such as Ethereum, often have block times of 10-15 seconds, which can introduce delays in transaction confirmations. To mitigate this, developers can use layer 2 scaling solutions, such as state channels and rollups, which allow transactions to be processed off-chain and settled on-chain periodically.

For example, state channels enable two parties to conduct numerous transactions off-chain, only recording the final state on the blockchain. This approach significantly reduces latency and transaction costs.

Here's an example of setting up a state channel:

```solidity
pragma solidity ^0.8.0;

contract StateChannel {
    address public player1;
    address public player2;
    uint256 public balance1;
    uint256 public balance2;
    bool public isOpen;

    constructor(address _player1, address _player2) {
        player1 = _player1;
        player2 = _player2;
        isOpen = true;
    }

    function closeChannel(uint256 finalBalance1, uint256 finalBalance2) public {
        require(msg.sender == player1 || msg.sender == player2, "Not authorized");
        balance1 = finalBalance1;
```

```
        balance2 = finalBalance2;
        isOpen = false;
    }
}
```

This contract sets up a basic state channel for two players to conduct off-chain transactions.

Another approach to reducing latency is using faster blockchains. Some blockchains, like Solana and Binance Smart Chain, offer significantly faster transaction times compared to Ethereum. By building games on these faster blockchains, developers can minimize delays and enhance the user experience.

Optimizing smart contract execution is also crucial for improving performance. Developers should write efficient code, minimize gas usage, and avoid complex computations within smart contracts. Regularly auditing and optimizing contracts can help identify and address performance bottlenecks.

For example, consider a gas-optimized NFT transfer function:

```
pragma solidity ^0.8.0;

contract OptimizedNFT {
    mapping(uint256 => address) public tokenOwners;

    function transferNFT(uint256 tokenId, address to) public {
        require(msg.sender == tokenOwners[tokenId], "Not the owner");
        tokenOwners[tokenId] = to;
    }
}
```

This function minimizes gas usage by using a simple mapping to track token ownership.

Implementing off-chain computation can further enhance performance. Off-chain computation involves processing complex game logic off-chain and only recording essential state changes on-chain. This approach reduces the computational load on the blockchain and improves responsiveness.

For instance, a game's matchmaking and ranking algorithms can be processed off-chain, with only the final match results recorded on-chain. This hybrid approach balances the security of the blockchain with the performance of off-chain computation.

Here's an example of recording match results on-chain:

```
pragma solidity ^0.8.0;

contract MatchResults {
    mapping(uint256 => string) public matchResults;

    function recordResult(uint256 matchId, string memory result) public {
        matchResults[matchId] = result;
```

                }
}

This contract records match results on-chain, while the matchmaking logic is handled off-chain.

Using content delivery networks (CDNs) can also improve performance by reducing latency for users distributed globally. CDNs cache and deliver content from servers closer to the user's location, speeding up load times for game assets and metadata. Integrating CDNs with decentralized storage solutions like IPFS can provide a balance between decentralization and performance.

Finally, continuous monitoring and optimization are essential for maintaining high performance. Developers should use performance monitoring tools to track latency, transaction times, and system load. Regularly analyzing this data helps identify areas for improvement and ensures that the game remains responsive.

In conclusion, overcoming latency and performance hurdles in NFT gaming involves using layer 2 solutions, faster blockchains, optimized smart contracts, off-chain computation, CDNs, and continuous monitoring. By implementing these strategies, developers can create more responsive and engaging NFT games that provide a better user experience.

18.4. Ensuring Game Continuity and NFT Persistence

Ensuring game continuity and NFT persistence is crucial for the longevity and reliability of NFT games. Players invest time, money, and effort into acquiring NFTs, and any disruption or loss of these assets can severely impact trust and engagement. This section explores strategies to ensure game continuity and NFT persistence.

One of the primary considerations for ensuring game continuity is using decentralized storage solutions. Traditional centralized servers pose a risk of data loss or unavailability due to server failures, cyberattacks, or administrative issues. Decentralized storage solutions like the InterPlanetary File System (IPFS) and Arweave provide a more reliable and resilient way to store NFT metadata and game assets.

For example, storing NFT metadata on IPFS ensures that the data is distributed across multiple nodes, reducing the risk of data loss. Here's an example of uploading metadata to IPFS:

```
const ipfsClient = require('ipfs-http-client');
const ipfs = ipfsClient({ host: 'ipfs.infura.io', port: '5001', protocol: 'https' });

async function uploadMetadata(metadata) {
    const { path } = await ipfs.add(JSON.stringify(metadata));
    return `ipfs://${path}`;
}

const metadata = {
```

```
    name: "Rare Sword",
    description: "A rare and powerful sword.",
    image: "ipfs://QmExampleHash",
    attributes: [
        { trait_type: "Power", value: 100 },
        { trait_type: "Durability", value: 80 }
    ]
};

uploadMetadata(metadata).then(console.log);
```

This script uploads metadata to IPFS and returns the IPFS link.

Another important aspect is implementing robust backup and recovery mechanisms. Regularly backing up game data and NFT records ensures that the game can be restored in case of data loss or corruption. Developers should store backups in multiple locations and use automated systems to manage backup schedules and recovery processes.

Smart contract immutability is another key factor in ensuring NFT persistence. Once deployed, smart contracts on the blockchain cannot be altered, providing a secure and permanent record of NFT ownership and transactions. Developers should thoroughly test and audit smart contracts before deployment to ensure they are secure and free of vulnerabilities.

Here's an example of a basic NFT contract with immutability:

```
pragma solidity ^0.8.0;

import "@openzeppelin/contracts/token/ERC721/ERC721.sol";
import "@openzeppelin/contracts/access/Ownable.sol";

contract ImmutableNFT is ERC721, Ownable {
    uint256 public tokenCounter;

    constructor() ERC721("ImmutableNFT", "IMNFT") {
        tokenCounter = 0;
    }

    function mintNFT(address recipient) public onlyOwner {
        _mint(recipient, tokenCounter);
        tokenCounter++;
    }
}
```

This contract mints NFTs with immutable ownership records on the blockchain.

Implementing decentralized governance can also enhance game continuity. Decentralized Autonomous Organizations (DAOs) allow the community to participate in decision-making processes, such as game updates, feature additions, and policy changes. This approach ensures that the game evolves in line with the community's interests and reduces reliance on a single entity.

Here's an example of a simple DAO contract for governance:

```solidity
pragma solidity ^0.8.0;

contract SimpleDAO {
    struct Proposal {
        string description;
        uint256 voteCount;
    }

    mapping(uint256 => Proposal) public proposals;
    uint256 public proposalCounter;

    function createProposal(string memory description) public {
        proposals[proposalCounter] = Proposal(description, 0);
        proposalCounter++;
    }

    function vote(uint256 proposalId) public {
        proposals[proposalId].voteCount++;
    }

    function getProposal(uint256 proposalId) public view returns (string memory, uint256) {
        Proposal memory proposal = proposals[proposalId];
        return (proposal.description, proposal.voteCount);
    }
}
```

This contract allows the community to create and vote on proposals, enabling decentralized governance.

Ensuring compatibility and interoperability with future technologies is another important consideration. As the blockchain and NFT ecosystems evolve, maintaining compatibility with new standards and platforms ensures that the game and its assets remain relevant and usable. Developers should design their systems to be flexible and adaptable to changes in the technology landscape.

In conclusion, ensuring game continuity and NFT persistence involves using decentralized storage, implementing backup and recovery mechanisms, deploying immutable smart contracts, adopting decentralized governance, and ensuring compatibility with future technologies. By following these strategies, developers can create reliable and resilient NFT games that maintain player trust and engagement.

18.5. Advanced Solutions in Blockchain Technology for Gaming

Blockchain technology offers a range of advanced solutions that can enhance the functionality, security, and user experience of NFT games. This section explores some of the cutting-edge technologies and techniques that developers can leverage to create innovative and robust NFT gaming experiences.

One of the most promising advancements in blockchain technology for gaming is the use of non-custodial wallets. Non-custodial wallets allow players to have full control over their private keys and assets without relying on a centralized entity. This approach enhances security and reduces the risk of hacks and data breaches.

For example, integrating a non-custodial wallet solution like MetaMask into an NFT game allows players to manage their assets securely and independently. Here's an example of connecting a non-custodial wallet to a game:

```
if (typeof window.ethereum !== 'undefined') {
    console.log('MetaMask is installed!');
}

async function connectWallet() {
    const accounts = await ethereum.request({ method: 'eth_requestAccounts' });
    console.log('Connected account:', accounts[0]);
}

document.getElementById('connect-wallet').addEventListener('click', connectWallet);
```

This script connects the game to a player's MetaMask wallet.

Another advanced solution is the implementation of zero-knowledge proofs (ZKPs). ZKPs enable players to prove ownership or specific attributes of their NFTs without revealing any additional information. This enhances privacy and security in transactions and interactions within the game.

For instance, a player could use a ZKP to prove they own a specific rare item without disclosing their entire inventory. This approach can be particularly useful in competitive games where players want to keep their strategies and assets confidential.

Cross-chain interoperability is another significant advancement. Projects like Polkadot and Cosmos facilitate communication and asset transfers between different blockchains, enabling a more interconnected and versatile gaming ecosystem. Developers can leverage these platforms to create games that utilize assets from multiple blockchains, enhancing gameplay possibilities and market reach.

Here's an example of using Polkadot for cross-chain interoperability:

```
// Sample Polkadot parachain contract interface
pragma solidity ^0.8.0;
```

```
interface IPolkadotParachain {
    function transferAsset(address to, uint256 amount) external;
    function receiveAsset(address from, uint256 amount) external;
}
```

This interface outlines the basic functions for transferring and receiving assets across Polkadot parachains.

Decentralized identity solutions are also gaining traction in the blockchain gaming space. Decentralized identifiers (DIDs) and verifiable credentials allow players to create and manage their digital identities securely and privately. These identities can be used across different games and platforms, providing a seamless and consistent user experience.

For example, a player could use a DID to sign in to multiple games, maintaining their reputation and achievements across different virtual worlds. This approach enhances interoperability and reduces the need for repetitive identity verification processes.

Here's an example of a simple DID integration:

```
const did = 'did:example:123456789abcdefghi';

async function authenticate() {
    const credentials = await fetch(`https://example.com/did/${did}/credentials`);
    console.log('Authenticated credentials:', credentials);
}

document.getElementById('authenticate').addEventListener('click', authenticate);
```

This script authenticates a player's DID and retrieves their credentials.

Advanced consensus mechanisms, such as Proof of Stake (PoS) and Delegated Proof of Stake (DPoS), offer improved scalability and energy efficiency compared to traditional Proof of Work (PoW) systems. These mechanisms can support higher transaction throughput and reduce the environmental impact of blockchain gaming.

For example, using a PoS-based blockchain like Ethereum 2.0 can significantly enhance the scalability and sustainability of an NFT game. Developers can design their games to take advantage of the faster and more efficient consensus process.

Tokenomics and game economy design are critical areas where advanced blockchain solutions can be applied. Creating balanced and sustainable in-game economies requires careful planning and innovative approaches. Developers can use automated market makers (AMMs) and decentralized exchanges (DEXs) to create dynamic and liquid markets for in-game assets.

For instance, a game could implement an AMM to allow players to trade in-game tokens seamlessly. This approach can provide consistent liquidity and fair pricing for in-game assets.

Here's an example of a simple AMM contract:

```solidity
pragma solidity ^0.8.0;

contract SimpleAMM {
    mapping(address => uint256) public balances;
    uint256 public totalSupply;

    function addLiquidity(uint256 amount) public {
        balances[msg.sender] += amount;
        totalSupply += amount;
    }

    function removeLiquidity(uint256 amount) public {
        require(balances[msg.sender] >= amount, "Insufficient balance");
        balances[msg.sender] -= amount;
        totalSupply -= amount;
    }

    function swap(uint256 inputAmount, uint256 outputAmount) public {
        require(balances[msg.sender] >= inputAmount, "Insufficient balance");
        balances[msg.sender] -= inputAmount;
        balances[msg.sender] += outputAmount;
    }
}
```

This contract implements a basic AMM for adding and removing liquidity and swapping tokens.

In conclusion, advanced solutions in blockchain technology, such as non-custodial wallets, zero-knowledge proofs, cross-chain interoperability, decentralized identity, advanced consensus mechanisms, and innovative tokenomics, offer significant enhancements for NFT gaming. By leveraging these technologies, developers can create more secure, scalable, and engaging gaming experiences that meet the evolving needs of players.

Chapter 19: Player Analytics and Data in NFT Gaming

19.1. Tracking Player Behavior in NFT Games

Tracking player behavior is essential in understanding how players interact with NFT games, identifying areas for improvement, and optimizing the gaming experience. This section explores the methods and tools used to track player behavior in NFT games.

One of the primary methods for tracking player behavior is through event logging. Event logging involves recording specific actions taken by players within the game. These actions can include in-game purchases, quest completions, interactions with other players, and usage of specific features. By analyzing these logs, developers can gain insights into player preferences and engagement patterns.

For example, a game might log events such as:

```
{
    "event": "purchase",
    "player_id": "12345",
    "item_id": "98765",
    "timestamp": "2024-07-04T12:34:56Z"
}
```

This JSON log entry records a player's purchase of a specific item at a particular time.

Heatmaps are another useful tool for tracking player behavior. Heatmaps visually represent where players spend the most time or interact the most within the game environment. By analyzing heatmaps, developers can identify popular areas, frequently accessed features, and potential bottlenecks or underutilized sections.

User flow analysis involves mapping out the paths players take through the game. This analysis helps developers understand the common sequences of actions, identify drop-off points where players leave the game, and optimize the game flow to enhance player retention and satisfaction.

For instance, a user flow diagram might show that many players exit the game after reaching a difficult level. By identifying this pattern, developers can adjust the level's difficulty or provide additional support to keep players engaged.

Cohort analysis groups players based on specific characteristics or behaviors and tracks their performance over time. This analysis helps developers understand how different segments of players interact with the game, which features are most appealing to specific groups, and how retention rates vary among cohorts.

A cohort analysis might reveal that new players who complete a tutorial have higher retention rates than those who skip it. This insight can guide improvements to the onboarding process.

In-game surveys and feedback mechanisms provide direct input from players about their experiences, preferences, and suggestions. Implementing periodic surveys or feedback prompts allows developers to gather qualitative data that complements quantitative analytics.

For example, an in-game survey might ask:

```
<form>
    <label for="experience">Rate your overall game experience:</label><br>
    <input type="radio" id="excellent" name="experience" value="excellent"> Excellent<br>
    <input type="radio" id="good" name="experience" value="good"> Good<br>
    <input type="radio" id="average" name="experience" value="average"> Average<br>
    <input type="radio" id="poor" name="experience" value="poor"> Poor<br>
    <button type="submit">Submit</button>
</form>
```

This form collects players' ratings of their game experience, providing valuable feedback.

Using analytics platforms and tools, such as Google Analytics, Mixpanel, or custom-built solutions, can streamline the process of collecting, analyzing, and visualizing player behavior data. These tools offer features like real-time tracking, segmentation, funnel analysis, and reporting, enabling developers to make data-driven decisions.

Tracking player behavior also involves monitoring social interactions and community engagement. Analyzing chat logs, forum discussions, and social media activity can provide insights into player sentiment, common issues, and community dynamics. This analysis helps developers address concerns, foster a positive community, and identify opportunities for community-driven content.

In conclusion, tracking player behavior in NFT games involves event logging, heatmaps, user flow analysis, cohort analysis, in-game surveys, and the use of analytics platforms. By leveraging these methods, developers can gain a comprehensive understanding of player interactions, optimize the gaming experience, and enhance player engagement and retention.

19.2. Utilizing Analytics for Game Improvement

Utilizing analytics is crucial for continuous game improvement in the dynamic environment of NFT gaming. By systematically analyzing player data, developers can identify areas for enhancement, optimize game mechanics, and deliver a better gaming experience. This section explores how analytics can be leveraged for game improvement.

One of the primary uses of analytics is to identify and address pain points in the player experience. By analyzing metrics such as player drop-off rates, session lengths, and level completion rates, developers can pinpoint where players are encountering difficulties or losing interest. This information helps prioritize areas for improvement.

For example, if analytics reveal a high drop-off rate at a specific game level, developers can investigate the cause and make adjustments, such as reducing the difficulty or providing additional guidance.

Balancing game mechanics is another critical application of analytics. By tracking player progression, win/loss ratios, and in-game economies, developers can ensure that the game remains challenging yet fair. Analytics help identify imbalances, such as overpowered items or characters, and guide adjustments to maintain a balanced gameplay experience.

Here's an example of tracking win/loss ratios:

```
{
    "event": "battle_result",
    "player_id": "12345",
    "result": "win",
    "timestamp": "2024-07-04T12:34:56Z"
}
```

This log entry records a player's win in a battle, contributing to the overall analysis of game balance.

Personalizing the player experience is another benefit of using analytics. By analyzing player behavior and preferences, developers can tailor content, rewards, and recommendations to individual players. Personalization enhances engagement and satisfaction by providing players with experiences that align with their interests and playstyles.

For instance, if a player frequently engages in crafting activities, the game can recommend related quests or items that enhance their crafting experience.

Improving user acquisition and retention strategies is essential for the growth of NFT games. Analytics can provide insights into which marketing campaigns, referral programs, or onboarding processes are most effective in attracting and retaining players. By analyzing metrics such as conversion rates, retention rates, and lifetime value, developers can optimize their strategies to maximize growth.

Here's an example of tracking user acquisition metrics:

```
{
    "event": "user_signup",
    "campaign_id": "campaign_123",
    "player_id": "12345",
    "timestamp": "2024-07-04T12:34:56Z"
}
```

This log entry records a new user signup attributed to a specific marketing campaign.

Enhancing in-game monetization is another key area where analytics can provide valuable insights. By tracking in-game purchases, spending patterns, and the effectiveness of different pricing strategies, developers can optimize their monetization models. Analytics help identify which items or bundles are most popular, the ideal pricing points, and opportunities for introducing new revenue streams.

For example, if analytics show that limited-time offers result in a significant increase in sales, developers can incorporate more time-limited promotions to boost revenue.

Monitoring community sentiment and feedback is vital for maintaining a positive player community. Analytics tools can aggregate and analyze feedback from various channels, including in-game surveys, social media, forums, and customer support interactions. Understanding player sentiment helps developers address concerns, implement requested features, and foster a supportive community.

Here's an example of collecting feedback through an in-game prompt:

```html
<form>
    <label for="feedback">Share your feedback:</label><br>
    <textarea id="feedback" rows="4" cols="50"></textarea><br>
    <button type="submit">Submit</button>
</form>
```

This form collects player feedback directly within the game.

Experimentation and A/B testing are powerful techniques for game improvement. By testing different versions of game elements, such as user interfaces, level designs, or reward structures, developers can determine which variations perform better. Analytics provide the data needed to evaluate the effectiveness of these experiments and make informed decisions.

Here's an example of setting up an A/B test:

```json
{
    "event": "ab_test",
    "test_id": "test_123",
    "variant": "A",
    "player_id": "12345",
    "result": "completed_level",
    "timestamp": "2024-07-04T12:34:56Z"
}
```

This log entry records a player's interaction with variant A of an A/B test.

In conclusion, utilizing analytics for game improvement involves identifying pain points, balancing game mechanics, personalizing experiences, optimizing user acquisition and retention, enhancing monetization, monitoring community sentiment, and conducting experimentation. By leveraging these analytics-driven insights, developers can continuously refine and enhance their NFT games, providing a more engaging and satisfying experience for players.

19.3. Data Security and Privacy in Player Analytics

Data security and privacy are paramount when handling player analytics in NFT gaming. Protecting players' personal information and ensuring compliance with data protection regulations are essential for maintaining trust and avoiding legal issues. This section explores best practices and strategies for ensuring data security and privacy in player analytics.

One of the fundamental principles of data security is data minimization. Only collect the data that is necessary for the intended purpose. By minimizing the amount of data collected, the risk of data breaches and privacy violations is reduced. For example, if player behavior analytics can be conducted without collecting personally identifiable information (PII), avoid gathering PII.

Here's an example of anonymizing data collection:

```
{
    "event": "level_complete",
    "player_id": "anon_12345",
    "level_id": "level_5",
    "timestamp": "2024-07-04T12:34:56Z"
}
```

This log entry records a player's completion of a level without collecting any PII.

Implementing strong encryption protocols is crucial for protecting data both in transit and at rest. Use encryption to secure data as it is transmitted between players' devices and the server, as well as when it is stored in databases. Encryption ensures that even if data is intercepted or accessed without authorization, it remains unreadable.

For example, using HTTPS for data transmission:

```
<form action="https://secure-game-server.com/submit" method="post">
    <input type="text" name="player_data" placeholder="Player Data">
    <button type="submit">Submit</button>
</form>
```

This form transmits player data securely using HTTPS.

Access control measures are essential to ensure that only authorized personnel can access sensitive data. Implement role-based access controls (RBAC) to restrict access based on the user's role and responsibilities. Regularly review and update access permissions to reflect changes in team roles or employment status.

Here's an example of an access control policy:

```
{
    "roles": {
        "admin": {
            "can_view": ["all_data"],
            "can_edit": ["all_data"],
```

```
            "can_delete": ["all_data"]
        },
        "analyst": {
            "can_view": ["analytics_data"],
            "can_edit": [],
            "can_delete": []
        }
    }
}
```

This policy defines different access levels for admin and analyst roles.

Compliance with data protection regulations, such as the General Data Protection Regulation (GDPR) in the European Union and the California Consumer Privacy Act (CCPA) in the United States, is critical. These regulations impose strict requirements on data collection, storage, and processing. Ensure that your data practices align with these regulations to avoid legal repercussions.

Here's an example of a GDPR-compliant data collection notice:

```html
<div class="data-notice">
    <p>We collect data to improve your gaming experience. Your data will be processed in accordance with our <a href="privacy-policy.html">Privacy Policy</a>. You have the right to access, rectify, and delete your data. For more information, contact us at [email address].</p>
    <button>Accept</button>
</div>
```

This notice informs players of their data rights and provides a link to the privacy policy.

Implementing data anonymization techniques can further enhance privacy. Anonymization involves removing or altering personal information so that individuals cannot be identified. Techniques such as data masking, pseudonymization, and aggregation help protect privacy while still allowing useful analytics.

For example, pseudonymizing player IDs:

```json
{
    "event": "item_purchase",
    "player_id": "pseudo_12345",
    "item_id": "98765",
    "timestamp": "2024-07-04T12:34:56Z"
}
```

This log entry pseudonymizes the player ID to protect their identity.

Regular security audits and vulnerability assessments are essential for identifying and addressing potential security weaknesses. Conducting these assessments helps ensure that security measures are effective and that any vulnerabilities are promptly addressed. Engaging third-party security experts can provide an unbiased evaluation of your security practices.

Implementing multi-factor authentication (MFA) adds an extra layer of security for accessing sensitive data and systems. MFA requires users to provide two or more verification factors, such as a password and a one-time code sent to their mobile device. This approach reduces the risk of unauthorized access.

Here's an example of enabling MFA for an admin login:

```html
<form action="/login" method="post">
    <input type="text" name="username" placeholder="Username">
    <input type="password" name="password" placeholder="Password">
    <button type="submit">Login</button>
</form>
<form action="/verify-otp" method="post">
    <input type="text" name="otp" placeholder="One-Time Password">
    <button type="submit">Verify</button>
</form>
```

This form includes an additional step for verifying a one-time password.

Educating employees and players about data security and privacy best practices is crucial. Providing regular training sessions and resources helps ensure that everyone understands the importance of data protection and how to implement it effectively.

In conclusion, ensuring data security and privacy in player analytics involves data minimization, encryption, access control, regulatory compliance, anonymization, regular security assessments, multi-factor authentication, and education. By implementing these best practices, developers can protect player data, maintain trust, and comply with data protection regulations.

19.4. Personalizing Player Experiences with Data

Personalizing player experiences using data is a powerful way to enhance engagement, satisfaction, and retention in NFT games. By leveraging player data, developers can tailor content, recommendations, and interactions to individual preferences and behaviors. This section explores strategies for personalizing player experiences with data.

One of the primary methods for personalization is using player profiles to store and analyze data about individual players. Player profiles can include information such as gameplay history, achievements, preferences, and in-game purchases. This data serves as the foundation for personalized experiences.

For example, a player profile might look like this:

```json
{
    "player_id": "12345",
    "username": "gamer01",
    "preferences": {
        "favorite_genre": "RPG",
        "preferred_language": "English"
    },
```

```
    "gameplay_history": [
        {"game_id": "game_1", "hours_played": 50},
        {"game_id": "game_2", "hours_played": 30}
    ],
    "achievements": ["First Victory", "Master Collector"],
    "in_game_purchases": ["Sword of Power", "Dragon Armor"]
}
```

This profile includes detailed information about the player's preferences, history, achievements, and purchases.

Recommending content based on player data is a key personalization strategy. By analyzing players' past behaviors and preferences, developers can suggest relevant games, items, quests, or events that align with their interests. Personalized recommendations enhance the player experience by providing tailored content that resonates with individual players.

For example, if a player frequently engages in crafting activities, the game could recommend new crafting recipes or materials:

```
<div class="recommendations">
    <h3>Recommended for You</h3>
    <ul>
        <li>New Crafting Recipe: Enchanted Sword</li>
        <li>Special Material: Dragon Scale</li>
        <li>Upcoming Event: Crafting Competition</li>
    </ul>
</div>
```

This section provides personalized recommendations based on the player's crafting activities.

Dynamic content adaptation is another effective personalization technique. Games can adjust the difficulty level, storylines, or in-game events based on the player's skill level, progress, and preferences. This approach ensures that players are continually challenged and engaged without becoming frustrated.

For instance, if a player is struggling with a particular level, the game could dynamically reduce the difficulty or provide additional hints:

```
<div class="dynamic-content">
    <p>We noticed you're having trouble with this level. Here are some hints to help you progress:</p>
    <ul>
        <li>Try using the Fire Spell against the Ice Monster.</li>
        <li>Explore the hidden cave to find a powerful weapon.</li>
    </ul>
</div>
```

This content adapts to the player's needs, providing assistance to enhance their experience.

Personalized in-game rewards can also enhance player engagement. By analyzing player data, developers can offer rewards that align with players' achievements, preferences, and playstyles. Personalized rewards create a sense of recognition and motivation, encouraging continued participation.

For example, if a player completes a challenging quest, the game could reward them with an item that suits their preferred playstyle:

```
{
    "reward": {
        "player_id": "12345",
        "item": "Epic Sword",
        "attributes": {
            "damage": 50,
            "special_ability": "Fire Damage"
        }
    }
}
```

This reward is tailored to the player's achievements and preferences.

Leveraging social data for personalization is another effective strategy. By analyzing players' social interactions, friendships, and community involvement, developers can create social experiences that enhance engagement. This includes suggesting friends to connect with, recommending social events, or highlighting community achievements.

For example, a game could recommend joining a guild based on the player's interactions and interests:

```
<div class="social-recommendations">
    <h3>Join a Guild</h3>
    <p>We think you'll enjoy being part of the "Dragon Slayers" guild. Join now to participate in exclusive quests and events!</p>
    <button>Join Guild</button>
</div>
```

This recommendation is based on the player's social interactions and interests.

Implementing real-time personalization can further enhance the player experience. By using data to adapt content and interactions in real time, developers can create a dynamic and responsive gaming environment. This includes adjusting in-game events, providing instant feedback, and delivering personalized notifications.

For example, if a player achieves a significant milestone, the game could instantly congratulate them and offer a reward:

```
<div class="real-time-notification">
    <p>Congratulations on reaching Level 50! You've earned a Legendary Chest as a reward.</p>
    <button>Claim Reward</button>
</div>
```

This notification provides immediate recognition and a personalized reward.

In conclusion, personalizing player experiences with data involves creating detailed player profiles, recommending content, dynamically adapting content, offering personalized rewards, leveraging social data, and implementing real-time personalization. By using these strategies, developers can enhance engagement, satisfaction, and retention, creating a more compelling and tailored gaming experience for players.

19.5. Ethical Data Usage in Blockchain Gaming

Ethical data usage is crucial in blockchain gaming, ensuring that players' rights and privacy are respected while leveraging data to enhance the gaming experience. This section explores the principles and practices of ethical data usage in blockchain gaming.

One of the foundational principles of ethical data usage is transparency. Developers must be clear about what data is being collected, how it will be used, and why it is necessary. Providing detailed and easily accessible privacy policies helps build trust and ensures that players are informed about data practices.

Here's an example of a transparency statement:

```
<div class="privacy-notice">
    <p>We collect data to improve your gaming experience. Your data will be processed in accordance with our <a href="privacy-policy.html">Privacy Policy</a>. You have the right to access, rectify, and delete your data. For more information, contact us at [email address].</p>
</div>
```

This notice informs players about data collection and their rights.

Consent is another critical aspect of ethical data usage. Players should have control over their data and provide explicit consent for data collection and processing. Implementing opt-in mechanisms for data collection and allowing players to revoke consent at any time ensures that data practices are respectful and compliant with regulations.

For example, an opt-in consent form might look like this:

```
<form>
    <label for="data-consent">I agree to the collection and processing of my data for improving the game experience.</label>
    <input type="checkbox" id="data-consent" name="data-consent">
    <button type="submit">Submit</button>
</form>
```

This form requires players to provide explicit consent for data collection.

Data minimization is an essential practice in ethical data usage. Collect only the data necessary for the intended purpose and avoid gathering excessive or irrelevant information. Minimizing data collection reduces the risk of data breaches and ensures compliance with privacy regulations.

For example, instead of collecting full names and addresses, a game might only collect necessary gameplay data:

```
{
    "player_id": "12345",
    "gameplay_data": {
        "level_completed": 10,
        "score": 5000
    }
}
```

This data is sufficient for analyzing gameplay without collecting unnecessary personal information.

Ensuring data security is crucial for protecting players' information. Implementing strong encryption, access controls, and regular security audits helps safeguard data from unauthorized access and breaches. Developers should adopt best practices for data security and stay updated on emerging threats.

For example, using HTTPS for secure data transmission:

```
<form action="https://secure-game-server.com/submit" method="post">
    <input type="text" name="player_data" placeholder="Player Data">
    <button type="submit">Submit</button>
</form>
```

This form ensures that data is transmitted securely.

Respecting players' rights to access, rectify, and delete their data is fundamental to ethical data usage. Providing mechanisms for players to view their data, request corrections, or delete their information ensures that they maintain control over their personal data.

For example, a data access request form might look like this:

```
<form>
    <label for="data-access">Enter your player ID to view your data:</label>
    <input type="text" id="data-access" name="data-access">
    <button type="submit">Submit</button>
</form>
```

This form allows players to request access to their data.

Using anonymization and pseudonymization techniques helps protect players' privacy while still allowing for useful analytics. By removing or obscuring personal identifiers, developers can analyze data without compromising individual privacy.

For example, pseudonymizing player IDs:

```
{
    "event": "item_purchase",
    "player_id": "pseudo_12345",
    "item_id": "98765",
```

```
    "timestamp": "2024-07-04T12:34:56Z"
}
```

This log entry pseudonymizes the player ID to protect their identity.

Implementing data governance frameworks helps ensure that data practices are ethical and compliant. Establishing policies, procedures, and accountability mechanisms for data management ensures that data is handled responsibly and transparently.

For example, a data governance policy might include:

```
{
    "policies": {
        "data_collection": "Collect only necessary data with explicit consent.",
        "data_security": "Implement encryption and access controls.",
        "data_access": "Provide mechanisms for players to access, rectify, and delete their data."
    },
    "accountability": {
        "data_protection_officer": "Jane Doe",
        "contact_email": "dpo@gameserver.com"
    }
}
```

This policy outlines data governance practices and accountability.

Promoting ethical AI and machine learning practices is also essential. When using AI for personalization or analytics, ensure that algorithms are fair, transparent, and free from bias. Regularly audit AI systems to identify and mitigate potential biases and ensure they operate ethically.

For example, an AI audit checklist might include:

```
{
    "audit_criteria": {
        "bias_detection": "Check for biased outcomes based on race, gender, or other attributes.",
        "transparency": "Ensure AI decision-making processes are understandable.",
        "fairness": "Verify that AI systems treat all players equitably."
    }
}
```

This checklist helps ensure that AI systems are audited for ethical practices.

In conclusion, ethical data usage in blockchain gaming involves transparency, consent, data minimization, security, respecting players' rights, anonymization, data governance, and ethical AI practices. By adhering to these principles, developers can protect players' privacy, build trust, and ensure compliance with data protection regulations.

Chapter 20: Case Studies and Real-World Applications

20.1. Analysis of Successful NFT Games

Analyzing successful NFT games provides valuable insights into the strategies and practices that contribute to their success. This section explores several case studies of successful NFT games, highlighting key factors that have driven their popularity and growth.

Case Study 1: Axie Infinity

Axie Infinity is one of the most well-known and successful NFT games, combining elements of traditional gaming with blockchain technology. Players collect, breed, and battle fantasy creatures called Axies, which are represented as NFTs. The game's success can be attributed to several factors:

1. **Play-to-Earn Model**: Axie Infinity introduced the play-to-earn model, allowing players to earn cryptocurrency (Smooth Love Potion, SLP) by playing the game. This model has attracted a large player base, particularly in countries where earning opportunities are limited.
2. **Strong Community**: Axie Infinity has built a strong and active community. Regular updates, events, and community engagement initiatives keep players invested and involved.
3. **Partnerships and Collaborations**: The game has formed partnerships with various platforms and organizations, enhancing its visibility and credibility.
4. **User-Friendly Interface**: Despite its blockchain-based nature, Axie Infinity offers a user-friendly interface that makes it accessible to both crypto-savvy players and newcomers.

Case Study 2: Decentraland

Decentraland is a virtual world where players can buy, sell, and develop virtual real estate. The game operates on the Ethereum blockchain and utilizes NFTs to represent land parcels and in-game assets. Key factors contributing to Decentraland's success include:

1. **Decentralized Governance**: Decentraland uses a Decentralized Autonomous Organization (DAO) to involve the community in decision-making processes. This decentralized governance model fosters a sense of ownership and participation.
2. **Virtual Economy**: The game has established a thriving virtual economy, allowing players to monetize their creations and participate in a vibrant marketplace.
3. **Interoperability**: Decentraland supports interoperability with other blockchain projects and platforms, expanding its ecosystem and user base.
4. **Creative Freedom**: Players have the freedom to build and create diverse experiences within the virtual world, attracting a wide range of users with different interests.

Case Study 3: CryptoKitties

CryptoKitties is one of the earliest and most popular NFT games, where players collect, breed, and trade virtual cats. Each CryptoKitty is a unique NFT with distinct attributes. The game's success can be attributed to several factors:

1. **Pioneering Concept**: CryptoKitties was one of the first games to demonstrate the potential of NFTs, capturing the interest of both gamers and the broader blockchain community.
2. **Simple Gameplay**: The game's simple and engaging gameplay mechanics made it accessible to a wide audience, including those new to blockchain technology.
3. **Viral Marketing**: CryptoKitties benefited from viral marketing and media coverage, rapidly increasing its visibility and user base.
4. **Collectibility**: The collectibility aspect of CryptoKitties, with each cat having unique traits and rarities, drove high engagement and trading activity.

Case Study 4: Gods Unchained

Gods Unchained is a blockchain-based collectible card game where players own and trade cards represented as NFTs. The game's success can be attributed to several key factors:

1. **Competitive Gameplay**: Gods Unchained offers a competitive and strategic gameplay experience, attracting players who enjoy collectible card games.
2. **True Ownership**: By utilizing NFTs, the game provides true ownership of in-game assets, allowing players to trade and sell their cards freely.
3. **Regular Updates**: The development team frequently releases updates, expansions, and balance changes, keeping the game fresh and engaging.
4. **Community Engagement**: Gods Unchained actively engages with its community through events, tournaments, and feedback channels, fostering a loyal player base.

Case Study 5: The Sandbox

The Sandbox is a decentralized virtual world where players can create, own, and monetize their gaming experiences. The game uses NFTs to represent land, assets, and experiences. Key factors contributing to The Sandbox's success include:

1. **User-Generated Content**: The Sandbox empowers players to create and share their own content, driving creativity and engagement.
2. **Monetization Opportunities**: The game provides various monetization opportunities, including selling creations, participating in events, and earning rewards.
3. **Partnerships and IP Collaborations**: The Sandbox has formed partnerships with popular brands and intellectual properties, attracting fans and expanding its user base.
4. **Active Community**: The game has built an active and supportive community, with regular events, contests, and community-driven initiatives.

In conclusion, analyzing successful NFT games like Axie Infinity, Decentraland, CryptoKitties, Gods Unchained, and The Sandbox reveals common factors such as innovative gameplay models, strong community engagement, decentralized governance, interoperability, and monetization opportunities. These case studies provide valuable insights for developers looking to create successful NFT games.

20.2. Lessons from Failed NFT Game Projects

Analyzing failed NFT game projects provides valuable insights into the pitfalls and challenges that developers should avoid. This section explores several case studies of failed NFT games, highlighting the key reasons for their lack of success and the lessons that can be learned.

Case Study 1: FOMO3D

FOMO3D was a controversial blockchain game that gained attention for its "exit scam" mechanics. Players purchased keys, and the last person to buy a key before a timer ran out would win the pot. Key reasons for the game's failure include:

1. **Ponzi Scheme Mechanics**: The game's structure resembled a Ponzi scheme, where early participants benefited at the expense of later ones. This unsustainable model led to ethical concerns and regulatory scrutiny.
2. **Lack of Long-Term Engagement**: The game's appeal was short-lived, relying on the novelty of its mechanics rather than offering sustained engagement or meaningful gameplay.
3. **Negative Publicity**: The controversial nature of FOMO3D attracted negative media coverage, damaging its reputation and deterring potential players.

Case Study 2: CryptoCelebrities

CryptoCelebrities allowed players to buy and trade virtual celebrities represented as NFTs. The game's downfall can be attributed to several factors:

1. **Limited Appeal**: The concept of buying and trading virtual celebrities had limited appeal and failed to capture a broad audience.
2. **Lack of Gameplay Depth**: CryptoCelebrities lacked engaging gameplay mechanics beyond the basic buying and selling of NFTs, leading to player attrition.
3. **Market Saturation**: The game launched during a period of market saturation, with numerous similar projects competing for attention and investment.

Case Study 3: BitconnectX

BitconnectX was an attempt to create a gaming platform on the back of the controversial Bitconnect cryptocurrency. The project failed due to several key reasons:

1. **Association with Bitconnect**: The association with Bitconnect, which was widely regarded as a Ponzi scheme, severely damaged the credibility of BitconnectX.

2. **Regulatory Issues**: Regulatory crackdowns on Bitconnect and similar schemes created legal and operational challenges for BitconnectX.
3. **Lack of Trust**: The gaming community and potential investors were wary of the project due to its connections with Bitconnect, leading to low adoption and support.

Case Study 4: EtherTulips

EtherTulips was a game where players could buy, trade, and battle virtual tulips. The game's failure can be attributed to several factors:

1. **Niche Appeal**: The concept of virtual tulips failed to resonate with a broad audience, limiting the game's appeal and player base.
2. **Poor User Experience**: EtherTulips suffered from a clunky user interface and technical issues, leading to a frustrating user experience.
3. **Lack of Marketing**: The game lacked effective marketing and community engagement strategies, resulting in low visibility and awareness.

Case Study 5: CryptoCountries

CryptoCountries allowed players to buy and trade virtual countries represented as NFTs. Key reasons for the game's failure include:

1. **Unsustainable Model**: The game's model relied on the continuous buying and selling of countries at increasing prices, which was unsustainable in the long term.
2. **Lack of Utility**: The virtual countries had no utility beyond ownership, offering little incentive for continued engagement or investment.
3. **Market Speculation**: The game's success was heavily dependent on speculative investment, leading to volatility and eventual decline.

Lessons Learned

1. **Sustainable Gameplay Mechanics**: Avoid Ponzi-like structures and speculative models that are unsustainable in the long term. Focus on creating engaging and meaningful gameplay experiences.
2. **Broad Appeal**: Ensure that the game's concept has broad appeal and can attract a diverse player base. Niche concepts may struggle to gain traction.
3. **User Experience**: Prioritize user experience by creating intuitive interfaces and addressing technical issues. A positive user experience is crucial for player retention.
4. **Trust and Credibility**: Build trust and credibility by avoiding associations with controversial projects and ensuring transparency in operations.
5. **Marketing and Community Engagement**: Invest in effective marketing and community engagement strategies to raise awareness and build a supportive player community.
6. **Utility and Value**: Provide utility and value for NFTs beyond ownership. Incorporate elements that encourage continued engagement and investment.

In conclusion, analyzing failed NFT game projects like FOMO3D, CryptoCelebrities, BitconnectX, EtherTulips, and CryptoCountries highlights the importance of sustainable gameplay mechanics, broad appeal, positive user experience, trust, marketing, and utility. By learning from these failures, developers can avoid common pitfalls and create more successful NFT games.

20.3. Innovative Use Cases of NFTs in Indie Games

Indie game developers are exploring innovative use cases of NFTs to create unique and engaging gaming experiences. This section highlights several case studies of indie games that have successfully integrated NFTs in novel ways, showcasing the potential of blockchain technology in the indie game industry.

Case Study 1: Neon District

Neon District is a cyberpunk-themed role-playing game (RPG) that integrates NFTs to represent characters, equipment, and other in-game assets. Innovative use cases in Neon District include:

1. **Customizable Characters**: Players can collect and customize characters with unique attributes and equipment, represented as NFTs. This allows for a high degree of personalization and ownership.
2. **Play-to-Earn Mechanics**: The game features play-to-earn mechanics, where players can earn cryptocurrency and valuable NFTs through gameplay, creating economic opportunities for players.
3. **Interoperability**: Neon District assets can be used in other compatible games and platforms, enhancing the value and utility of NFTs beyond the game itself.

Case Study 2: MyCryptoHeroes

MyCryptoHeroes is a blockchain-based RPG where players collect and train historical heroes, represented as NFTs. Key innovative use cases in MyCryptoHeroes include:

1. **Hero Ownership**: Players own their heroes as NFTs, which can be traded, sold, or used in various game modes. This ownership creates a strong sense of investment and engagement.
2. **Decentralized Governance**: The game features a decentralized governance system, allowing players to participate in decision-making processes and influence the game's development.
3. **Collaborative Gameplay**: MyCryptoHeroes encourages collaboration through guilds and alliances, where players can work together to achieve common goals and earn rewards.

Case Study 3: CryptoSpaceX

CryptoSpaceX is a strategy game that combines space exploration with blockchain technology. Innovative use cases in CryptoSpaceX include:

1. **Explorable NFTs**: Players can explore and discover new planets, each represented as an NFT with unique resources and attributes. These explorable NFTs add depth and excitement to the gameplay.
2. **Resource Management**: The game incorporates resource management mechanics, where players collect and trade resources from different planets, creating a dynamic in-game economy.
3. **Cross-Game Integration**: CryptoSpaceX assets can be integrated with other blockchain games, allowing players to use their resources and planets across multiple gaming experiences.

Case Study 4: Axie Infinity

Axie Infinity, though widely recognized, started as an indie game and showcases several innovative NFT use cases:

1. **Breeding and Genetics**: Players can breed Axies, each with unique genetic traits represented as NFTs. This breeding system creates endless possibilities for new and rare Axies.
2. **Marketplace Integration**: Axie Infinity features a built-in marketplace where players can buy, sell, and trade Axies and other in-game assets. This marketplace facilitates a vibrant player-driven economy.
3. **Scholarship Programs**: The game has inspired scholarship programs where experienced players lend Axies to new players, who can then earn rewards and share profits. This model promotes community growth and inclusivity.

Case Study 5: Gods Unchained

Gods Unchained is a blockchain-based collectible card game with several innovative NFT use cases:

1. **True Ownership of Cards**: Each card in Gods Unchained is an NFT, giving players true ownership and the ability to trade or sell their cards freely. This ownership model enhances the value and appeal of rare cards.
2. **Immutable Game Rules**: The use of blockchain technology ensures that the game's rules and card attributes are immutable, providing transparency and fairness in gameplay.
3. **Tournaments and Competitions**: Gods Unchained regularly hosts tournaments and competitions, where players can win valuable NFTs and cryptocurrency, adding excitement and competitive elements to the game.

Lessons Learned

1. **Personalization and Ownership**: Allowing players to customize and own their in-game assets as NFTs creates a strong sense of investment and engagement.
2. **Economic Opportunities**: Integrating play-to-earn mechanics and marketplaces enables players to earn rewards and participate in a dynamic in-game economy.
3. **Interoperability**: Designing NFTs that can be used across multiple games and platforms enhances their utility and value.

4. **Decentralized Governance**: Involving players in decision-making processes through decentralized governance fosters a sense of community and ownership.
5. **Innovative Gameplay Mechanics**: Incorporating unique gameplay mechanics, such as breeding, exploration, and resource management, adds depth and excitement to the gaming experience.

In conclusion, innovative use cases of NFTs in indie games like Neon District, MyCryptoHeroes, CryptoSpaceX, Axie Infinity, and Gods Unchained demonstrate the potential of blockchain technology to create unique and engaging gaming experiences. By leveraging these innovative use cases, indie developers can differentiate their games and attract a dedicated player base.

20.4. Corporate and Big Studio Approaches to NFT Gaming

Corporate and big studio approaches to NFT gaming differ from indie developers in terms of scale, resources, and strategies. This section explores several case studies of corporate and big studio NFT games, highlighting their approaches and the key factors contributing to their success.

Case Study 1: Ubisoft - Quartz

Ubisoft, a major game studio, launched Quartz, a platform for integrating NFTs into its games. Key aspects of Ubisoft's approach include:

1. **In-Game NFTs**: Ubisoft Quartz allows players to earn, buy, and sell NFTs within its games. These NFTs, known as Digits, include unique cosmetic items like weapons and skins.
2. **Environmental Considerations**: Ubisoft has emphasized the use of energy-efficient blockchain technology, such as Tezos, to minimize environmental impact.
3. **Player-Centric Approach**: The platform focuses on enhancing player experience by providing true ownership and the ability to trade in-game items.

Case Study 2: Electronic Arts (EA)

Electronic Arts (EA) has explored integrating NFTs into its sports franchises, such as FIFA and Madden NFL. Key aspects of EA's approach include:

1. **Collectible NFTs**: EA plans to introduce collectible NFTs representing players, teams, and moments from sports history. These NFTs can be traded and used within the game.
2. **Enhanced Fan Engagement**: By leveraging NFTs, EA aims to enhance fan engagement through unique and limited-edition collectibles.
3. **Integration with Existing Ecosystems**: EA is integrating NFTs into its existing ecosystems, ensuring a seamless transition for players.

Case Study 3: Square Enix

Square Enix has announced plans to incorporate NFTs into its game franchises, such as Final Fantasy and Dragon Quest. Key aspects of Square Enix's approach include:

1. **Story-Driven NFTs**: Square Enix focuses on creating NFTs that enhance storytelling and world-building within its games. These NFTs may include unique characters, items, and lore.
2. **Partnerships with Blockchain Platforms**: Square Enix collaborates with established blockchain platforms to develop and implement its NFT strategies.
3. **Player Ownership**: The company aims to provide players with true ownership of in-game assets, allowing them to trade and monetize their collections.

Case Study 4: Atari

Atari, a pioneering game company, has embraced NFTs through various initiatives, including the Atari Token and partnerships with blockchain platforms. Key aspects of Atari's approach include:

1. **Virtual Real Estate**: Atari has invested in virtual real estate within platforms like Decentraland, allowing players to buy, sell, and develop Atari-themed experiences.
2. **NFT Collectibles**: Atari has released NFT collectibles representing classic games, characters, and memorabilia. These NFTs appeal to both gamers and collectors.
3. **Brand Revival**: By leveraging NFTs, Atari aims to revive its brand and engage a new generation of players.

Case Study 5: Zynga

Zynga, a major mobile game developer, has announced plans to integrate NFTs into its games. Key aspects of Zynga's approach include:

1. **NFT-Driven Gameplay**: Zynga plans to create games where NFTs play a central role in gameplay, offering unique experiences and rewards.
2. **Mobile Integration**: As a leading mobile game developer, Zynga focuses on making NFTs accessible and engaging for mobile gamers.
3. **Community Building**: Zynga aims to build strong communities around its NFT games, leveraging social features and community-driven content.

Lessons Learned

1. **Resource Allocation**: Big studios have the resources to invest in robust NFT integration, ensuring seamless and scalable implementations.
2. **Brand Leverage**: Leveraging well-established brands and franchises can attract a large player base and generate interest in NFT initiatives.
3. **Environmental Considerations**: Addressing environmental concerns by using energy-efficient blockchain technologies is crucial for gaining player support.

4. **Partnerships and Collaborations**: Collaborating with blockchain platforms and technology providers can enhance the development and implementation of NFT strategies.
5. **Player-Centric Approaches**: Focusing on enhancing player experience, ownership, and engagement is key to successful NFT integration.

In conclusion, corporate and big studio approaches to NFT gaming, as demonstrated by Ubisoft, EA, Square Enix, Atari, and Zynga, involve leveraging resources, established brands, environmental considerations, partnerships, and player-centric strategies. These approaches highlight the potential for large-scale NFT integration and the benefits it can bring to both players and developers.

20.5. Future Directions and Experimental Concepts in NFT Gaming

The future of NFT gaming holds exciting possibilities and experimental concepts that can revolutionize the industry. This section explores potential future directions and innovative ideas that could shape the next generation of NFT games.

1. Metaverse Integration

The concept of the metaverse, a collective virtual shared space, is gaining traction. NFT gaming can play a significant role in the development of the metaverse by providing interoperable assets and experiences across different virtual worlds. Players could own NFTs that are usable in multiple games and platforms, creating a seamless and immersive experience.

2. AI-Generated Content

Integrating artificial intelligence (AI) with NFTs can lead to the creation of unique, procedurally generated content. AI algorithms can generate personalized in-game assets, quests, and storylines based on players' preferences and behaviors. These AI-generated NFTs can provide endless possibilities for customization and exploration.

3. Dynamic NFTs

Dynamic NFTs are tokens that can change and evolve based on in-game events and player interactions. For example, an NFT representing a character could gain new abilities, attributes, and appearances as the player progresses through the game. Dynamic NFTs add depth and personalization to the gaming experience.

4. Decentralized Autonomous Worlds (DAWs)

Decentralized Autonomous Worlds (DAWs) are fully decentralized game worlds governed by smart contracts and DAOs. In DAWs, players have full control over the game environment, rules, and economy. This concept empowers players to shape the virtual world collaboratively and democratically.

5. NFT-Driven Ecosystems

Future NFT games could feature complex ecosystems where every in-game asset, from characters to resources, is an NFT. These ecosystems can create intricate economies with players engaging in various roles, such as crafting, trading, and governance. NFT-driven ecosystems offer a high degree of player autonomy and interaction.

6. Virtual Reality (VR) and Augmented Reality (AR) Integration

Combining NFTs with VR and AR technologies can enhance immersion and interactivity. Players can interact with their NFTs in virtual or augmented environments, creating a more engaging and realistic experience. For example, players could showcase their NFT collections in virtual galleries or use AR to visualize in-game assets in the real world.

7. Cross-Game Quests and Events

Cross-game quests and events involve collaboration between multiple games and platforms. Players can participate in quests that span different virtual worlds, earning rewards and NFTs that are usable across games. This approach fosters a sense of interconnectedness and expands gameplay possibilities.

8. Sustainable NFT Practices

As environmental concerns continue to grow, future NFT gaming projects will likely prioritize sustainability. Developers can adopt energy-efficient blockchain technologies, implement carbon offset programs, and promote eco-friendly practices to minimize the environmental impact of NFT gaming.

9. Gamified DeFi (GameFi)

Gamified decentralized finance (GameFi) combines elements of gaming and DeFi to create new financial opportunities for players. Players can earn, stake, and lend NFTs and in-game tokens within the game, participating in a gamified DeFi ecosystem. GameFi adds a financial layer to the gaming experience, making it more engaging and rewarding.

10. Real-World Asset Integration

Integrating real-world assets with NFTs can create unique and valuable experiences. For example, players could own NFTs representing real estate, art, or collectibles that have both virtual and physical value. This integration blurs the lines between the virtual and real worlds, offering new avenues for investment and interaction.

Experimental Concepts

1. **NFT-Based AI Companions**: AI-powered NFT companions that learn and evolve with the player, providing personalized assistance and interaction.
2. **Time-Limited NFTs**: NFTs that exist for a limited time, offering exclusive and ephemeral experiences that create urgency and excitement.
3. **Quantum NFTs**: Leveraging quantum computing to create NFTs with unique properties and behaviors that are not possible with classical computing.

4. **Biofeedback Integration**: Incorporating biofeedback devices to create NFTs that respond to players' physiological states, such as heart rate and stress levels.
5. **NFT-Driven Storytelling**: Collaborative storytelling where players' NFTs influence the narrative and outcome of the game's story.

In conclusion, the future of NFT gaming is filled with innovative possibilities, from metaverse integration and AI-generated content to decentralized autonomous worlds and sustainable practices. By exploring these future directions and experimental concepts, developers can create groundbreaking and immersive NFT gaming experiences that redefine the industry.

www.ingramcontent.com/pod-product-compliance
Lightning Source LLC
Chambersburg PA
CBHW071913210526
45479CB00002B/405